Teaching Content Area Reading Skills

A Modular Preservice and Inservice Program

Harry W. Forgan

Charles T. Mangrum II

University of Miami

CHARLES E. MERRILL PUBLISHING COMPANY
A Bell & Howell Company
Columbus, Ohio 43216

The Charles E. Merrill
Comprehensive Reading Program
Arthur W. Heilman, Consulting Editor

To Ruth Ann and Jane
Whose encouragement, help, and loyalty make every under-
taking—and all of life—a joyous pursuit.

Published by
Charles E. Merrill Publishing Company
A Bell & Howell Company
Columbus, Ohio 43216

This book was set in Times Roman.
The Production Editor was Jan Hall.
The cover was designed by Will Chenoweth.

Library of Congress Catalog Card Number: 75–40531

International Standard Book Number: 0–675–08597–7

4 5 6 7 8 9—81 80 79 78 77

PRINTED IN THE UNITED STATES OF AMERICA

Acknowledgments

The authors are grateful to the many preservice and inservice teachers in Florida who field-tested the modules and made suggestions for improvements. We wish to thank the University of Miami students who reviewed the modules and made many valuable criticisms and suggestions. George Mitchell and Ann Ebersole of the University of Miami are thanked for publishing the field trial edition of the modules.

Special thanks is extended to Marilyn Neff and Millie Augustine of the Dade County Board of Public Instruction, and to Evelyn Searls of the University of South Florida, for their valuable reactions and suggestions for some of the modules. Teachers and administrators in the following counties in Florida who provided feedback concerning the modular program also deserve recognition for their valuable comments: Dade, Lee, Alachua, Clay, Collier, Hardee, Marion, Martin, Orange, Baker, Broward, Brevard, Taylor, Hendry, DeSoto, Charlotte, and Glades.

A special note of appreciation is extended to Edward Fry for developing the Graph for Estimating Readability, and to Nativadad Santos for developing the Classification Scheme for Reading Questions. Both of these devices should prove valuable to content area teachers and we appreciate the opportunity to share them with suggested ways for their effective use. Jan Hall and Fred Kinne of Charles Merrill Publishing Company are also acknowledged for their contributions and patience.

Finally, we appreciate the valuable support of our families. Our children, Jennifer, Jimmy, Mykel, and Mark, were patient even though they could not understand why it took so long to write one book. Our wives, Ruth Ann and Jane, typed the many rough drafts and the final draft, and provided the necessary encouragement and support to accomplish this task.

Harry Forgan and Charles Mangrum

Table of Contents

Overview

There are three basic reasons why you need to acquire the competencies in this modular program. First, there is dissatisfaction with the present reading achievement levels of secondary students who live in a world in which reading is so important. Second, it is not possible for elementary school teachers to help students develop all the necessary reading skills for different types of content area materials. Elementary school children simply are not capable of developing some of the higher level reading skills and specialized vocabulary required for reading content area materials. Third, it is generally agreed that the teachers who are the most effective in helping students read specialized content materials are the teachers of the content areas.

The purpose of this modular program is to enable you to help students read your content area materials. This does not mean that as content area teachers you are expected to teach beginning reading skills. We recognize that content teachers are mainly responsible for helping students to meet the objectives of particular subject areas. The competencies stressed in these modules do not give you additional responsibilities, but rather enable you to be more effective as you implement the responsibilities you presently have.

Ten Basic Competencies

This program is designed to help you accomplish the ten reading competencies required of content area teachers. When you are able to perform them, you will be doing your part to help students read content area materials and thus be more likely to succeed in your classes. Specifically, you are expected to help students read content area materials by performing the following tasks:

1. Students cannot be expected to read materials which are written above their reading levels. Therefore, you need to be able to determine the readability of your written material to avoid

frustrating your students with reading requirements they cannot handle.

2. You will frequently need to supplement the available materials and prepare written materials for your students. In order to do this you must be able to write and alter materials at specified readability levels. As a result your resources for teaching will be increased and more appropriate for your students.

3. Often a variety of reading materials are used to teach basic concepts in content area courses. Before assigning materials to students you must be sure the materials are suitable in reading level. You need to determine which materials are suitable for particular students.

4. Many reading skills are needed to read specialized materials. After becoming aware of the reading skills which are necessary in your content area, you must determine which reading skills the students have or have not acquired. You need reading skills tests to diagnose the needs of students in your content area.

5. All content areas have a specialized vocabulary. Teachers are expected to help students develop and expand word meanings at different levels. To do so, you will need guidelines and activities for teaching the specialized vocabulary of your area.

6. A student is not reading unless he is comprehending. Oftentimes students need help in comprehending subject area materials. You must be able to help students develop strategies which will help them comprehend the specialized reading materials in your content area.

7. Different types of study strategies are appropriate for different content areas. Since content area teachers themselves have employed study strategies, they are the most qualified persons to help students develop appropriate strategies for the specific area. You must be aware of your strategies and share them with your students.

8. Students often encounter long and difficult words when reading content area materials. You are not expected to teach the beginning word recognition skills, but you should be able to help students develop a strategy for pronouncing multisyllable words which may at first appear unfamiliar to them.

9. There are many students who know how to read, but are reluctant to read. You should be able to use a strategy that will increase their motivation.

10. Just because students are reluctant to read does not mean they are reluctant to learn. There are some students who are far behind in reading and need assistance in order to succeed in content areas. Every content teacher is responsible for identifying and referring problem readers, and for adapting instruction so problem readers can succeed. You are expected to help problem readers survive—and learn—in your classroom while they are overcoming their reading problems.

The Modular Format

You will probably notice the format of this book is different from other textbooks you have used. The title states that this is a *modular program.* A module is a self instructional package designed to assist the learner in accomplishing certain objectives. An objective consists of what you are able to do, know, and/or feel after instruction that you may not have done, known, and/or felt before instruction. The ten modules in this book are self instructional packages to enable you to achieve the ten basic tasks required of content area teachers. You will find there is a separate module for each of the ten major competencies that you need to help students read content materials.

In examining the modules you will notice each module includes the following components: Prospectus, Pre-test, Branching Program Alternatives for Pre-test Responses, several Enabling Elements, Post-test, Answers to Post-test, and a Selected Bibliography. Since you may be expected to complete the modules independently, let us take a closer look at each one of these parts.

The *Prospectus* provides an overview of the module. It includes the rationale for accomplishing the objectives of the module. After reading the rationale, you will understand why the module might be of value to you as a content area teacher. The terminal and specific objectives are also listed in the Prospectus. The terminal objective indicates the behavior you are expected to perform in the classroom. This behavior is indicated in more detail by the clearly and precisely defined specific objectives. The Prospectus also includes a description of the resources and time required to do the module so you will be able to plan its completion. Any special materials that may be required for completing the module are specified along with an estimated completion time for the most important activities.

After reading the Prospectus, turn to the Pre-test to determine if there are any objectives you have accomplished. The Pre-test is a simple yes-no checklist designed for self-evaluation. If you feel you can perform the behavior which is asked for in the Pre-test, choose YES. If you have any doubt in your mind, choose NO.

The *Branching Program Alternatives for Pre-test Responses* is designed to provide the direction you need to go through the modules. The Branching Program will tell you which Enabling Elements are designed to help you accomplish specific objectives. The Branching Program tells you what to do for each response you made on the Pre-test. The modules then take into account your individual differences in that you only work to accomplish the objectives which you have not yet developed.

A major part of the modules are *Enabling Elements*. Each Enabling Element consists of a restatement of the specific objective, and Enabling Activities which are designed to help you accomplish that specific objective. You will notice that some of the activities in every Enabling Element suggest that you read a study guide. Study guides include the background information that you need to accomplish the objectives. In addition to the background information, many of the study guides include practicum exercises so you can actually put your new skills to work. The study guides make the modules relatively self-contained since the reader is not referred to other resources to accomplish the objectives.

A *Post-test* is included for each of the ten modules. You will notice the Post-test items are based on the objectives and are used to determine whether or not you have accomplished the objectives. Post-test items vary in format. You will find that some of the items require you to list or describe, while others are simulation type activities requiring you to apply your newly developed skills.

The *Answers to the Post-test* are provided in each module. You can check your responses with the Answers as a method of self-evaluation. The results of your self-evaluation can then be used to determine if you have accomplished the objectives. If so, you can go on to the next module. If not, you may want to return through some of the Enabling Elements as directed.

A *Selected Bibliography* is included after each module. In some cases you may want more information or would like to consult other sources for different ideas. The references which are included in the bibliography have been selected because they are the ones we feel are the most helpful and readily available to content area teachers.

Instructions and Flowchart for Completing the Ten Modules

Your instructor may have specific suggestions for completing the modules in this book. If not, we suggest beginning with Module 1. The following Instructions and Flowchart will explain the recommended procedure for completing each module. After completing Module 1, complete the remaining modules in any sequence according to your needs as a content area teacher. We hope you enjoy the modules and accomplish the objectives.

1. Read the Prospectus to determine if this module meets your specific professional needs. If the module meets your specific needs, continue reading.

2. Self-administer the Pre-test and follow the Branching Program to complete the objectives which you have not accomplished.

3. Complete the Enabling Elements in sequence. Use the Study Guides and Activities as appropriate.

4. When you have completed all activities for your selected objectives, take the Post-test to determine if you have met the evaluative criteria.

5. If satisfactory performance was not obtained, return to previous Enabling Activities as needed or consult your instructor. Retake the appropriate Post-test items.

6. When the module has been completed, you may wish to examine the Selected Bibliography for additional information or study.

FLOWCHART

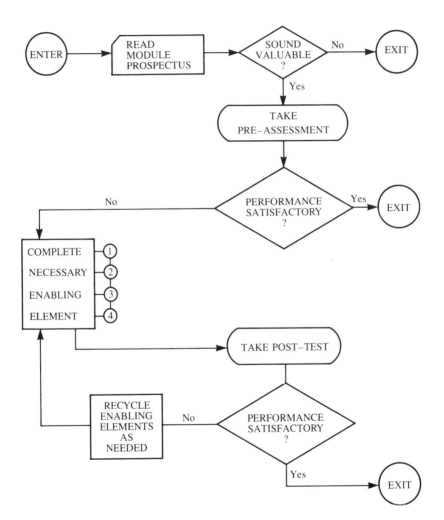

You can keep records of your progress with a checklist of terminal objectives.

Checklist of Terminal Objectives

_____ *Module 1.* You will determine the readability level of passages selected from major reading sources in your content area.

_____ *Module 2.* You will write materials at specified readability levels and alter the readability levels of passages related to your content area.

_____ *Module 3.* You will use an Informal Suitability Survey to determine the suitability of content area materials.

_____ *Module 4.* You will use reading skills tests to determine if students have acquired the reading skills related to your content area.

_____ *Module 5.* You will be able to introduce and expand word meanings in your subject area.

_____ *Module 6.* You will prepare a lesson plan that uses the Introspective Comprehension Strategy to improve the comprehension achievement of students in your subject area.

_____ *Module 7.* You will become acquainted with three study strategies; you will describe and apply the SQ3R Study Strategy.

_____ *Module 8.* You will determine the word pronunciation strategies used by students and help them use a strategy for pronouncing multisyllable words.

_____ *Module 9.* You will acquire and use the provided strategy for motivating reluctant readers.

_____ *Module 10.* You will identify problem readers and factors which may be interfering with their responsiveness to reading tasks and adapt your instructional procedures to help problem readers succeed in your content areas.

Module 1

Determining Readability Levels of Content Area Materials

CONTENTS

Prospectus

Rationale

As a teacher you will need to select materials for your students to read in conjunction with the course assignments. These materials may include textbooks, newspapers, magazines, and pamphlets. One of the criteria you should use for selecting these materials is readability. Readability is concerned with the difficulty of materials to be read.

This module is designed to help you use Fry's Graph for Estimating Readability. The graph is useful for determining the reading level of materials and thus for matching materials with students' reading levels.

Objectives

TERMINAL OBJECTIVE: You will determine the readability level of passages selected from major reading sources in your content area.

Specific Objectives:

1. You will list the two major factors that influence the readability of material and the two major uses of readability formulas.
2. You will state the five procedures for using Fry's Graph for Estimating Readability to determine the reading level of specified passages.
3. You will use Fry's graph to estimate readability levels of (1) textbooks, (2) articles, and (3) selections with less than 100 words.

Resources and Time Required

Most of the materials required for completing this module are provided. You will also need textbooks, newspaper or magazine articles, and other written materials such as handouts which you commonly use in teaching your classes. The estimated time to complete the starred core Enabling Activities is three to four hours.

Directions: For each question, choose the word that indicates your belief regarding your competency. If you are in doubt, choose NO.

1. There are two major factors which influence the readability of written material and two major uses of readability formulas. Can you state the two major factors influencing the readability of written material and list the two major uses of readability formulas?   YES NO

2. Edward Fry developed the Graph for Estimating Readability. Do you know how to use Fry's graph to determine the readability level of written material?   YES NO

3. Have you used Fry's graph to estimate readability levels of (1) textbooks, (2) articles, and (3) selections with less than 100 words?   YES NO

Branching Program Alternatives for Pre-test Responses

1. If you can state the two major factors which influence the readability of written material and list the two major uses of readability formulas, you are ready for Enabling Element 2. If not, Enabling Element 1 will provide you with this information.

2. If you know how to use Fry's Graph for Estimating Readability, you are ready for Enabling Element 3. If not, Enabling Element 2 is designed to develop this competency.

3. If you are skillful in using Fry's graph to estimate readability levels of (1) textbooks, (2) articles, and (3) selections with less than 100 words, you have completed the objectives of this module and are ready for the Post-test. If you need to practice, or use Fry's graph to estimate readability levels of different types of written materials such as textbooks, articles, *or* other selections with fewer than 100 words, do the appropriate sections in Enabling Element 3.

Enabling Element 1
Factors Influencing Readability

Specific Objective 1

You will list the two major factors that influence the readability of material and the two major uses of readability formulas.

Enabling Activities

*1. Read Study Guide 1, "Factors Influencing Readability." Identify the two factors that influence readability and the two major uses of readability formulas.

2. Reflect upon your own reading and ask, "What makes some selections more difficult for me to comprehend?"

3. Ask your students, "Why are some materials easier to read than others?" Have you identified other factors which may make some material more difficult than others?

4. Why should you learn about the factors that influence readability and the formulas that are available to determine it? How can this information help you as a teacher? Discuss these questions with your colleagues.

5. Most of the readability formulas developed today are for the English language; however, applications are growing. Locate the Klare article, "Assessing Readability," in the Selected Bibliography for this module if you want to learn about formulas which are available to measure materials which are written in any of the following foreign languages: French, Dutch, Spanish, Hebrew, German, Hindi, Russian, or Chinese.

---

*Indicates core Enabling Activities

Study Guide 1
Factors Influencing Readability

Readability is the objective measure of the difficulty of a book or article. Generally readability levels are reported in terms of grade level and therefore, one might find a textbook written at the ninth-grade level, fourth-grade level, and so forth. Readability should be a major concern of teachers because students are expected to gather information and develop new skills via reading. Teachers then need to know the factors which influence readability and ways of determining readability.

History

Factors which influence readability have been the subject of scholarly study for thousands of years. According to Klare, "Lorge tells of word and idea counts made by Talmudists in 900 A.D. so that they could use frequency of occurrence to distinguish from usual senses [meanings]" (1963, p. 30).

Although the study of readability has been underway for many years, little progress was made until statistical techniques were developed. Such techniques made it possible to identify important readability factors and to construct formulas for estimating passage difficulty. According to Klare (1963) early studies revealed many factors that were related to readability. Klare reports that Gray and Leary, for example, identified 289 factors influencing readability, twenty of which were significantly related to readability.

Several dozen readability formulas have been developed over the years. Many of the earlier formulas were complex and required the user to count a number of variables. Later research revealed the two most important factors influencing readability of commonly printed materials in the United States are sentence length and word difficulty.

Today, the more commonly accepted and widely used formulas use sentence length and word difficulty for estimating reading level. Examples of this method are the Spache Readability Formula (1953) for primary grade materials and the Dale-Chall Readability Formula (1947, 1948) for materials in grades four through sixteen. Because the Spache and Dale-Chall formulas require considerable time, in the last few years researchers have developed short-cut tables or charts which facilitate the use of the Spache and Dale-Chall formulas. Others such as Edward Fry

(1968) have developed alternative formulas based upon the same factors but which are simply and quickly applied. Of the less time-consuming formulas, Fry's Graph for Estimating Readability is one of the most commonly accepted.

Uses and Limitations of Readability Formulas

Readability formulas are usually used for two purposes— estimating reading difficulty, or preparing and altering written material. Estimates of reading level are useful to a teacher interested in reading assignments or in selecting textbooks and other commonly used written materials. The formulas are also helpful when material must be written or altered for low or high achievement students. Both teachers and librarians should be familiar with at least one readability formula.

Readability formulas do not measure noncontent influences such as the use of slang, satire, poetry, concepts, multiple meanings, or reader interest. This is a limitation all users must keep in mind when applying the formulas to reading materials.

Common Formulas

For use in the primary grades, the Spache Readability Formula is the most commonly accepted. Developed in 1953, the formula uses two factors to estimate reading level: average sentence length and percentage of difficult words. Through use and study this formula has been demonstrated to be valid and reliable for estimating reading level of written material; however, it is complex and time-consuming.

For grades four through sixteen the Dale-Chall Readability Formula is widely used. This formula first appeared in 1947. Like the Spache, it uses sentence length and word difficulty for estimating reading level. While it is considered to be one of the more accurate readability formulas, it is complex and time-consuming.

Fry's Graph for Estimating Readability is an outgrowth of a need for a simple and efficient technique for estimating reading difficulty. Fry's graph uses the traditional factors of sentence length and word difficulty to determine readability. However, with Fry's graph word difficulty is estimated through a count of syllables rather than through the cumbersome and lengthy technique of comparing every word to a list of words to determine its difficulty. Fry (1969, pp. 534–538) reports that the Fry Graph for Estimating Readability correlates 0.90 with the Spache Readability Formula and 0.94 with the Dale-Chall Readability Formula. These high correlations indicate considerable consistency between formulas and support the wide acceptance and use of Fry's graph.

Now you know that word difficulty and sentence length are the two major factors influencing readability and that readability formulas are usually used for estimating reading level or preparing and altering reading material. You are ready to learn how to use Fry's Graph for Estimating Readability. If you know how to use Fry's graph, go directly to Enabling Element 3. If not, or if you are rusty on the procedure, Enabling Element 2 will serve as a review.

Enabling Element 2
How to Use Fry's Graph for Estimating Readability

Specific Objective 2

You will state the five procedures for using Fry's Graph for Estimating Readability to determine the reading level of specified passages.

Enabling Activities

*1. Read Study Guide 2, "How to Use Fry's Graph for Estimating Readability" and familiarize yourself with the procedures for estimating readability.

*2. Make a list of the five procedures for using Fry's graph.

3. Do you need more practice in counting syllables? If so, read these words out loud and decide on the number of sound units that you hear. Check your responses with those listed on page 26 of this Enabling Element.

very _____   basketball _____   calendar _____
telephone _____   hopeful _____   vocal _____
desk _____   six _____   any _____
environment _____ matches _____   school _____
pencil _____   shouldn't _____   let's _____

*4. When counting the number of sentences in a 100-word passage, the last sentence is often not a complete sentence. The proportion of the last sentence must be determined if this is the case. What proportion (in a decimal) is each one of the following sentences?

    a. The last sentence contains eight words, four of which are in the 100-word count.

    b. The last sentence is fifteen words, and you are using four of the words as a part of the 100-word selection.

*Indicates core Enabling Activities

      c. The last sentence includes thirty-two words, and you are using nine of these in your 100-word passage.

Check your responses with those listed on page 26 of this Enabling Element.

*5. Let us suppose you find the readability estimate of a selection is tenth grade. What is the range of the true estimate of readability? Check your response with the answer on page 26.

*6. According to Fry's graph, what is the readability of a selection with the following counts:

      a. 128 syllables in five sentences
      b. 156 syllables in seven sentences
      c. 160 syllables in ten sentences

Check your response with the answers on page 26 of this Enabling Element.

Study Guide 2
How to Use Fry's Graph for Estimating Readability

Fry's graph was developed to serve as a quick, easy, usable technique for estimating the reading difficulty of written material for grades 1 through college. The graph incorporates two factors: average sentence length and total number of syllables for estimating reading level. Locate and examine Fry's graph (see pg. 19, Figure 1).

As you examine Fry's graph, notice the top heading is, "average number of syllables per 100 words." The numerals at the top of the graph then refer to the number of syllables contained in a 100-word selection. A 100-word selection with short words may contain as few as 108 syllables, while a 100-word selection with long words may contain as many as 172 syllables. If a 100-word selection contains fewer than 108 syllables or more than 172 syllables, Fry's graph cannot be used.

Look at the left side of the graph and notice the statement, "average number of sentences per 100 words." A 100-word selection may contain 3.6 (long sentences) to twenty-five sentences (short sentences). If a 100-word selection has fewer than 3.6 sentences or more than twenty-five sentences, Fry's graph cannot be used.

*Indicates core Enabling Activities

Figure 1
Graph For Estimating Readability*

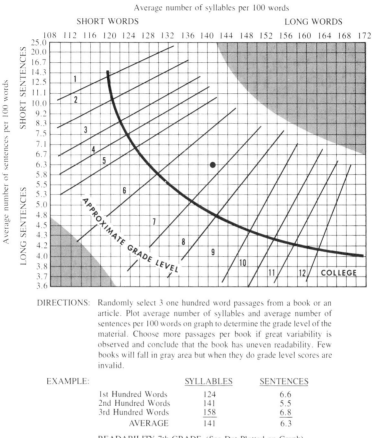

Average number of syllables per 100 words

DIRECTIONS: Randomly select 3 one hundred word passages from a book or an article. Plot average number of syllables and average number of sentences per 100 words on graph to determine the grade level of the material. Choose more passages per book if great variability is observed and conclude that the book has uneven readability. Few books will fall in gray area but when they do grade level scores are invalid.

EXAMPLE:		SYLLABLES	SENTENCES
	1st Hundred Words	124	6.6
	2nd Hundred Words	141	5.5
	3rd Hundred Words	158	6.8
	AVERAGE	141	6.3

READABILITY 7th GRADE (See Dot Plotted on Graph)

As you look at the center of the graph, you will notice that grade level bands range from first grade to college. Also notice some of the areas of the graph are gray because grade level scores in these areas are invalid.

Now that you have carefully examined Fry's Graph for Estimating Readability, you are ready for directions on how to use the graph. Refer to the graph as you read these directions.

_____

*By Edward Fry. Reprinted from the *Journal of Reading,* April, 1968, and *Reading Teacher,* March, 1969. Reproduction permitted—no copyright.

Directions for Estimating Readability Using Fry's Graph

Fry (1972, pp. 231–33) provides the following directions (partially adapted by the authors) for obtaining reading level estimates:

1. *Select a representative passage from written material for which you wish to know the reading level.* Count 100 words in the sample, skipping all proper nouns, dates, and numerals. As a general rule of thumb, skip words that are capitalized (American, European, Kent State University). Make sure you begin counting at the beginning of a sentence. Do not count the words in a title or heading.

2. *Count the number of sentences in the 100-word passage.* If the final sentence does not end at the end of your 100 words, determine what proportion of the sentence you are including in the 100-word count. Estimate the last sentence to the nearest tenth. For example, if the final sentence in a 100-word count has sixteen words, and eight of these are in the 100-word count, the final sentence would be counted as 0.5 sentences. For additional practice, see Enabling Activity 4.

3. *Count the number of syllables in the 100-word passage.* For example: *though*—one syllable; *counted*—two syllables; *determine*—three syllables; *appropriate*—four syllables. Keep in mind that when a word is pronounced there will be a syllable for each vowel sound. Remember that proper nouns, dates, and numerals are not counted. For additional practice, see Enabling Activity 3.

4. *Refer to Fry's graph* (see Figure 1). Notice the grid of intersecting lines. The vertical lines represent average number of syllables per 100 words. The horizontal lines represent the average number of sentences per 100 words. Where any two intersecting vertical and horizontal lines meet, approximate grade levels are revealed. Record the level of your selection at this time. According to Fry, most of the intersecting points will fall near the curved line. If the intersecting point falls in the gray area, conclude that the results are invalid and select another 100-word sample and refigure.

5. *Remember that these are estimates of readability.* Fry (1972) states that these estimates are probably within one year of true estimates of readability.

Illustrations of Each Step

Let us suppose you desire to use the following selection, "Teachers Don't Want to be Labeled" (pg. 21) with your students to help them realize that each person has strengths and weaknesses rather than being totally gifted, average, or slow. After reading the article, you want to know at what reading level it is written in order to determine whether or not you can actually require it to be read by your students.

Step 1: Select a Representative 100-Word Selection. Usually the first 100 words in a selection are used if they are fairly representative of the selection. In counting the first 100 words in this particular selection, you should skip *Kent State University* because all proper nouns are excluded from the 100-word count. Likewise, if any numerals appeared, they would not be counted.

If you use the first 100 words of this article, you will find the 100th word is *or,* which is in the first sentence of the second paragraph. Again we remind you to not count titles in your word count.

Step 2: Count the Number of Sentences. The second step in using Fry's graph is to count the number of sentences in the 100-word selection. The one-hundreth word does not always end the selection; therefore, it is necessary to determine the proportion of the last sentence which is included in the 100-word count.

Teachers Don't Want
To Be Labeled*

By Harry W. Forgan

When teaching a course on tests and measurements at Kent State University recently, I decided to administer an adult group intelligence test to the class. I wanted the students to "feel" what it was like to take such a

---

*Reprinted with permission from the *Phi Delta Kappan,* vol. LV, no. 1, September 1973, pg. 98.

test and realize what items we use to measure intelligence. I also thought they might be more aware of the short time it takes to obtain a number which is regarded as very important by many educators.

The students were told not to write their names on the test papers, but rather to use a code such as their house number, physical measurements, or any less obvious symbol. I explained that I really didn't have faith in IQ scores; therefore, I didn't want to know their IQs.

The administration of the test required only 50 minutes. The students seemed to enjoy taking it and chuckled at some of the tasks they were expected to perform. I had to laugh myself when I saw some of them looking at their hands and feet when responding to items concerning right and left.

Upon scoring the test I found that the lowest IQ was 87 and the highest 143. The mean IQ for the 48 students was 117. I was not astonished by the 87, even though all of the students had successfully completed the general education course and student teaching at Kent State and were ready to graduate by the end of the term. After all, IQ tests have many limitations.

Then I got an idea. I decided to prepare a report for each student, writing his code on the outside and ''IQ 87'' on the inside of each. I folded and stapled each paper—after all, an IQ is confidential information!

At the next class period I arranged all of the folded papers on a table at the front of the room. I wrote the range and the average IQ on the chalkboard. Many students snickered at the thought of somebody getting an 87. The students were eager and afraid as I began by explaining the procedures for picking up their papers. I made a point of telling them not to tell others their IQ score, because this would make the other person feel as if he too had to divulge his ''total endowment.'' The students were then directed to come up to the table, row by row, to find their coded paper. I stood sheepishly—ready to laugh out loud as I watched the students carefully open their papers and see''IQ 87.'' Many opened their mouths with astonishment and then smiled at their friends to indicate they were extremely happy with their scores.

There was dead silence when I began to discuss the implications of the IQ scores. I explained that in some states a person who scores below 90 on an IQ test is classified as a slow learner. The fact that group intelligence tests should not be used to make such a classification was stressed. I also emphasized the fact that *someone* in this class could have been classified as a slow learner and placed in a special class on the basis of this test.

I told how many guidance counselors would discourage a child with an 87 IQ from attending college. Again I emphasized the fact that one person in this room was ready to graduate from college having passed several courses in history, biology, English, and many other areas.

I then went on to explain that the majority of elementary and secondary school teachers believe in ability grouping. This is usually done on the basis of intelligence tests, so I explained that I would like to try ability grouping with this class—again to see "how it feels." Some students objected right away, saying that "I did not want to know their IQ scores." I calmed them by saying it would be a worthwhile learning experience and assured them that I really didn't believe in IQ scores.

I told the students not to move at this time, but I would like all of those with an IQ below 90 to come to the front so they could sit nearer to me for individual help. I told the students who had an average IQ (between 90-109) to go to the back of the room and then take the seats in the middle of the class. The students with an above average IQ were asked to go to the side of the room and take the seats in the back because they really didn't need much extra help.

"O.K., all those who got an IQ below 90 can come to the front of the room." The students looked around to find those who scored below 90. I said that I knew there was an 87 and maybe a couple of 89's. Again, there was dead silence.

"O.K., all those students whose IQ is between 90-109 go to the back of the room." Immediately, to my amazement, 8 or 10 students picked up their books and headed for the back of the room. Before they could get there I said, "Wait a minute! Sit down! I don't want to embarrass you, but you would lie and cheat—the same way we make our students lie and cheat—because you don't want to be classified as 'slow.' I wrote 'IQ 87' on every paper!"

The class erupted. It was in an uproar for about five minutes. Some of the women cried. Some indicated that they needed to use the restroom. All agreed it was a horrifying and yet valuable experience.

I asked them to do one thing for me: Please don't label kids. Because we are all "gifted," "average," and "slow," depending on the task at hand. They promised.   □

In our 100-word sample there are three complete sentences and part of another sentence. Specifically, the fourth sentence contains a total of thirty-one words, of which twenty-seven are in our 100-word count. In total then we have three 27/31 sentences. The fraction 27/31 can be changed to a decimal by dividing thirty-one into twenty-seven. In doing so, we find the decimal is 0.87, which is rounded off to the nearest tenth

(0.9). Thus, our sentence count for the 100-word selection is 3.9. In actuality, you need not do the division; the fraction can be estimated.

Step 3: Count the Number of Syllables. Teachers seem to prefer different ways of counting the number of syllables in a 100-word selection. Two procedures are illustrated below. Choose the one which is easier for you.

Procedure A. Read the selection subvocally and put a slash to indicate the number of syllables in each word. Keep in mind it is not necessary to divide the words into syllables. Simply note how many syllables are in each word. After making slashes for each syllable, count the number of syllables in each line and record this number to the right of the line. Add the number of syllables in each line to determine the total number of syllables in the 100-word selection. An illustration follows:

	Syllables
When teaching a course on tests and measurements at Kent	12
State University recently, I decided to administer an adult group	16
intelligence test to the class. I wanted the students to "feel"	16
what it was like to take such a test and realize what items we use	18
to measure intelligence. I also thought they might be more	15
aware of the short time it takes to obtain a number which is	16
regarded as very important by many educators.	16
The students were told not to write their names on the test	13
papers, but rather to use a code such as their house number,	15
physical measurements or /100 words/ any less obvious symbol.	7
Total	144

Procedure B. Assume each word in the 100-word selection has one syllable (that's true!) and simply make slashes for or count the second, third, fourth syllable in each word. Remember to add your subtotal to 100 to determine the total number of syllables in the 100-word selection. An illustration follows:

	Syllables
When teaching a course on tests and measurements at Kent	3
State University recently, I decided to administer an adult group	8
intelligence test to the class. I wanted the students to "feel"	5
what it was like to take such a test and realize what items we use	3
to measure intelligence. I also thought they might be more	5

aware of the short time it takes to obtáin a numbér which is   _3_
regaŕded as veŕy impórtaŕt by maŕy edúcátoŕs.   _9_

    The studeŕts were told not to write their names on the test   _1_
papeŕs, but rathéŕ to use a code such as their house numbéŕ,   _3_
physícál measúŕemeŕts, or /100 words/ any less obvious sym-   _4_
bol.

Subtotal   _44_

+100=   _144_

A word of caution! Do not be surprised if your syllable counts vary from other teachers who are evaluating the same selection. Variances are expected because people have different dialects or different ways of pronouncing the same words. For example, when saying the word *history,* some people say *his' to ri* and others say *his' tri.* Webster says both pronunciations are acceptable. Slight differences in syllable counts do not make a significant difference when using Fry's graph.

Step 4: Refer to Fry's Graph. Locate the number which indicates the number of syllables at the top of Fry's graph. For our sample look at the 144. Place your finger on the vertical line under the 144. Locate the number which indicates the number of sentences at the left-hand side. We have 3.9 sentences in the selection, which is in the middle of 3.8 and 4.0. Place your finger on that area and follow it over to the line which indicates 144 syllables. Notice the grade level band on which the two points intersect. This is the reading level estimate (ninth-grade). Remember that lines which intersect in the gray areas always reveal invalid scores.

Step 5: Remember, This Is an Estimate! Since the estimate for readability when using Fry's graph is within one year of the true estimate, our ninth grade sample has a true range of grades eight through ten. If your students read at these levels, you may be able to use the article with them. If not, you can read it to them or alter it to a lower reading level.

    You learn by doing! Now that you know how to use Fry's Graph for Estimating Readability, it is time to actually try it. Go to Enabling Element 3 to locate specific directions and practice activities for estimating readability levels of (1) textbooks, (2) articles, and (3) selections with less than 100 words. After using Fry's graph several times you will be able to determine the readability of a selection within five to ten minutes.

Answers to Enabling Activities 3-6

3. very   (2)
   telephone   (3)
   desk   (1)
   environment   (4)
   pencil   (2)
   basketball   (3)
   hopeful   (2)
   six   (1)

   matches   (2)
   shouldn't   (2)
   calendar   (3)
   vocal   (2)
   any   (2)
   school   (1)
   let's   (1)

4. a. $4/8 = 0.5$
   b. $4/15 = 0.26$
   c. $9/32 = 0.3$

5. The true estimate is ninth, tenth, or eleventh - grade reading level.

6. a. Seventh grade

   b. Ninth grade

   c. Invalid estimate (Another sample would have to be used to find the reading level.)

Enabling Element 3
Using Fry's Graph to Determine Readability

Specific Objective 3

You will use Fry's graph to estimate readability levels of (a) textbooks, (b) articles, and (c) selections with less than 100 words.

Enabling Activities

*1. Read Study Guide 3, *Using Fry's Graph to Determine Readability Levels.* It is designed to acquaint you with specific directions that are necessary to use the graph with different types of written materials.

*2. Do Practicum Exercises 1 and 2 to develop skill in determining readability levels of textbooks. This skill will be valuable when you evaluate textbooks for use and also as you determine the readability levels of your present texts. Check your response for Practicum Exercise 1 with the answers listed on pages 35–36 of this Enabling Element.

*3. Do Practicum Exercises 3 and 4 to practice evaluating the readability levels of articles. Check your answer for Exercise 3 with those on page 37 of this Enabling Element.

*4. Do Practicum Exercises 5 and 6 to develop skill in using Fry's graph to estimate the readability of selections which are less than 100 words. Check your response for Exercise 5 on page 38 of the Enabling Element.

5. You may want to duplicate Fry's graph for each of your students and teach them how to use the graph. Many secondary students can learn how to use Fry's graph and thus help you determine the readability of many of your written materials. Of course, you will want to check their work.

---

*Indicates core Enabling Activities

Study Guide 3
Using Fry's Graph to Determine Readability Levels

You can use Fry's graph to estimate the readability of several types of written materials. This Study Guide is designed to provide specific directions and practice activities for using Fry's graph to estimate readability of (1) textbooks, (2) articles, and (3) selections with less than 100 words. Refer to Enabling Element 2 for general directions.

Using Fry's Graph with Textbooks

If you want to determine the readability level of a textbook, you will need to select a minimum of three 100-word passages. One of the selections should be from the beginning of the book, one from the middle of the book, and one from the last third of the book. Be sure to choose selections which are self-contained and do not refer to charts or illustrations.

Follow the directions in Enabling Element 2 to determine the number of syllables and sentences in each selection. After doing so, find the *average* number of syllables and sentences by adding the three passages together and dividing by three. For an example:

100-Word Passages		Syllables	Sentences
First 100 Words		124	6.6
Second 100 Words		141	5.5
Third 100 Words		158	6.8
	Sums	423	18.9
	Averages	141	6.3

Go to the graph and plot the average number of sentences and syllables to estimate readability. In the preceding example you will note the average readability is seventh grade.

Now it is your turn.

Practicum Exercise 1

Determine the average readability of the following three passages randomly selected from the beginning, middle, and end of a hypothetical basic health book.

1. Count 100 words in each representative passage. Always begin counting at the beginning of a sentence and do not count the title, proper nouns, or numerals.
2. Count the number of syllables in each passage.
3. Count the number of sentences in each passage.
4. Determine the reading level of each passage.
5. Determine the average reading level of the health textbook by finding the average number of syllables and sentences. Use these averages as you refer to Fry's graph.
6. Check your answers with the answers on pages 35-37 of this Study Guide.

Rabies

Syllables

Since bites by cats, dogs, or any wild animal always present the danger of infection with rabies, a biting animal should never be killed unless unavoidable as a matter of safety. It should be caught and held for observation for at least fifteen days, in order to determine whether it develops rabies.

If it is necessary to kill the animal at the time of the biting, the carcass should be sent to the state public health laboratory for an examination of its brain. If the laboratory finds the animal was rabid, it is essential that treatment be initiated at once. /100 words/

Total

Headache

Syllables

The term *headache* is such a part of our everyday vocabulary that is has become almost synonymous with any unpleasant situation or problem. But in a medical sense the term quite literally means a head pain or an aching head, and is a symptom rather than itself an actual disease condition.

Hence, headache can suggest the possibility of a great many underlying conditions. Perhaps one of the better known types is the throbbing, devastating headache that sometimes accompanies a hangover. This differs from the type known as tension headache, associated with figuring out one's income tax, since they arise from /100 words/ different causes.

Total

Heat Stroke

Syllables

The most important feature of heat stroke, which is some- _____
times also referred to as sunstroke, is the extremely high body _____
temperature which accompanies it. It is a far more serious _____
condition than heat exhaustion. _____
    Heat stroke occurs more often in males than in females and _____
is more common in elderly people and in those addicted to _____
alcohol. Physical exertion is a definite contributing factor; and _____
an attack is much more likely to occur when the humidity is high _____
than when it is low, even at the same temperature. _____
    The underlying cause of heat stroke is intimately con- _____
nected with a cessation /100 words/ of sweating, accounting for _____
the excessive rise in body temperature.

Total   _____

	Number of Sentences	Number of Syllables	Reading Level	True Estimate Range
"Rabies"	_____	_____	____	_____
"Headache"	_____	_____	____	_____
"Heat Stroke"	_____	_____	____	_____
Sums	_____	_____		
Averages	_____	_____	____	_____

The answers are at the end of Enabling Element 3. If you are correct, continue reading. If not, repeat procedures one through six and determine why not. Remember that your syllable count may vary by a few syllables due to dialect differences.

Practicum Exercise 2

Now try a real exercise. Randomly select at least three 100-word passages from a textbook used in your teaching area. Determine the average grade level reading ability necessary for reading this material. A chart such as follows may be helpful.

	Number of Sentences	Number of Syllables	Reading Level	True Estimate Range
First 100-Word Passage	_____	_____	____	_____

	Number of Sentences	Number of Syllables	Reading Level	True Estimate Range
Second 100-Word Passage	_____	_____	_____	_____
Third 100-Word Passage	_____	_____	_____	_____
Sums	_____	_____		
Averages	_____	_____	_____	_____

Here are some follow-up questions you may want to ask yourself. Does the readability estimate match the reading levels of my students? If yes, then you have chosen textual material suitable for your students. If no, you may want to consider changing textual material. Is the readability range among passages less than two years for grades seven through nine and three years for grades ten through twelve? If yes, the range of reading levels should not overtax your students' reading ability. If not, many passages may frustrate your students and it may be advisable to consider changing the textual material.

A word of caution! Sometimes a book is found with great variability either in sentence length or syllable count for all passages. If this is the case, randomly select additional sample passages; average the number of syllables and sentences; and plot as before. If the same variability occurs, conclude that the book has uneven readability and consider changing texts. This type of material is the most frustrating.

Now you know how to determine the readability level of textbooks in your subject area. Read on and you will learn how to evaluate journal articles.

Using Fry's Graph with Articles

Teachers often wish to use articles from magazines, newspapers, or other sources. They need to know if the reading levels of the materials are appropriate for their students.

The directions for using Fry's graph in Study Guide 2 can be followed exactly if the articles contain at least 100 words. One representative 100-word selection is sufficient to determine the readability unless the article is unusually long. For longer articles two or three randomly selected passages will provide a more valid estimate.

Practice your skill in using Fry's graph by determining the readability of the following article.

Practicum Exercise 3

1. Count the number of sentences per 100 words.
2. Count the number of syllables per 100 words excluding proper nouns, dates, numerals, and title.
3. Refer to Fry's graph.
4. Check your answers on the last page of this Study Guide. If you have the correct answer, go to the next Practicum Exercise. If not, check to see if your numbers for syllables and sentences match ours. If not, recount your syllables and sentences and repeat step number 3. Do not expect your syllable count to be exactly the same as ours because of dialect differences; however, the syllable count should vary by only a few syllables.

New Target for Lib: TV Kiddie Cartoon

Syllables

Women's lib may have a new battle to fight–Saturday morning cartoon shows. According to researchers at the University of Michigan, cartoons still are entrenched firmly in traditional male-female sex roles.

This conclusion was drawn by analyzing 20 programs from such series as "Fat Albert," "Underdog," and "The Flintstones." Males were seen in 42 job roles while females appeared in only nine. Only six of the 31 cartoon women had jobs outside the home; whereas in reality, 50 percent of all American women are in the labor force.

Perhaps the time has come for women's lib to analyze all television shows to determine if this is how children develop stereotype of sex roles. /100 words/

Total

Practicum Exercise 4

Put your new skill into action by selecting an article you have used or would like to use with your classes. Follow the directions to estimate the readability level.

Selections with Less Than 100 Words

Sometimes teachers want to evaluate selections which are less than 100 words in length. This is particularly true for essay test questions, math problems, directions to an activity, or brief articles. Fry's graph can still be useful; however, the directions must be adapted because the graph is based on 100-word selections. The following procedures should be used:

1. Count the total number of words in the selection and round down to the nearest ten. For an example, if there are forty-four words in your selections, use only the first forty to make a count of the number of syllables and sentences.

2. Count the number of syllables and sentences in the selected words.

3. Multiply the total number of sentences and syllables by the number in the Conversion Chart (below) which corresponds with the number of words in your selection.

Conversion Chart for Fry's Graph
For Selections with Less Than 100 Words

If the number of words in the selection is:	Multiply the number of syllables *and* sentences by:
30	3.3
40	2.5
50	2.0
60	1.67
70	1.43
80	1.25
90	1.1

4. Refer to Fry's graph to find the grade level band which indicates the readability level.

The following essay questions are used to demonstrate these directions.

Essay Questions   Syllables

1. To what extent do you believe it is possible for people   _16_
   of different races, religions, or political beliefs to live   _18_
   together in harmony? What suggestions can you make   _14_
   to help people become more tolerant?   _10_

2. It is often said communism develops fastest in those   _16_
   countries where people do not have the basic neces-   _13_
   sities of life. Why do you think this might /60 words/   _10_
   be possible?

   Total   _97_

In counting the words you will find a total of sixty-two, Rounding this down to the nearest ten, you will be using sixty words in our sample. There are ninety-seven syllables and 3.8 sentences in the sixty words. Both of these numbers are then multiplied by 1.67 to convert them to a scale of 100 words. Thus, we have 162 syllables and 6.3 sentences which indicate the readability of eleventh-grade level.

Practicum Exercise 5

A sample math problem follows. Notice there are only seventy-six words in this selection. Estimate the readability by following these directions:

1. Count the number of words and round down to the nearest ten.

2. Count the number of syllables and sentences in the selected words.

3. To base your estimate on a 100-word passage, find the appropriate number on the Conversion Chart.

4. Multiply the appropriate number times the number of sentences and syllables.

5. Plot these numbers on Fry's graph to obtain an estimate of readability. Check your answers at the end of this Study Guide.

Math Problem

Syllables

You can compare ratios if each ratio has the same second _____
number. Let's suppose three boys jog every morning. Mark _____

jogs two miles in 20 minutes, Jim jogs one mile in 8 minutes, _____
and Bob jogs six miles in 40 minutes. You can compare their _____
speeds by writing ratios to show the number of miles they _____
jogged compared to the time required. To find out who jogged _____
the fastest, change each ratio to an equal ratio /70 words/ that has _____
40 as the second number.

Total   _____

Record your answers and check them with the ones at the end of the
Study Guide.

_____ Nearest ten (number of words used in determining readability)
_____ Number of syllables ×   _____   =   _____
_____ Number of sentences ×   _____   =   _____
_____ Estimate of readability

Practicum Exercise 6

If you do not use it, you will lose it! Retain your newly acquired
skill by determining the readability of selections from textual material in
your content areas. Find the readability levels of essay questions and
other material containing less than 100 words. Many times students fail
tests because the questions are written at reading levels which are too
difficult.

If you can use Fry's graph to determine the readability levels of
textbooks, articles, and selections containing less than 100 words, you
are ready for the Post-test. You have acquired some new skills which
will help you select appropriate materials for your students. In addition,
you will be able to use this information as you write and alter reading
levels of different materials. Module 2 will show you how this is done.
Pass the Post-test and go on to Module 2!

Answers to Enabling Activities in Enabling Element 3

Practicum Exercise 1

The average reading level of the three health book selections,
"Rabies," "Headache," and "Heat Stroke," is college level. This was
found by finding the average number of sentences (4.5) and the average
number of syllables (165), and then locating the intersecting point on the
graph.

	Number of Sentences	*Number of Syllables	Reading Level	True Estimate Range
"Rabies"	4.0	161	12th grade	11- College
"Headache"	4.9	170	College	12- College
"Heat Stroke"	4.6	163	12th grade	11- College
Sums	13.5	494		
Averages	4.5	165	College	12- College
(divided by 3)				

Rabies

Syllables

Since bites by cats, dogs, or any wild animal always _14_
present the danger of infection with rabies, a biting animal _18_
should never be killed unless unavoidable as a matter of safety. _19_
It should be caught and held for observation for at least fifteen _16_
days, in order to determine whether it develops rabies. _16_

If it is necessary to kill the animal at the time of the biting, _20_
the carcass should be sent to the state public health laboratory _17_
for an examination of its brain. If the laboratory finds the animal _22_
was rabid, it is essential that treatment be initiated at once. /100 _19_
words/

Total _161_

Headache

Syllables

The term *headache* is such a part of our everyday vocabu- _14_
lary that is has become almost synonymous with any unpleasant _19_
situation or problem. But in a medical sense the term quite _19_
literally means a head pain or an aching head, and is a symptom _17_
rather than itself an actual disease condition. _16_

Hence, headache can suggest the possibility of a great _15_
many underlying conditions. Perhaps one of the better known _17_
types is the throbbing, devastating headache that sometimes _14_
accompanies a hangover. This differs from the type known as _16_
tension headache, associated with figuring out one's income _17_
tax, since they arise from /100 words/ different causes. _6_

Total _170_

---

*Caution: Remember dialects make a difference in syllable counts. Check your syllable counts with the ones listed below if there is a great variance.

Heat Stroke

	Syllables
The most important feature of heat stroke which is some-	13
times also referred to as sunstroke is the extremely high body	17
temperature which accompanies it. It is a far more serious	18
condition than heat exhaustion.	8
Heat stroke occurs more often in males than in females and	14
is more common in elderly people and in those addicted to	17
alcohol. Physical exertion is a definite contributing factor; and	21
an attack is much more likely to occur when the humidity is high	19
than when it is low, even at the same temperature.	14
The underlying cause of heat stroke is intimately con-	15
nected with a cessation /100 words/ of sweating, accounting for	7
the excessive rise in body temperature.	
Total	163

Practicum Exercise 3

The article, "New Target for Libs: TV Kiddie Cartoons," contains 6.0 sentences and 151 syllables in the 100-word passage; therefore, the readability is ninth-grade level. The true estimate of readability is from eighth-grade level to tenth-grade level. If your syllable count varies check it line by line with the one below.

New Target for Lib: TV Kiddie Cartoon

	Syllables
Women's lib may have a new battle to fight—Saturday	11
morning cartoon shows. According to researchers at the Uni-	14
versity of Michigan, cartoons still are entrenched firmly in	9
traditional male-female sex roles.	9
This conclusion was drawn by analyzing 20 programs	13
from such series as "Fat Albert," "Underdog," and "The	6
Flintstones." Males were seen in 42 job roles while females	9
appeared in only nine. Only six of the 31 cartoon women had	16
jobs outside the home; whereas in reality, 50 percent of all	16
American women are in the labor force.	8
Perhaps the time has come for women's lib to analyze all	15
television shows to determine if this is how children develop	18
stereotype of sex roles. /100 words/	7
Total	151

Practicum Exercise 5

__70__ Nearest ten
__97__ Number of syllables × __1·43__ = __139__ syllables
__4·7__ Number of sentences × __1·43__ = __6·7__ sentences
__7ᵗʰ__ Estimate of readability

If your syllable count is extremely different, check it line by line with the one below.

Math Problem

Syllables
You can compare ratios if each ratio has the same second __17__
number. Let's suppose three boys jog every morning. Mark __13__
jogs two miles in 20 minutes, Jim jogs one mile in 8 minutes, __10__
and Bob jogs six miles in 40 minutes. You can compare their __11__
speeds by writing ratios to show the number of miles they __16__
jogged compared to the time required. To find out who jogged __14__
the fastest, change each ratio to an equal ratio /70 words/ that has __16__
40 as the second number.

                                                    Total __97__

Post-test

Directions: Read each of the following statements and complete each Post-test item.

1. State the two most important factors which influence the readability of written material.

2. List the two major uses of readability devices such as Fry's Graph for Estimating Readability.

3. Write the five directions for estimating readability when using Fry's Graph for Estimating Readability.

4. Use Fry's graph to determine the reading level of the following selection, "The International Date Line."

The International Date Line

Syllables

The International Date Line is often referred to as the _____
Sunday-Monday line. It follows approximately the 180th meri- _____
dian, on opposite sides of which the reckoning of the date _____
differs by one complete day. If you travel from west to east, _____
standard time advances one hour for each fifteen degrees which _____
is 1/24 of a circle of longitude around the earth. In passing _____
around the earth completely, you gain 24 hours or one complete _____
day. If you travel from east to west it is necessary to turn your _____
clock back one hour for each fifteen degrees of longitude; thus, _____
you lose 24 hours in passing completely around the earth. _____

Total _____

_____ Number of sentences
_____ Number of syllables
_____ Readability level

5. Decide if the following directions for using Fry's graph are true or false.

_____ a. Skip all proper nouns when selecting a 100-word passage.

_____ b. The estimate of readability is probably within one-half year of the true estimate of readability.

_____ c. Syllable counts by various people may differ slightly.

_____ d. If the intersecting points fall in the gray areas of the graph, the results are invalid.

_____ e. Count only complete sentences when counting the number of sentences in the 100-word count.

6. What adaptations would you make if you wanted to use Fry's graph with selections less than 100 words?

7. What adaptations are necessary when using Fry's graph to determine the readability levels of textbooks?

Answers to the Post-test

1. The two most important factors which influence the readability of written material are:

   a. sentence length

   b. vocabulary (or word difficulty)

2. The two major uses of readability formulas such as Fry's Graph for Estimating Readability are:

   a. estimating reading level

   b. preparing or rewriting material

3. The general procedures for estimating the reading level of any material when using Fry's Graph for Estimating Readability are:

   Step 1. Select a representative 100-word passage.

   Step 2. Count the number of sentences.

   Step 3. Count the number of syllables.

   Step 4. Plot the number of sentences and syllables on Fry's graph to obtain an estimate of readability.

Step 5. Remember that the true estimate is in a range of one
year either direction.

4. The selection, "The International Date Line" has:

_5_ number of sentences

_143_ number of syllables

_9th_ readability level

You can check your syllable count by comparing it line by line
with the sample below.

The International Date Line

	Syllables
The International Date Line is often referred to as the	9
Sunday-Monday line. It follows approximately the 180th meri-	12
dian, on opposite sides of which the reckoning of the date	16
differs by one complete day. If you travel from west to east,	15
standard time advances one hour for each fifteen degrees which	15
is 1/24 of a circle of longitude around the earth. In passing	16
around the earth completely, you gain 24 hours or one complete	14
day. If you travel from east to west it is necessary to turn your	18
clock back one hour for each fifteen degrees of longitude; thus,	15
you lose 24 hours in passing completely around the earth.	13
Total	143

5. a. true
   b. false
   c. true
   d. true
   e. false

6. Count the words and round down to the nearest ten. To base
   your selection on a scale of 100 words, find the appropriate
   number on the Conversion Chart. Multiply this number times
   the number of syllables and sentences.

7. Make sure you include a minimum of three 100-word selections
   randomly selected from the beginning, middle, and end of a
   textbook. The readability level is found by averaging the
   number of syllables and sentences in the selections.

If you have completed all Post-test items with 100 percent accuracy, you are ready for another module. If not, refer to the appropriate Study Guides for clarification of your difficulty. If you cannot clarify the difficulty, contact your instructor.

Final Comment

If you have completed this module with 100 percent accuracy, congratulations! You have now acquired a useful set of skills that will enable you to more adequately meet the needs of the students you teach. One word of caution, however. Your new knowledge is of no value unless you use it to help students cope with their reading assignments. This module does not test your intentions or application of readability skills; these qualities are dependent upon your professional and ethical responsibility.

Selected Bibliography

Dale, E., and Chall, J. S. "A Formula for Predicting Readability." *Educational Research Bulletin,* 1948, *27* (1), 11–20.

Dale E., and Chall, J. S. "A Formula for Predicting Readability: Instructions." *Educational Research Bulletin,* 1947, *27* (2), 37–54.

Fry, E. "A Readability Formula that Saves Time." *Journal of Reading,* 1968, *11* (4), 513–16, 575–78.

Fry, E. "The Readability Graph Validated at Primary Levels." *The Reading Teacher,* 1969, *22* (3), 534–38.

Fry, E. *Reading Instruction for Classroom and Clinic.* New York: McGraw-Hill, 1972.

Johnson, R. E., and Vardian, E. B. "Reading, Readability and Social Studies." *The Reading Teacher,* 1973, *26* (2), 483–88.

Kennedy, K. "Reading Level Determination for Selected Texts." *The Science Teacher,* 1974, *41,* 26–27.

Klare, G. R. "Assessing Readability." *Reading Research Quarterly,* 1974, *10,* 62–102.

Klare, G. R. *The Measurement' of Readability.* Ames, Iowa: Iowa State University, 1963.

Klare G. R. "Table for Rapid Determination of Dale-Chall Readability Scores." *Educational Research Bulletin,* 1952, *31* (2), 43–47.

Lorge, I. "Readability Formulas—An Evaluation." *Elementary English,* 1949, *36* (2), 86–95.

Spache, G. D. "A New Readability Formula for Primary Grade Reading Materials." *Elementary School Journal,* 1953, *53* (3), 410–13.

Spaulding, G. D. "A New Readability Formula for Primary Grade Reading Materials." *Elementary School Journal,* 1953, *53* (3), 410–13.

Stone, C. "Measuring Difficulty of Primary Reading Material: A Constructive Criticism of Spache's Measure." *Elementary School Journal,* 1957, *36* (10), 36–41.

Williams, R. T. "A Table for Rapid Determination of Revised Dale-Chall Readability Scores." *The Reading Teacher,* 1972, *26* (10), 158–65.

Module 2

Preparing Materials at Specified Readability Levels

CONTENTS

Rationale

Teachers often select reading material from magazines, newspapers, pamphlets, and other materials for their students to read. These materials are usually valuable but sometimes the readability level is above the reading level of the students. To make this material useful, skill in altering readability is necessary.

Over the term of a school year, teachers prepare many tests, course syllabi, worksheets, summaries, and other instructional aids for their students. It is essential for these materials to be prepared at the reading level suitable for most if not all students. Therefore it is necessary when teachers write material that they be able to control readability. This module is designed to help you write and alter materials to make them appropriate for your students.

Objectives

TERMINAL OBJECTIVE: You will write materials at specified readability levels and alter the readability levels of passages related to your content area.

Specific Objectives:

1. You will state the two major reasons for writing and altering materials for specified readability levels.
2. You will take a specified passage at the twelfth-grade reading level and alter the passage for a student with a sixth-grade reading level.
3. You will select a topic from your content area and write a 100-word passage at the fifth-grade reading level.

Resources and Time Required

Most of the materials required for completing this module are provided; however, it will be valuable to have some of your content area materials available. Gather sample test items, handouts you have prepared, magazine or newspaper articles, and various content area textbooks so they are ready for use. Module 1 should be completed before this module is begun. The estimated time for completing the starred Enabling Activities in this module is three to four hours.

Pre-test

Directions: For each question, determine the word that indicates your belief regarding your competency. If you are in doubt, choose NO.

1. Many educators believe it is important for teachers to be able to write and alter materials for specified reading levels. Can you state two reasons why these skills are necessary?   YES   NO

2. Readability formulas can be used to alter the reading level of materials. Can you alter materials in your content area to change the reading level?   YES   NO

3. Content teachers must frequently write test items and handouts for their students. Can you use Fry's graph to write materials at specified reading levels?   YES   NO

Branching Program Alternatives for Pre-test Responses

1. If you can state the rationale which explains why teachers should be able to write and alter materials for specified readability levels, you are ready for Enabling Element 2. If not, Enabling Element 1 will provide you with this information.

2. If you can alter materials in your content area to lower reading levels, you do not need to complete Enabling Element 2. Enabling Element 2 is very helpful if you do not know how to rewrite materials to change reading levels.

3. If you can use Fry's graph for preparing materials at specified readability levels, you are ready for the Post-test. If not, Enabling Element 3 is designed to help you develop this competency.

Enabling Element 1
Reasons for Preparing Materials for Specified Reading Levels

Specific Objective 1

You will state the two major reasons for writing and altering materials for specified readability levels.

Enabling Activities

*1. Read Study Guide 1, "Reasons for Preparing Materials for Specified Readability Levels." Identify the major reasons why teachers must be able to develop skill in writing and altering materials for particular reading levels.

2. Talk with some of your students and colleagues. Do they believe it is necessary for teachers to write materials at specified readability levels? Is Raths (1964) correct in saying that one responsibility assumed by good teachers is that of preparing curriculum materials?

3. Hold a discussion with one of your classes. Ask the students why they sometimes fail tests or neglect to complete assignments. See if they mention the fact that they did not understand the test items or directions. Probe to determine what caused the lack of understanding. Is the readability level of the materials one of the factors?

*4. Teachers are often cautioned to avoid "talking over the heads" of their students. Likewise, students do not like teachers who "talk down" to them. Discuss the implications for preparation of materials.

5. Some teachers believe standards are being lowered when reading levels of materials are lowered. Evaluate this argument.

---

*Indicates core Enabling Activities

49

Study Guide 1
Reasons for Preparing Materials for Specified Readability Levels

According to Raths (1964), one responsibility of a good teacher is that of preparing materials for students. All teachers recognize the inadequacies of available materials for meeting the individual needs of each student; thus they need supplemental materials. Teachers prepare handouts, review sheets, test items, directions for assignments and activities, and summaries from magazines and newspaper articles. Since students must be able to read these materials, it is imperative that teachers be skilled in writing the materials at appropriate reading levels.

We often hear of teachers who cannot understand why their students failed an examination after hours of teaching and reviewing. Some teachers claim the students know the answers the day before the test, but on the day of the test they do not seem to know a thing! When one examines the test items it is relatively easy to understand why students failed.

This same problem arises if assignment sheets, course outlines, summaries, or other handouts are written at levels which are too difficult for the students to read. Both teachers and students become frustrated because they are not communicating. Teachers are often warned about talking above the levels of their students and of course this same caution should be kept in mind concerning written communication.

We are not suggesting content teachers should lower their course standards. Rather they should do a more effective job of communicating with their students so that high standards can be achieved in the course. Just as students do not like teachers to talk down to them, neither do they enjoy materials which insult their reading capabilities. Likewise, students do not want to be confused by materials which are too difficult to understand. Somewhere between these two extremes clear communication is possible. Clear communication makes the achievement of subject area objectives possible. Teachers are advised to identify appropriate objectives and then do an effective job of preparing handouts, course outlines, assignment sheets, and so forth. Also, if the test items that are used to evaluate student knowledge are appropriate for the students' reading levels, then the objectives of the course are evaluated rather than the students' reading abilities. The level of written communication should be adapted so it is appropriate to help the students attain standards which are appropriate to their capabilities.

In addition to developing skill in writing materials, teachers should develop competency in altering materials that are valuable but are written above the reading levels of the students. For example, many excellent textbooks are written two or more years above the grade level of intended use. We are not suggesting that content teachers rewrite all their textbooks at lower readability levels. Certainly this is impossible! We are saying, however, that until authors and publishers begin to evaluate the readability of textbooks and make them more readable, teachers must be able to alter some of the textual materials if they desire to use them.

Just as important is the fact that although there are many supplemental materials available concerning the different content areas, they often are written above the reading levels of students. For example, if you find a newspaper or magazine article which illustrates an important concept but is too difficult for your students to read, you can alter the materials to an appropriate reading level. If you develop competency in altering materials, you will have more resources available for use with your classes.

In summary, if you develop skill in writing at specified readability levels, you will be confident that your students can read the materials you prepare. If you develop skill in altering readability, more resources will be useful for your classes. Your use of these skills will result in more appropriate reading materials in your classroom, which will in turn enable more of your students to accomplish the objectives of your content area. If you desire these competencies go on to Enabling Element 2 to learn how to alter materials and to Enabling Element 3 to develop skill in writing materials at specified readability levels.

Enabling Element 2
Altering Reading Levels of Subject Area Materials

Specific Objective 2

You will take a specified passage at the twelfth-grade reading level and alter the passage for a student with a sixth-grade reading level.

Enabling Activities

*1. Read Study Guide 2, "Altering Reading Levels of Materials," and identify the steps in the altering procedure.

*2. Do Practicum Exercise 1 which asks you to rewrite the eighth grade passage, "Florida," for a student with a sixth grade instructional reading level. Check your response with the one at the end of this Enabling Element.

3. Select a passage from a magazine or newspaper article in your subject area and alter the passage for a student in your class who reads two years below the level of the material.

4. Select an editorial from the newspaper or a short selection from a magazine and rewrite the selection to a lower or higher reading level.

5. Check the reading level of your essay test items. Alter them if necessary.

6. Try this if you have problems communicating with your students. Record one of your lectures. Select a 100-word unit and use Fry's graph to determine the listening level. Is it necessary to alter your oral communication?

7. You probably have a particularly good pamphlet that you have not shared with your students because you thought it was too difficult for them. Select some 100-word passages and rewrite

*Indicates core Enabling Activities

52

them to lower reading levels. Ask your students to read the rewritten passages. If the material is now readable, you may want to rewrite the remainder of the pamphlet and some of the other materials you have been storing simply because they are too difficult for your students to read in their present form.

Study Guide 2
Altering Reading Levels of Materials

The readability level of material can be altered by increasing or decreasing the reading difficulty of the material. This Study Guide emphasizes lowering the readability level. It is the authors' experience that although many content area resource materials are available for students who are reading above grade level, the supply of lower level material is very limited.

It is easy to rewrite materials to a lower reading level. This is accomplished by changing sentence length and word difficulty as necessary. Remember, sentence length and word difficulty are the two most important factors influencing the readability of materials.

Read the following selections. The first was written at the eighth-grade level and the second was written at the fourth-grade level. As you read the two selections you will notice the content is the same. Try to determine what changes were made to lower the second selection to a fourth-grade reading level.

Selection 1:   Eighth-Grade Reading Level

A glance at the advertisements in magazines leaves no doubt as to the interest of people in their weight. The dictators of fashion have made us weight conscious. And now the writers of advertisements are trying to convince the thin and fat alike that if they will only buy this exercising machine, this or that drug, or eat certain foods, a beautiful figure will result. They promise to make us look like, or at least desire to be like, the model that is pictured in the advertisement. They usually fail to point out that each person is different.

Selection 2:   Fourth-Grade Reading Level

Do you ever read magazines? If so, you have probably noticed all the advertisements about weight. Most people are interested in their weight.

The people who determine what is in style make us attach importance to weight. Now advertisers are doing the same thing. Some will tell you to buy an exercise machine. Others try to sell drugs to reduce or gain weight. Special food or liquid diets are often suggested, too. All of the advertisements try to make us want to be like the model in the picture. Yet each person is different. The advertisements do not say this.

What are the differences in the two selections?

1. _____

2. _____

If you look closely at the two selections, you will notice one difference is that more sentences were used in the last selection. In fact, the fourth-grade selection has eleven sentences as compared to the five sentences found in the eighth-grade selection. When you add more sentences and decrease the length of the existing sentences, you reduce the number of complex ideas per sentence that the student must comprehend. Understanding is facilitated because the ideas are offered in smaller doses.

Another difference in the two selections is that the fourth-grade selection includes fewer difficult words. The words *conscious, dictators, fashion,* and *pictured* have been replaced by synonyms which are shorter words. This generally reduces the number of syllables and thereby lowers the reading level. The fourth-grade selection has 137 syllables and the eighth-grade selection has 140 syllables.

How to Alter Readability of Written Materials

Revising the sentence structure of the selection is perhaps the easier of two procedures for altering the readability level. Often good materials include long sentences with many details used to express the thought or idea. Consider the following descriptive sentence.

In general each flower consists of a floral axis upon which are borne the necessary organs of reproduction (stamen and pistils) and usually accessory organs (sepals and petals), which may serve both to attract pollinating insects and to protect the essential organs.

When reading this sentence, the reader must process and organize many different facts:

1. Each flower consists of a floral axis.
2. The necessary organs of reproduction are borne on the floral axis.
3. The necessary organs of reproduction are stamens and pistils.
4. Sepals and petals are also borne on the floral axis.
5. Sepals and petals are accessory organs.
6. Sepals and petals attract pollinating insects.
7. Sepals and petals protect the essential organs.

To lower the readability it is necessary to introduce the facts in many sentences rather than in one long complex sentence. This aids the reader's organization of facts and usually improves comprehension because the facts are introduced in shorter doses. For example, the above sentence might be written as follows:

> In general each flower consists of a floral axis. The necessary organs of reproduction, stamens and pistils, are borne upon the floral axis. The floral axis also contains sepals and petals. Sepals and petals are important because they attract pollinating insects and protect the essential organs.

Did you find this easier to understand? Probably so, because the thoughts concerning the parts of a flower were presented in four sentences rather than in one. As you read, you had an opportunity to process each fact in a separate sentence rather than having to separate the complex sentences to notice each fact. The need to "run that by again," does not occur.

The second procedure for lowering readability is to decrease the number of syllables by substituting shorter words for longer words. A dictionary or thesaurus is helpful when changing words in the selection; however, you will find it difficult to find synonyms for some basic words. For example, stamens and pistils do not have any easier synonyms. The emphasis in such a case should be on changing the sentence length rather than on changing the vocabulary. This is not to say that it is not necessary to change some vocabulary words; but overall it is easier to lower the readability level by increasing the number of sentences.

A Special Note

When altering the readability of selections it is not essential that the word count be exactly the same. Often the word count is increased or decreased when changing vocabulary and sentence length. Remember that the goal is to alter the selection so your students can read and understand it, not to get an exact amount of words. If the word count in the altered selection is less than 100 words, simply follow the directions for using Fry's graph with selections containing fewer than 100 words. (Enabling Element 3, Module 1)

When changing a selection to a specified reading level, follow these directions:

1. Look at Fry's Graph for Estimating Readability. Locate the band containing the grade level to which you wish to change the material.
2. Determine (a) the number of possible sentences used at the desired reading level and (b) the number of syllables that are possible at that desired level.
3. Alter the material to the desired level by using the number of sentences and syllables as a guide. Remember that the easier way to change readability is to change the number of sentences, although it is usually necessary to change some vocabulary words, too.

Practicum Exercise 1

Now that you know the procedure for altering reading levels, try your skill on the following selection entitled "Florida." Presently the selection is written at the eighth-grade level because it has eight sentences and 151 syllables. Rewrite "Florida" at the sixth-grade level by increasing the number of sentences and syllables. Remember to use Fry's graph as your guide to determine the number of sentences and syllables which are possible at the sixth-grade reading level. Check your response with the sample at the end of this Enabling Element.

Florida

In 1565 the Spanish founded St. Augustine, the oldest permanent European settlement on the North American mainland. Most of Florida is young even though the state contains the country's oldest city. Cape Kennedy, a symbol of the space age, is the launching site of space vehicles. Walt Disney World is changing rolling, citrus-clad hills around Orlando, and attracting tens of thousands of tourists. Miami Beach entertains thousands of visitors.

Annually the woodlands of northern Florida are a rich resource of pulpwood. The orange groves of central Florida produce much of the country's orange crop. The vegetable fields of southern Florida produce fresh vegetables—corn, beans, and tomatoes—which are sent to the colder parts of the country in the winter.

Rewrite "Florida."

Practicum Exercise 2

Now it is time to try your hand at changing the reading level of the content material which most students in your classes use frequently. Follow this procedure:

1. Select a 100-word passage from a commonly used teaching material.
2. Count the number of syllables and sentences and determine the reading level with Fry's graph.
3. Decide upon the readability level you want for the material.
4. Look at Fry's graph to determine the number of sentences and syllables that are included in the readability level you desire.
5. Change the selection by increasing or decreasing the number of sentences and/or number of syllables.

After doing this a few times, you will probably be able to change a 100-word selection in five to ten minutes. Again, do not feel we are implying that you should rewrite all your textbooks and supplemental materials. Certainly this is impossible! Yet, this skill in altering reading levels is beneficial. Perhaps you will be able to use this skill to alter test items, handouts, assignments, and magazine and newspaper articles which may be valuable but too difficult for your students to read.

Sample Answer for Practicum Exercise 1

The selection "Florida" presently contains eight sentences and 151 syllables; thus, it has a readability at the eighth-grade level. To apply the procedures for rewriting material at the sixth-grade level, you would:

1. Look at Fry's graph to determine how many sentences and syllables are used in 100-word selections at the sixth-grade level. There can be between 4.3 and eleven sentences in a sixth-grade selection *depending upon the number of syllables* in the selection. For example, if there were only 112 syllables, you could use 4.5 sentences. However, if there are 146 syllables, you will need eleven sentences.

2. Since the selection "Florida" has eight sentences, you should consider reducing the number of syllables. Six possible changes in syllables are as follows:

Present Word	Synonym
annually (4)	yearly (2)
contains (2)	has (1)
permanent (3)	lasting (2)
symbol (2)	sign (1)
attracting (3)	getting (2)
woodlands (2)	woods (1)

3. Increasing the number of sentences from eight to eleven makes a difference too.

The selection reads as follows when you have eleven sentences and 143 syllables (sixth-grade level).

Florida

In 1565 the Spanish founded St. Augustine. This is the longest lasting European settlement on the mainland of North America. Most of Florida is young even though it has the country's oldest city. Cape Kennedy, a sign of the space age, is the launching site of space vehicles. Walt Disney World is changing rolling, citrus-clad hills around Orlando. Disney World is getting tens of thousands of tourists now. Miami Beach entertains thousands of visitors.

Yearly the woods of northern Florida are a rich source of pulpwood. Orange groves of central Florida produce much of the country's orange crop. Vegetable fields of southern Florida produce fresh vegetables. Corn, beans, and tomatoes are sent to colder parts of the country in the winter season.

Enabling Element 3
Writing Materials at Specified Readability Levels

Specific Objective 3

You will select a topic from your content area and write a 100-word passage at the fifth-grade reading level.

Enabling Activities

*1. Read Study Guide 3, "Writing Materials at Specific Readability Levels." It provides detailed directions and examples of how you can write materials at particular reading levels.

*2. Use Fry's graph to check a few of your test items. At what readability levels did you write them? If the readability level is too high, prepare new questions at a lower readability level. You may administer both forms of the test and compare the results.

3. Work together with members of your content area to identify important concepts, ideas, or other knowledge. Have each member select a few topics and then prepare a handout at a low reading level. If the members of your department cooperate, you will have many low level reading materials on your most important topics.

4. Check the readability levels of some of the items on a standardized test in your area. Should standardized test makers also be able to write at particular readability levels? Is this one reason why some students do poorly on standardized tests?

5. The next time you prepare a course outline or assignment sheets, follow the directions for writing materials at specified readability levels. Observe and compare the reactions of your students.

*Indicates core Enabling Activities

Study Guide 3
Writing Materials at Specified Readability Levels

Teachers have the responsibility of preparing specialized material for students, such as test items, assignments, and handouts with supplemental information. Since students must be able to read these prepared materials, it is essential that the reading levels of the materials are appropriate.

How to Write at Particular Reading Levels

Perhaps the easiest procedure for writing materials at specified reading levels is to write as if you were talking to your students. After doing so, check the readability using Fry's graph. If the readability level is appropriate, there will be no need to alter it. If the reading level is too difficult, you can follow the procedures for altering materials which were suggested in Study Guide 2. Let's examine each of these procedures in more depth.

Step 1. Write the Materials as if You Were Talking. Rather than suggesting that you look at Fry's graph first, it is suggested that you write the materials as if you were talking to your students. Most teachers find it difficult to control the number of sentences and syllables as they write because their most important concern is that of expressing an idea or direction. After the ideas are well organized, it is possible to go back and see if the length of the sentences and syllables needs to be changed. First say what you want to say, and then alter the readability level if the material is too difficult.

Step 2. Check the Reading Level by Using Fry's Graph. Follow the appropriate directions which were given in Module 1 to find out the readability level of your materials. If you use Fry's graph several times you will develop a sense of the reading difficulty of written material and a sense for the adjustments which are necessary.

Step 3. Alter the Readability Level if Necessary. If adjustments are necessary, the procedures suggested in Study Guide 2 for altering the readability levels can be followed. Remember to (1) look at Fry's graph to identify the band containing the level to which you wish to raise or lower the material, (2) determine the number of sentences and syllables that are possible for the desired reading level, and (3) alter the materials accordingly. You may want to recheck the readability of the selection if you are still in doubt of the level. Remember that it is not essential to have the same word count in the altered selections.

Let's take an example. Suppose you teach social studies and must prepare an examination. Write the following questions as if you were talking to your students (in other words, as in giving an oral examination). Your next step is to use Fry's graph to determine the readability level of the questions.

Sample Test Items

Essay Questions
    1. What effects do you think Europe's great population growth in the nineteenth century had on the population growth of the United States during the same period?
    2. What are the Soviet planners doing to overcome the hazards of the droughts which are so prevalent throughout the grassland areas of southern USSR?

True and False
    1. Penetration of the interior of Africa was a relatively easy matter for the explorers because of the continent's many navigable rivers.

Short Answers
    1. Name an area in northern Eurasia where farming is not an important occupation because there is no month which is free of frost, hence, where it is too cold for food crops to be grown except in sheltered places.

In determining the readability level of the test items you will notice there are 102 words (remember to skip all proper nouns and numerals) in the four sample questions. In counting the syllables and sentences you will find there are 157 syllables and three 36/38 sentences, or approximately 4.0 sentences. According to these facts, the readability level is twelfth grade.

Let us suppose most of your students are reading at the eighth-grade level. If you will examine the eighth-grade band on Fry's graph, you will notice that seven sentences and 152 syllables indicate approximately eighth-grade level. This means you must change the number of sentences from four to seven, and also decrease the syllable count by five. After making these revisions, the questions may appear as follows:

Essay Questions

    1. Europe had a great population growth in the nineteenth century. What effects do you think Europe's growth had on the population growth of the United States in the same period?

    2. Droughts are common throughout the grassland areas of southern USSR. What are Soviet planners doing to overcome the hazards of the droughts?

True and False

    1. Appropriate. Leave as is. Remember that the readability of the test items on one test will vary. You should concentrate on changing the test items that are too difficult.

Short Answer

    1. In some places the weather is too cold to grow food crops except in sheltered places. Name an area in northern Eurasia where farming is not an important occupation because there is no month which is free of frost.

Practicum Exercise

You learn by doing. Write some test items, directions for an assignment, or prepare a handout which you need at this time. In doing so, try to write the material at the grade level which is most appropriate for most of your students. If possible, you may want to work with one of your colleagues to develop a series of handouts on topics which are extremely important to all students.

Final Comment

You have developed new skills which will enable your students to learn more in your content area. If you will use the suggestions for altering and writing materials several times, they will become automatic. If not, chances are your students will continue to be frustrated by the written materials in your area. The decision is yours.

Post-test

Directions: Read each of the following statements and complete each Post-test item. One hundred percent accuracy is expected.

1. State the two major reasons why teachers should be able to write and alter materials for specified readability levels.
2. Rewrite the following selection, "The Comma," so it has sixth-grade readability. In its present form, "The Comma" contains 100 words, six sentences, 166 syllables, and is twelfth-grade readability.

The Comma

When speaking to someone, you are communicating information or ideas from your mind to his. If you communicate effectively, you control the flow of information and ideas in such a way that the listener can follow you easily. You do this by using changes in stress and pitch and by using pauses. Likewise, you use punctuation to control the flow of information in writing. Punctuation separates one sentence or thought from another, thus keeping the relationship among parts of the sentence clear and distinct. The comma is especially useful for this purpose, so remember to use commas to separate thoughts.

3. Describe the three procedures which are necessary to write materials at the fifth-grade readability level.

Answers to the Post-test

1. One of the responsibilities of teachers is that of preparing written materials such as tests, handouts, directions to assignments and so forth. If the students are expected to read the materials, teachers must write them at appropriate reading

levels so communication is possible. Teachers should be able to alter selections so they will have more resources available for teaching their classes.

2. If you have rewritten the passage on ''The Comma'' on a sixth-grade reading level and can substantiate the reading level using Fry's Graph for Estimating Readability, you have successfully completed Post-test item number 5. Remember that your selection need not contain exactly 100 words, but rather be at the sixth-grade level. A sixth-grade sample revised selection on ''The Comma'' follows. (nine sentences and 139 syllables)

The Comma

When speaking to someone, you are relaying ideas and information. The ideas go from your mind to his. If you are communicating well, you control the flow of thoughts in such a way that the listener can follow easily. You can do this by using changes in stress and pitch. Pauses can be used, too. When you write, you use commas to control the flow of thoughts. Commas are used to separate one thought from another in a sentence and thus make the sentence clear. The comma is really useful for this purpose. You can use commas to separate thought units.

3. Three procedures which are necessary to write materials at the fifth-grade level are:

   a. Write the selection as if you are talking to your students.

   b. Use Fry's graph to check the readability level.

   c. Alter the selection if necessary by changing the number of sentences and syllables. At the fifth-grade level you can have approximately five to twelve sentences (depending upon the number of syllables) and approximately 108 to 146 syllables (depending upon the sentence length).

Selected Bibliography

Abramowitz, J. *Follett Basic Learning Program*. Chicago: Follett, 1964.

Botel, M., and Granowsky, A. "A Formula for Measuring Syntactic Complexity: A Directional Effort." *Elementary English*, 1972, *49*, 513–16.

Endicott, A. L. "A Proposed Scale for Syntactic Complexity." *Research in the Teaching of English*, 1973, *7*, 5–12.

Flesch, R. *The Art of Readable Writing*. New York: Collier Books, 1951.

Fry, E. "A Readability Formula that Saves Time." *Journal of Reading*, 1968, *11*, 513–16, 575–78.

Jacobson, M. D. "Reading Difficulty of Physics and Chemistry Textbooks." *Educational and Psychological Measurement*, 1965, *25*, 449–57.

Klare, G. R. "The Role of Word Frequency in Readability." *Elementary English*, 1968, *45*, 12–22.

Koenke, K. "Another Practical Note on Readability Formulas." *Journal of Reading*, 1971, *15*, 203–8.

Kulm, G. "Sources of Reading Difficulty in Elementary Algebra Textbooks." *The Mathematics Teacher*, 1973, *66*, 649–52.

McCuaig, S. M., and Hutchings, B. "Using Fry's Graph to Describe the Variation of Readability." *Journal of Reading*, 1975, *18*, 298–300.

McLeod. J. "The Estimation of Readability of Books of Low Difficulty." *The British Journal of Educational Psychology*, 1962, *32*, 112–18.

Morris, J. O. *Make Yourself Clear!* New York: McGraw-Hill, 1972.

Raths, L. E. "What is a Good Teacher?" *Childhood Education*, 1964, *40*, 451–56.

Rogers J. R. "A Formula for Predicting the Comprehension Level of Material to be Presented Orally." *The Journal of Educational Research*, 1962, *56*, 218–20.

Smith, R., and Barrett, T. *Teaching Reading in the Middle Grades*. Reading, Mass: Addison-Wesley, 1974.

Spache, G. D. *Good Reading for Poor Readers*. 9th ed., rev. Champaign, Illinois: Garrad, 1974.

Module 3

Determining Suitability of Content Area Materials

CONTENTS

Prospectus

Rationale

One factor which influences student achievement in content areas is the suitability of the textbooks or other commonly required written materials. Materials can be classifed as suitable if the student can recognize 95 percent of the words and comprehend 75 percent of what he reads. Just as there is not one golf club suitable for all the various shots on the golf course, neither is there one textbook suitable for all the various students in a typical class. One task of the content teacher is to determine the suitablity of available materials so that pupils are capable of handling assignments.

This module is designed to teach you how to construct, administer, score, and interpret an Informal Suitability Survey for your content classes. An Informal Suitablility Survey is a device which consists of a sample reading selection, accompanying motivation statement, and comprehension questions. The Informal Suitability Survey can be used to determine the suitability or appropriateness of the materials you have available and help you match these to your students. The result should be students who can read their assignments and therefore succeed in content areas.

Objectives

TERMINAL OBJECTIVE: You will use an Informal Suitability Survey to determine the suitability of content area materials.

Specific Objectives:

1. You will describe an Informal Suitability Survey and state the major purpose for using one with your class.

2. You will construct an Informal Suitability Survey by selecting a representative passage of 200 words; writing a motivation statement; and preparing five comprehension questions consisting of three factual questions, one vocabulary question, and one inference question.

3. You will administer and score an Informal Suitability Survey following the procedures described in this module.

4. After scoring an Informal Suitability Survey, you will state the specific implications of the findings for assignments that require reading.

Resources and Time Required

You will need textbooks or other commonly required reading materials used in your subject area to complete this module. Paper is needed for developing an Informal Suitability Survey. If you have completed Module 1 on readability, you may want to refer to it for determining the reading difficulty level of your subject area material. It is not, however, essential to have completed Module 1 on readability prior to this module. The estimated time to complete the starred core Enabling Activities is three to four hours.

Directions: For each question, determine the word that indicates your belief regarding your competency. If you are in doubt, choose NO.

1. Before you can develop an Informal Suitability Survey, you must realize what it contains and why you might use it. Can you describe an Informal Suitability Survey and state the reasons for using one in subject area classes?   YES   NO

2. The materials needed to construct an Informal Suitability Survey are commonly available. Do you have a collection of selections and accompanying motivation statements and comprehension questions? Have you developed an Informal Suitability Survey using these materials?   YES   NO

3. If you want to implement the concept of an Informal Suitability Survey in your classes, you must learn how to administer and score one. Can you administer and score an Informal Suitability Survey to determine the suitability of required reading materials?   YES   NO

4. The results of any evaluative procedure are useless if they are not interpreted. Do you know how to interpret and use the results from an Informal Suitability Survey?   YES   NO

Branching Program Alternatives for
Pre-test Responses

1. If you cannot describe an Informal Suitability Survey and state the purpose for applying the concept of one in your classroom, Enabling Element 1 will help you acquire this information. If you can describe an Informal Suitability Survey and state its major purpose, you are ready for Enabling Element 2.

2. You are in great shape if you have a selection with accompanying motivation statement and comprehension questions to be used in determining the suitability of your textbooks. Enabling Element 2 is designed to help you develop these materials into an Informal Suitability Survey if you have not done so.

3. If you have already administered and scored an Informal Suitability Survey to determine the suitability of materials for your students, you need not do Enabling Element 3. This element is designed for those who have never administered and scored such a device. Procedures for both individual and group administration are presented.

4. Your answer to this question is very important. The implications from an Informal Suitability Survey are essential for increasing your effectiveness as a teacher. Do Enabling Element 4 if you have any doubts. If you already know the implications you are ready for the Post-test.

Enabling Element 1
The Informal Suitability Survey

Specific Objective 1

You will describe an Informal Suitability Survey and state the major purpose for using one with your class.

Enabling Activities

*1. Read Study Guide 1, "The Informal Suitability Survey." Determine what an Informal Suitability Survey is and the value of using such surveys.

2. Teaching is both satisfying and frustrating. Think of those things that frustrate you most. Does the fact that some students cannot read the textbook or other required material frustrate you? If so, are you committed to doing something about it?

3. Consider the students who cannot read your textbook or other commonly required reading materials. How do they feel when you make an assignment? How do they feel when others are sharing information gleaned from the reading assignments? How do they respond?

4. Discuss why there is such a wide range of reading achievement among secondary students. Make a list of possible reasons. Module 10, "Identifying and Helping Problem Readers," can be used to verify your ideas.

5. Look at the students in your classes to notice the range in their heights. If a standard size of clothing were required, it would be inappropriate for many students. Is there any reason to believe that mental abilities will not vary as do physical characteristics?

* Indicates a core Enabling Activity

Study Guide 1
The Informal Suitability Survey

The first task in bowling is to find a ball which fits. Bowlers move from one rack of balls to another to find a ball which is suitable to them. Others go to the expense of having the holes drilled to fit their own fingers, thumb, and span. It is a fact that one bowling ball simply is not suitable for all bowlers.

Such is the case with textbooks or other commonly required reading materials which are used in content area classes. The materials are too difficult for some students and suitable for others. This is true because within a classroom, one-third of the students read below their current grade level, one-third at the grade level, and one-third above their current grade level. The range of reading levels of a typical seventh-grade class is between third and eleventh grade and this range increases as students advance in grade level.

The wide range in reading achievement is to be expected because of the heterogeneous nature of school populations. Students vary in height, weight, attitudes, and mental ability to mention just a few factors. Textbooks, on the other hand, vary in readability less than the group of students served in any subject area classroom. The difference between the students' reading levels and the book reading level produces an instructional problem for subject area teachers. One text is simply not suitable for every student.

Description of an Informal Suitability Survey

For each student in their classes, content teachers must determine the suitability of textbooks or other required reading material. A useful technique to identify the suitability of a textbook and/or other written material is the Informal Suitability Survey. *An Informal Suitability Survey is an informal device which can be used to determine if students can handle selected content area reading material.*

An Informal Suitability Survey consists of a representative selection from some commonly required content area material. In addition, a motivation statement and comprehension questions accompany the selection. To develop the Informal Suitability Survey, the teacher (1) selects a representative selection from commonly required reading materials, (2) writes the motivation statement to provide a purpose for reading the selection, and (3) prepares comprehension questions covering vocabulary, facts, and inferences in order to check the students' understanding of the selection. The teacher then administers the Informal Suitability Survey to students to determine if the textbook is appropriate in terms of their reading capabilities. For example, the speech or language arts teacher might use the following Informal Suitability Survey.

Sample Informal Suitability Survey

Name _____   Date _____

Source _____

Circle One: Suitable Unsuitable

Motivation Statement: Many students like to find jobs and of course all of you will probably be employed some day. Read the following selection to answer the question, "How do I prepare for a job interview?"

Selection:

Preparing for the Job Interview

An interview is a meeting between two or more parties to exchange information. The purpose of a job interview is to provide opportunities for the employer and prospective employee to exchange information. The employer desires to know if the applicant possesses the necessary capabilities and qualities to handle certain responsibilities. The candidate wants to know if the responsibilities, working conditions, and salary are suitable for his needs.

There are two different ways employers interview prospective candidates. In the *open ended* interview the employer generally begins by saying, "Tell me a little bit about yourself." The prospective employee then has the responsibility of informing the employer of his strengths and capabilities as a person. The *closed* interview technique is different in that the employer has many specific questions which he asks. For example, he may ask questions about your grades in school, family background, previous responsibilities and interests.

In preparing for a job interview, you should try to learn about the job so you have questions to ask. You may want to discuss the type and responsibilities of the work with your family, friends, or people who have similar jobs. Make a list of the important questions you have.

Another step in preparing for an interview is simply "know yourself." Be prepared to give the interviewer a concise picture of your interests and capabilities. Evaluate yourself to determine those things you do well and the characteristics you have which others seem to like.

Make the appointment for the interview and then plan to arrive a few minutes early. Promptness is generally considered very important by most employers. Evaluate your personal appearance to see if you are creating the image you desire. Usually, simple, conservative clothing is just right for an interview. Be ready to greet the employer with a smile/300th word/ and simply be yourself!

Comprehension Questions:
V = Vocabulary, F = Factual, I = Inference
   1. (V) What does *prospective* mean?
   2. (F) What is the major purpose of a job interview?
   3. (F) What three things should you do in preparing for a job interview?
   4. (F) What information does an employer usually like to have about an applicant?
   5. (I) Why do you suppose some employers like to use the open ended interview technique?

As you can see, an Informal Suitablity Survey is a sampling technique to determine if the materials you are considering for use with the students are appropriate. The above selection consists of a 300-word passage; however, you may want to use 200-, 400-, or even 500-word selections. If you have many materials available, you can construct a series of Informal Suitability Surveys and then match the materials to the students. If only one textbook is available, you may need to determine the students who are capable of reading the text and then make adaptations for other students.

As mentioned in Module 1, you can also match materials to students by comparing readability levels of the materials to the students' reading levels. Of course, to do so you must have the reading scores for all your students. Often these scores are either not available or invalid. Students have many different reading levels, depending upon their interests and the background information that they may possess on any specific topic. For example, a student who is very interested in math may be able to read higher level books because he knows the specialized vocabulary and symbols and he is highly motivated. This same student may read social studies books at a level two or three years lower because he does not have the same interest and/or a good background in social studies. Using the Informal Suitability Survey, then, is a more valid technique than using readability formulas for matching specific materials to your students. Enabling Element 2 will help you construct an Informal Suitability Survey.

Enabling Element 2
Constructing an Informal Suitability Survey

Specific Objective 2

You will construct an Informal Suitability Survey by selecting a representative passage of 200 words, writing a motivation statement, and preparing five comprehension questions consisting of three factual questions, one vocabulary question, and one inference question.

Enabling Activities

*1. Read Study Guide 2, "Constructing an Informal Suitability Survey." This Study Guide provides the necessary directions to help you make your own Informal Suitability Surveys.

*2. Select a 200-word passage which is representative of the textbook used most often in the classroom and write a motivation statement and five comprehension questions as directed in Study Guide 2.

*3. Evaluate your questions. When writing the factual questions, did you select significant facts? What about your question concerning vocabulary? Is the vocabulary word one which is essential to the meaning of the selection? Is your inference question one which requires knowledge from the selection as well as information from the reader's background of experiences?

4. What are the advantages of having ten questions as compared to five? Try checking comprehension with ten questions as compared to five. Are there differences in your findings?

*5. Discuss why it is important to provide a statement to motivate the reader. What are the advantages of presenting questions before asking students to read the selection? Are there implications for introducing all reading assignments?

---

*   Indicates core Enabling Activities

76

Study Guide 2
Constructing an Informal Suitability Survey

When developing an Informal Suitability Survey remember the final product consists of (1) a representative reading selection from any textual material commonly used in the class, (2) a motivation statement giving the student a purpose for reading the selection, and (3) comprehension questions to determine if the students understand the reading selection. Specific instructions for constructing an Informal Suitability Survey follow.

Step 1:   Select a Representative Passage

Select a representative passage from your textbook or other frequently assigned reading materials. The length of the passage will vary with the grade level and nature of the materials. Generally a 200-word passage is preferred; however, if it is difficult to find 200 consecutive words (as in some math books) you can use a 100-word selection. For longer textbooks, you may want to develop a 300- or 400-word selection, or two 200-word passages. The selections need not contain exactly 200, 300, or 400 words, but it is necessary to mark the 200th, 300th, or 400th word for scoring purposes. The important fact to remember is that an Informal Suitability Survey uses samples from your textual material; therefore, it is essential that the selection is a representative self-contained sample of the material being considered for use.

Select two or three passages of 200 words if you are surveying the suitability of a major textbook. The extra passages can be used as alternate forms of the Informal Suitability Survey for students whose scores you doubt.

Skip all proper nouns and numerals when counting words for your passages. Proper nouns are not counted because they are usually introduced to students when regular reading assignments are made. Numerals are not counted because they are not words. Mark the 200th, 300th, or 400th word by making a slash after it.

Step 2:   Write a Motivation Statement

Write a motivation statement for each passage to provide the students with a purpose for reading. The motivation statement usually consists of two sentences. The first sentence is a general statement concerning the topic of the representative passage. This sentence provides the reader with a frame of reference for reading the selection. The second statement is a question or command which states what the reader should be trying to learn. For example, a motivation statement for the following passage on becoming a naturalized citizen might read as follows:

> People who were not born in the United States but who desire to become United States citizens can become naturalized citizens. Read this selection to determine the requirements for becoming a naturalized citizen.

The motivation statement provides the student with a frame of reference and purpose for reading and thus insures his attention and concentration to the selection.

Step 3:   Prepare Five Comprehension Questions

Once you have selected the passage and your motivation statement is prepared, you will need to write questions for checking comprehension. You will need five questions for this purpose. Specifically, you should write one vocabulary question, three factual questions, and one inferential question. If you have long selections of 400 words or more, it may be desirable to have ten comprehension questions (two vocabulary, six factual, and two inferential).

Vocabulary questions are designed to test the students' understanding of a word used in a selection. Generally the vocabulary questions include words that are used in the selection but whose meanings are not necessarily obvious in the selection. The factual questions require answers that are directly stated in the passage. Factual questions might concern the sequence of events, main idea, or significant details. The inferential question requires some knowledge from the selection as well as some thinking on the part of the reader as he relates the selection to his experiences. A good inferential question requires that the reader use the information presented in the passage and combines it with his experiences in order to answer the question.

Samples of the three types of questions are given below. The following 200-word selection is typical of selections found in social studies textbooks. Use these examples as a guideline for preparing your own.

Becoming a Naturalized Citizen

People who desire to become naturalized citizens of the United States must be at least eighteen years old. The applicant must be able to sign a petition in his own handwriting. He must demonstrate skill in reading, writing, and speaking the English language unless physically unable to do so. Those applicants who have been residing in the United States for 20 years are exempted from the English proficiency examination.

A person who desires to become a naturalized citizen must be of good moral character and well-disposed to the good order and prosperity of the United States. There are residence requirements which must be met before filing a petition to become a citizen. The petition must have two credible citizen witnesses who have personal knowledge of the applicant's character, residence, and loyalty. The applicant must demonstrate knowledge and understanding of the fundamentals of history and form of government in the United States.

Naturalization is denied to any person who within 10 years has been subversive, including Communists or others who favor totalitarian government, and who were members of a prescribed organization, unless the petitioner was under 16 or forced under duress.

As with other federal statutes, there are exceptions to the guidelines stated above. Of course, the guidelines are subject to change by the /200th word/ Congress of the United States.

Factual Questions

Essay:

1. How old must a person be before he can apply to become a naturalized citizen? (18)
2. Name two proficiencies a person must have to become a naturalized citizen. (Skill in using the English language and knowledge of United States history and government.)
3. How many character references must an applicant have? (2)

Multiple choice:
1. Circle the letter which indicates how old a person must be to be eligible to become a naturalized citizen.
   a. Seventeen   c. Twenty
   (b.) Eighteen   d. Twenty-one

2. Circle the letter which indicates the two proficiencies a person must have to become a naturalized citizen.

   a. Knowledge of English and science

   b. Knowledge of the government of the United States and communistic government

   (c.) Knowledge of English and the history and government of the United States

   d. Knowledge of English and mental health

3. Circle the letter which indicates how many character references an applicant needs.

   (a.) Two   c. Ten

   b. Four   d. Sixteen

Vocabulary Questions

Essay:

1. What does *well-disposed* mean in the selection? (Committed to; in favor of; inclined towards)

2. What does subversive mean? (Tendency to destroy or overthrow)

Multiple choice:

1. As used in the above selection, *well-disposed* means:

   a. to get rid of   c. unfavorable towards

   (b.) inclined towards   d. sanitary

2. Circle the letter which indicates the meaning of *subversive*.

   a. communist   c. tendency to disagree

   (b.) tendency to overthrow   d. tendency not to believe

Inferential Questions

Essay:

1. Why is it necessary for the applicant to have certain proficiencies? (He must know the form of government because he will be

under its rules and regulations. He must know English so he can communicate with others in the country.)

2. Why must a person be at least eighteen years old to become a naturalized citizen? (By the time a person is eighteen years old he should be able to make important decisions, and he should have had opportunities to develop and exhibit good moral character.)

3. Why can a person become a naturalized citizen without demonstrating skill in reading and writing English? (This is true if the person has lived in the United States for 20 years. If he has been able to communicate in some fashion for this long in the United States, it can be assumed he will be able to continue communicating; therefore, proficiency testing is not needed.)

Multiple choice:

1. An applicant must have certain proficiencies in order to become a naturalized citizen because:

   a. He should know the forms of government under which he will be living, and the language he needs to communicate most effectively so that he can be a productive citizen.

   b. United States citizens are at a higher intellectual level than citizens in other countries; therefore, all citizens must have certain proficiencies to maintain the high standards found in the United States.

   c. Knowledge of English and history is important so that the person will not feel like a foreigner in his own country.

   d. Good moral character and knowledge of English and government are important because the United States already has a high rate of crime and illiteracy.

When evaluating the sample questions, notice how:

1. The factual questions concern details which are important to the comprehension of the selection.

2. The vocabulary questions include words that are used, but whose meanings are not necessarily obvious in the selection.

3. The inferential questions require knowledge from the selection as well as thought; the student must relate the selection to his background of experiences.

It is necessary for you to determine the format of your questions. Essay and short-answer items usually require more memory; however, multiple-choice items might be more feasible when administering and grading the selection for large groups.

Practicum Exercise

Are you ready to prepare an Informal Suitability Survey for your students? You can do so by following these steps:

1. Select a representative 200-word passage. Make sure the passage is self-contained in that it does not refer to pictures or illustrations. Skip all proper nouns and numerals as you count the 200 words. If the selection does not end with the 200th word, mark the 200th word by making a slash after it.

2. Write a motivation statement to provide a specific purpose for reading.

3. Prepare five questions to check comprehension: one vocabulary, one inferential, and three factual.

After you have developed an Informal Suitability Survey, go on to Enabling Element 3, which explains how to administer and score this device.

Enabling Element 3
Administering and Scoring an
Informal Suitability Survey

Specific Objective 3

You will administer and score an Informal Suitability Survey following the procedures described in this module.

Enabling Activities

*1. Read Study Guide 3, "Administering and Scoring an Informal Suitability Survey," for directions in this method.

*2. Administer an Informal Suitability Survey to an individual and to a small group of students. Which procedures seem better suited to your purpose? What are the advantages and limitations of administering the Informal Suitability Survey to an individual? Group?

3. List the ways in which comprehension is affected by (1) insertions, (2) substitutions, and (3) omissions.

4. If your instructor has a tape of a student reading a selection, practice recording the word recognition errors.

*5. If a student reads a 300-word selection, makes fourteen word recognition errors, and misses one of the five comprehension questions, is the material suitable? Check your response with the Summary Scoring Guide.

*6. If you administer a selection individually and find that the student can recognize the words perfectly, but fails to answer three of the five comprehension questions, can you consider the material suitable? Check your response with the Summary Scoring Guide.

7. Make a chart to record the results of the Informal Suitability Survey.

*Indicates core Enabling Activities

Study Guide 3
Administering and Scoring an
Informal Suitability Survey

An Informal Suitability Survey can be administered to individuals or groups of students. Content area teachers are advised to administer the survey to the entire class initially, and then administer the survey individually to students who did extremely poor or had doubtful results.

Before administering an Informal Suitability Survey, it is necessary to have copies of the selection available. First type the survey on a master or ditto. Begin by placing the motivation statement on the top of the master and follow with the selection. It is also necessary to prepare dittoed copies of the questions. When all the materials are available, the survey can be administered as follows:

Group Administration

1. Be sure to have at least fifteen to thirty minutes available for the test. In addition, suggest work for those who might finish early so they do not disturb others.

2. Explain to the students you want to determine how well they can read the textual material used in your course. Indicate that grades will not be given, but rather the results will be used to help you determine useful material for teaching the course.

3. Distribute the selection and questions to the students and ask them to keep the materials face down on their desks. When all the students have a copy of the selection, read the motivation statement to them and tell them they can have as much time as they need to read the selection. When they have finished reading the selection, tell them to answer the comprehension questions. If you do not want them to refer back to the selection when answering the questions, collect the selections and then distribute the questions. In most instances, however, students are able to refer to the text when studying; thus, it is recommended the students be permitted to refer to the selection when answering the questions. The decision is yours.

4. Your major responsibility for step 4 is observing the students to make sure they are taking the test seriously rather than simply marking the answers randomly without reading the selection. Other observations you can make are: (1) the rates at which different students finish, (2) the attitudes of the students toward the task, and (3) reading habits such as head movements and finger pointing.

5. Check the papers to find how many of the questions were answered correctly and refer to the scoring guide to determine for whom the selection is suitable or unsuitable.

Individual Administration

The individually administered Informal Suitability Survey requires more time; but it is also more informative because in addition to the silent reading, you listen to the students read orally. You may want this opportunity to listen and talk with some students who puzzle you. If so, follow these directions:

1. Make sure you can spend seven to ten minutes with the student in a quiet place.

2. Tell the student you want to determine how well he can read the textbook and/or other required reading material used in your class.

3. Read the motivation statement to the student and ask the student to read the selection silently. Tell the student you are going to ask him questions after he has read the selection.

4. When the student has completed the silent reading of the selection, ask the five comprehension questions that you have prepared. Put a check mark after the question if the student's response is incorrect and leave it blank if the correct response is given. If there is more than one part to the answer, you may give partial credit.

5. After checking comprehension, tell the student you would like him to read the selection out loud. As the student is reading the selection, follow along on your copy. Your task is to notice his word recognition errors within the 200, 300, or 400 words. You

will need to put a check mark on your copy of the selection if the
student makes the following errors:

a. substitution—If the student says or substitutes one word for
   another word, put a check mark over the word he should
   have said. If a student makes an error on a proper noun or
   numeral, do not mark it because proper nouns or numerals
   were not counted in the passage.

b. omission—If the student omits a word or entire sentence,
   put a single check mark over the omitted word or sentence.
   Again do not count proper nouns or numerals as errors. If the
   student omits them, simply pronounce them. Count single or
   multi-word omissions as one error.

c. pronunciations—If the student hesitates when attempting to
   pronounce a certain word (other than a proper noun or
   numeral), ask him to try, allowing at least five seconds. Tell
   him the word and put a check mark over the word if you must
   pronounce it for him.

d. insertions—If the student inserts a word, put a check mark
   in the space where the word was inserted.

As you administer the Informal Suitability Survey to an individual,
you should observe his reading habits and obtain a feeling for his attitude
toward reading. Specifically, you can notice:

a. Is the student relaxed and comfortable when reading?

b. Is it necessary for him to use his finger or some other marker
   to keep his place?

c. Does he read word by word, or in phrases?

d. How much confidence and enthusiasm are displayed?

6. Refer to the scoring guide to determine the suitability of the
   selection.

Criteria for Scoring an Informal Suitability Survey

One criterion for classifying materials as suitable is that the student
should comprehend at least 75 percent of what he reads. This is not to
say that you expect students to comprehend only 75 percent of what they
read. But if the students are able to comprehend 75 percent of what they
read, their comprehension will increase if you: introduce specialized

vocabulary words (Module 5), help with comprehension (Module 6), teach a study strategy (Module 7), and provide specific purposes for reading (Module 9). The other criterion for classifying materials is that students recognize 95 percent of the words.

Scoring Surveys Administered to Groups

Informal Suitability Surveys typically have five questions; thus, if the student misses one question his score for comprehension is 80 percent. Two questions would be 60 percent, and so forth. A selection then can be considered as unsuitable if the student misses two or more of the five questions. If the student misses only one, or one and a half, the material can be designated as suitable. The authors realize missing one and a half questions out of five is equal to 70 percent; however, they have found there is no significant difference between 70 percent and 75 percent when determining suitability, especially when only five questions are used.

If ten questions are used in checking comprehension, the selection can be considered as unsuitable if a student missed *more than* three of the ten questions. If the student misses three questions or less the material can be considered suitable.

Scoring Surveys Administered Individually

When an Informal Suitability Survey is administered individually, two scores are necessary. The word recognition errors (omissions, insertions, substitutions, and words the teacher must pronounce) are recorded and must be scored. The general guideline for scoring the word recognition errors is that students should be able to recognize 95 percent of the words for the selection to be considered suitable. This does not mean teachers only want students to recognize 95 percent of the words, but this is a base from which the teacher builds. The teacher will introduce vocabulary (Module 5) and help needful students pronounce multisyllable words (Module 8) before asking the students to read the selection.

You probably realize now why proper nouns and numerals were not marked as word recognition errors. In selecting the passage for the Informal Suitability Survey you did not count proper nouns because these are usually introduced by the teacher in making reading assignments. Likewise, numerals were not counted because they are not words. Since the criterion for word recognition is that the student must recognize 95 percent of the words, only errors on words which were included in the word count can be considered. You should now also understand why you were directed to mark the 200th, 300th, or 400th word in the selection. When marking word recognition errors you only mark errors up to these lengths. If the selection is longer, do not mark errors past these word limits.

If a 200-word selection is used the students can make as many as ten word recognition errors and the material is still classified as suitable. If a 100-word selection is used the student can make only five word recognition errors for the material to be classified as suitable. A student may make as many as fifteen word recognition errors on a 300-word selection, twenty on a 400-word selection, and so forth. Of course the same criterion for comprehension which was described earlier is used to determine the suitability of an individually administered Informal Suitability Survey.

If the survey was administered individually it is likely that both scores would indicate the selection is suitable or unsuitable; however, it is also possible that a score on word recognition may indicate suitable and the score on comprehension indicate unsuitable or vice versa. Keep in mind comprehension is the more important criterion because reading is the meaningful interpretation of printed symbols. However, if the student scores below the suggested criteria (75 percent comprehension and 95 percent word recognition) for either word recognition or comprehension, the selection should be considered unsuitable. The following Summary Scoring Guide, Figure 2, can be used as you determine suitability of materials.

Keeping Records of Results from Informal Suitability Surveys

You may want to keep a record of the results from your Informal Suitability Surveys. You can do so by making a chart which includes the names of your students and the materials that you surveyed. You can mark a *U* by the student's name under each type of material if you found it to be unsuitable. An *S* can be written by the student's name under the material if you found it to be suitable. A chart like this is especially

Figure 2

Summary Scoring Guides For
Informal Suitability Surveys

Group Administration (Comprehension Only)

Suitable	*Unsuitable*
5 *Questions* – 3½ – 5 correct	5 *Questions* – 0 – 3 correct
10 *Questions* – 7 – 10 correct	10 *Questions* – 0 – 6 correct

Individual Administration (Word Recognition and Comprehension)

Suitable	*Unsuitable*
Comprehension 5 *Questions* – 3½ – 5 correct 10 *Questions* – 7 – 10 correct	Comprehension 5 *Questions* – 0 – 3 correct 10 *Questions* – 0 – 6 correct

Word Recognition		Word Recognition	
Number of words	Errors	Number of words	Errors
100	0- 5	100	6 or more
200	0-10	200	11 or more
300	0-15	300	16 or more
400	0-20	400	21 or more
500	0-25	500	26 or more

Remember—Errors made when pronouncing proper nouns and numerals are not counted as word recognition errors. If the survey was administered individually, the scores for *both* comprehension and word recognition must meet the criteria for suitability for the material to be classified as suitable.

helpful if you administer a series of Informal Suitability Surveys to determine the appropriateness of the different materials which you have available for use. As mentioned earlier, it is very unlikely that you will find one type of material which is suitable for all students. Your chart will guide you as you select suitable materials for different students. A sample chart follows.

Figure 3

Suitability of Materials

Names of Students	Names of Materials			
1.				
2.				
3.				
4.				
5.				
6.				
7.				
8.				
9.				
10.				
11.				
12.				
13.				
14.				
15.				
16.				
17.				
18.				
19.				
20.				
21.				
22.				
23.				
24.				
Total				

Code: U = Unsuitable
      S = Suitable

Enabling Element 4
Implications from an
Informal Suitability Survey

Specific Objective 4

After scoring the Informal Suitability Survey, you will state the specific implications of the findings for assignments that require reading.

Enabling Activities

*1. Read Study Guide 4, "Implications From An Informal Suitability Survey." Determine specific classroom practices that are desirable as you use the results of suitability surveys.

2. Let's assume the textbook you wanted to use is unsuitable for most of the students. What can you do? Brainstorm with your colleagues. Include the librarian in this discussion.

3. Hopefully, the text will be suitable for most of your students. What are the practices you should be implementing to help these students better comprehend the material?

4. The next time you visit a materials display or talk with sales representatives from various publishing firms, ask what low level reading materials they have available for your content area. Publishers generally try to market materials which teachers demand. If many teachers begin to request materials at different reading levels, publishers will make more materials available.

*5. Are you beginning to see how the modules in this textbook are interrelated? You can review Module 1 on determining readability levels as you evaluate textbooks and materials for their potential use. Module 2 provides suggestions for preparing teacher-made materials which are appropriate for your classes. This module helps you determine the suitability of selected

*Indicates core Enabling Activities

materials. As you progress through the modules, correlate the competencies you are developing.

Study Guide 4
Implications from an
Informal Suitability Survey

In considering the implications from an Informal Suitability Survey we must remember the purpose of the instrument. As stated in Study Guide 1 of this module, such a survey is an informal device which can be used to determine if students can handle selected content area reading material. After administering the survey you know whether the textual material is suitable or unsuitable for the different students. What are the implications of your findings?

What You Should Do If the Material Is Suitable

If the textbook or other required material is suitable you have a responsibility to introduce the specialized vocabulary words and especially the proper nouns which may cause difficulty. Module 5 on word meanings has specific suggestions for helping students develop the meanings of words. See Module 8 for ways of helping students pronounce long words.

When introducing assignments, be sure to provide students with purposes for reading. When you prepared a motivation statement in constructing your Informal Suitability Survey, you were actually providing the students with a purpose for reading. Module 9, "Motivating Reluctant Readers," has detailed examples for providing purposes as you introduce reading assignments.

Another way in which you can help the students get more from their textual materials is to continually remind them to use appropriate study strategies. Module 7 includes suggested study strategies and ways that you can demonstrate these to your students.

If the textbooks you are using include material that requires new or infrequently used reading skills, such as interpreting cartoons or graphs, discuss these materials in class. Also point out the special aids which may be available in the textbook: index, appendices, or glossary.

As you know, it is impossible to find the perfect textbook. Be prepared to suggest other resources to those students who are not challenged by the material you are using. Students generally like to be shown special interest; they will value your suggestions and appreciate your concern.

What You Can Do If the Textbook Is Unsuitable

If you have other resources available for use, you may want to develop other Informal Suitability Surveys to find out if these materials are suitable for your students. An Informal Suitability Survey is relatively easy to construct and is very economical in terms of time. Perhaps you and the other members of your department can develop a series of these surveys for matching materials to the students' capabilities. Check with the librarian to see if there are materials available of which you are unaware.

If other materials are not available, you may want to talk with the department chairman or librarian to see if new books are being ordered which cover the same concepts but are written at a lower readability level. Many publishing companies are beginning to publish books which include the same information, but are written at different reading levels. Write query letters to some of your favorite publishers to see what materials are available. Of course, if the textbook is unsuitable for most of your students, you will want to consider selecting new textbooks. Remember to determine the readability of textual materials which you are considering.

If you do not have any suitable materials for some of the students, perhaps you can have some of the better readers read the most important parts of the text on a tape to which other students can listen. Many times students are able to understand better through listening than reading.

There are many ways of gathering information rather than reading. If you use audio-visual materials in your class you can help the students develop concepts by seeing and hearing. In addition to using many audio-visual aids, you can provide more involvement activities during class sessions. Students generally enjoy role playing, simulation activities, and group discussions.

Feel free to read some of the most difficult parts of the textual materials to your students. This will provide an opportunity for the students to listen and learn, and at the same time be able to notice your model of reading. If you use expression by varying your rate, volume, and pitch, you can make the textbook come alive. Also, remember to use the illustrations, charts, and tables which are in the textbook.

You may want to develop some handouts which are appropriate for the students. The suggestions in Module 2 will be valuable for this purpose. Some teachers like to develop the handouts with their classes and then put them on a ditto. The latter procedure can be especially valuable when concluding a unit of study. The title of the handout might concern "big ideas" or "things to remember" about the topic being studied.

Perhaps the most important fact to keep in mind is that students who are having difficulty reading can survive in the content areas if you make these adaptations. Many times poor readers are labeled as lazy, uninterested, turned off, and slow. If you read the article, "Teachers Don't Want to Be Labeled," which was used as a sample in Module 1, you will realize that everyone is slow, average, gifted, interested, and uninterested, depending on the task at hand. Students and adults generally avoid those tasks that are difficult or frustrating. Just because you have students who are reluctant to read does not mean they are reluctant to learn. Module 10, "Identifying and Helping Problem Readers," has even more suggestions for you. Commit yourself to this challenge rather than "writing off" those who cannot read.

Post-test

Directions: The following questions are designed to test your accomplishment of the objectives in this module. Check your responses with the answers on the following pages to determine if you have met the objectives of this module. You can recycle as necessary after checking your responses.

1. Describe an Informal Suitability Survey and state the major purpose for using one in your classes.

2. Outline and explain the three major procedures involved in constructing such a survey.

3. List the major procedures for administering the survey as a group test.

4. What information can you get from an individually administered survey that cannot be obtained when you administer one to a group?

5. Let us suppose you are a math teacher and you individually administered the following 200-word Informal Suitability Survey to John who was absent the day you administered the survey to the group. Is the selection suitable?

Solving Math Problems Stated in Paragraph Form

The first step in solving mathematical problems which are written in paragraph form is to read the problems carefully to determine what you are supposed to find. After knowing this, reread the problem to find the relevant or irrelevant facts. For example, sometimes problems include facts which are not necessary to find the answer to the problem. The fact that Mrs. Jones waited in line for 12 minutes may be interesting, but it does not help you determine how much change she should receive considering her purchase.

The next step is to decide what process you must use to find the answer. Remember that sometimes it is necessary to use two or three processes in order to answer the question. For example, if it says that Mrs. Jones bought three cans of milk at 19 cents a can, you must multiply the cost of the milk and then add this to the other groceries. Of course it would be necessary then to subtract the total cost from the amount given to find how much change she should receive.

After you have done the computation, you should ask yourself if the answer makes sense. If it does not, check your computation and question the process that you used./200 words

Comprehension Questions:
V = Vocabulary, F = Factual, I = Inference

   a. (F) What is the first step in doing math problems that are stated in paragraph form?
   b. (V) What does *irrelevant* mean?
   c. (F) What are ways of checking your answer?
   d. (F) After you determine the question the question that is asked and the relevant facts, what is the next step to solve the math problem?
   e. (I) Why are irrelevant facts sometimes included in math problems that are stated in paragraph form?

John's Answers to the Comprehension Questions:

   a. The first step in doing a math problem which appears in paragraph form is to determine what you are supposed to find.
   b. *Irrelevant* means uninteresting.
   c. You can check your answers by questioning the process you used or by redoing the computation.
   d. Decide what process you should use to find the answer.
   e. The book tries to get you mixed up. The teacher is trying to fool you.
   6. Given the above information concerning John, state three things you should do as his instructor.
   7. If John scored 100 percent when you administered an Informal Suitability Survey to the class as a group, what are your responsibilities?

Answers to the Post-test

1. An Informal Suitability Survey consists of a representative selection from textual material you are planning to use; accompanying motivation statement; and questions to check comprehension. It is designed to determine if students can handle selected textual material.

2. The major procedures involved in constructing a survey are as follows:
   a. Select a 200-word passage which is representative of the reading material in a commonly used textbook or other written material. Skip all proper nouns and numerals when counting the 200 words and then mark the 200th word with a slash. (The selection may be more than 200 words.)
   b. Write a motivation statement to give the students a purpose for reading.
   c. Write three factual questions, one vocabulary question, and one inferential question.

3. The procedures for administering a survey as a group test are as follows:

   Prepare dittoed copies of the selection including a motivation statement. Also make copies of the accompanying questions. Make sure you have fifteen to thirty minutes available. Tell the students you want to determine how well they can read the selection so that you can identify useful teaching materials. Distribute the selection and questions. Have the students read it and answer the questions. Collect and score the test items.

4. Information concerning the student's skill in recognizing words while reading orally is obtained when a survey is administered individually.

5. John's word recognition and comprehension errors for this selection indicate the selection is unsuitable. He made eleven word recognition errors in this 200-word selection and missed two or more of the five questions.

6. You might have some of the better students read parts of the textual material on tape. You may be able to find this same information presented in a textbook which has a lower readability level. Finally, you may put a problem on the board and explain the same procedures which were described in the selection. Perhaps John can listen to you and can understand it even though he is not able to read it by himself and understand it.

7. If the material were suitable, you would still have to introduce new vocabulary words and provide the student with a purpose for reading.

Final Comment

The use of the Informal Suitability Survey technique will help you determine the appropriateness of instructional materials for your students and thus lessen the likelihood of frustrated readers in your classes. The results should yield a higher number of completed reading assignments. Now that you understand the concept of an Informal Suitability Survey, you should be able to administer one without extensive preparation. For example, you can take a book off a shelf, read a selection rapidly, mentally note a motivation statement and comprehensive questions, and administer the survey. Duplication of materials may not always be necessary.

If you have completed all the Post-test items with accuracy, you are ready for another module. If not, refer to the appropriate Enabling Element for clarification of your difficulty. If you cannot clarify the difficulty, contact your instructor.

Selected Bibliography

Cushenbery, D. C. *Remedial Reading in the Secondary School.* West Nyack, New York: Parker, 1972.

Emery, R. C., and Houshower, M. B. *High Interest-Easy Reading for Junior and Senior High School Reluctant Readers.* Champaign, Illinois: National Council of Teachers of English, 1965.

Hafner, L. E. *Improving Reading in Middle and Secondary Schools: Selected Readings.* 2d ed. New York: Macmillan, 1974.

Johnson, M. S. and Kress, R. A. "Informal Reading Inventories." *Reading Aids Series,* Newark, Delaware: International Reading Association, 1965.

Karlin, R. *Teaching Reading in High School.* 2nd ed. Indianapolis: Bobbs-Merrill, 1972.

Marksheffel, N. D. *Better Reading in the Secondary School.* New York: Ronald Press, 1966.

Mavrogenes, N. A.; Winkley, C. K.; Hanson, E.; and Vacca R. J. "Concise Guide to Standardized Secondary and College Reading Tests." *Journal of Reading,* 1974, *18,* 12–22.

Rakes, T. A. "A Group Instructional Inventory." *Journal of Reading,* 1975, *18,* 595–98.

Schubert, D. G., and Torgenson, T. L. *Improving the Reading Program.* Dubuque, Iowa: William C. Brown, 1972.

Shepherd, D. L. *Comprehensive High School Reading Methods.* Columbus, Ohio: Charles Merrill, 1973.

Smith, E. D.; Guice, B. M.; and Cheek, M. C. "Informal Reading Inventories for the Content Areas: Science and Mathematics." *Elementary English,* *49,* 1972.

Stine, D. E. "Tenth Grade Content—Fourth Grade Reading Level." *Journal of Reading,* 1971, *14,* 559–61.

Strang, R.; McCullough, C. M.; and Traxler, A. E. *The Improvement of Reading.* 4th ed. New York: McGraw-Hill, 1967.

Thomas, E. L., and Robinson, H. A. *Improving Reading in Every Class: A Sourcebook for Teachers.* Boston: Allyn and Bacon, 1972.

Umans, S. *New Trends in Reading Instruction.* New York: Teachers College Press, 1963.

Module 4

Diagnosing Reading Skill Needs in Content Areas

CONTENTS

Prospectus

Rationale

Students often fail in content areas because they have not acquired the reading skills which are essential for success in these areas. If teachers are aware of the skills needed for effective reading in their content area, they can help students master these skills and thereby increase the students' likelihood of success in subject areas.

An essential step in helping students become effective readers of content area materials is diagnosing their reading needs. The focus of this module is on determining if students have acquired the reading skills that are necessary for success in specific subject areas. The module is not designed to make content area teachers "reading teachers." Content teachers are not responsible for teaching beginning reading skills. However, content teachers can and should help students develop related vocabulary, comprehension, study strategies, higher level word pronunciation skills, and specialized reading skills that are a natural part of their subject areas. Detailed descriptions of the reading skills for various content areas are presented in this module along with practical suggestions for constructing, administering, scoring, and using the results of reading skills tests.

The suggestions for diagnosis provided in this module can be implemented as a routine part of the daily program. The ideas do not require extensive but rather minimal instructional changes. These minor changes will enhance your understanding of the interests and motivation of your students.

Objectives

TERMINAL OBJECTIVE: You will use reading skills tests to determine if students have acquired the reading skills related to your content area.

Specific Objectives:

1. You will state the reading skills which are necessary to read materials in your content area.

2. You will construct reading skills tests to determine the reading skill needs of students in your content area classes.

3. You will administer, score, and use the results from reading skills tests in your content area.

Resources and Time Required

In completing this module you will need textbooks and other commonly required reading materials used in your subject area. Paper is needed for developing the reading skills tests. If you have completed Modules 1 and 2 concerning readability, you may want to have Fry's graph available to check and perhaps alter the readability level of your test items; however, it is not essential to have completed Modules 1 and 2 before doing this module. The estimated time to complete the starred core Enabling Activities is three to five hours.

Directions: For each question, determine the word that indicates your belief regarding your competency. If you are in doubt, choose NO.

1. All content areas require some special reading skills due to the nature of the material. Can you state the reading skills which are necessary to read materials in your subject area classes? YES NO

2. Content area teachers are responsible for teaching the specialized reading skills which are necessary to read subject area materials. The first step in teaching is to determine the needs of students. Have you constructed a battery of reading skills tests to determine the reading skill needs of students in your content area? YES NO

3. After you develop or obtain reading skills tests, you must use them with your students. Can you administer, score, and use the results from reading skills tests in your content area? YES NO

Branching Program Alternatives for Pre-test Responses

1. You are ready for Enabling Element 2 if you already know the skills needed to read materials in your content areas. If you are uncertain of the reading skills required for your content area, you will find Enabling Element 1 very valuable.

2. Enabling Element 2 is designed to help you construct reading skills tests to determine which students have or have not accomplished the skills needed for reading your content area materials. If you have a battery of reading skills tests go on to Enabling Element 3. If not, Enabling Element 2 will be valuable because it includes specific instructions and many model tests.

3. Suggestions for administering, scoring and using the results of reading skills tests are presented in Enabling Element 3. Do this Enabling Element if you need practical ideas for actually using the reading skills tests to provide for the individual needs of your students. If you can already do so, you are ready for the Post-test.

Enabling Element 1
Skills Necessary for
Reading Content Area Materials

Specific Objective 1

You will state the reading skills which are necessary to read materials in your content area.

Enabling Activities

*1. Read Study Guide 1, "Skills Necessary for Reading Content Area Materials." Determine the reading skills which students need to read successfully in your content area.

2. Read the separate skill lists for the different content areas in Study Guide 1. Are there similar skills which are needed to read in all content areas? What are the differences?

3. State some examples of reading skills needed for success in content areas. After doing so, state why it is impossible for children to develop all the reading skills during the elementary school years (grades one through six.)

4. Evaluate your own reading. Do you continue to develop more skill in reading? Discuss the implications with your colleagues.

*5. Look through various textbooks and written materials which you commonly use with your students. Find specific examples of the reading skills needed for success in your content area. For example, look for specialized vocabulary and symbols. Note any tables, diagrams, charts, or illustrations. Consider the skills and knowledge that are necessary to use specialized reference materials in your content area. You will be able to use some of these materials and ideas as you actually construct skill tests.

*Indicates core Enabling Activities

Study Guide 1
Skills Necessary for Reading
Content Area Materials

In addition to determining if the students can read textbooks and other commonly required reading materials, many content teachers want to know if the students have developed the specific reading skills which are necessary to succeed in their content area. For example, most content teachers have the following reading-related questions about their students:

1. Can they use textbooks correctly? That is, the table of contents, index, list of illustrations, appendices, bibliography, and/or the glossary.

2. Can the students read and interpret tables, graphs, diagrams, and cartoons?

3. Do the students recognize and understand the specialized vocabulary of the content area?

4. Can the students use reference materials: encyclopedias, almanacs, *Reader's Guide to Periodical Literature,* dictionary, and supplemental reference books?

5. Do the students know the meanings of special symbols and formulas?

6. Are the students using appropriate study skills and habits?

7. Can the students outline and take notes?

8. Can the students use a flexible rate of reading?

9. Can the students evaluate what they read?

10. Can the students read to note the main ideas, significant details, sequence of events, and conclusions?

Of course, these reading skills vary in importance and use in different content areas. A mathematics teacher is more concerned about whether students can interpret symbols than about taking notes and outlining. Each content area teacher's task then is to be aware of the reading skills that are necessary for success in her area. After doing so, it is possible to construct simple skill tests to determine the reading needs of the students in each content area.

Listed below are general lists of reading skills required to read material in different content areas: art, business education, English language arts, foreign languages, health, homemaking, industrial arts, mathematics, music, physical education, science, social studies, and speech and drama. Read the list which includes the reading skills that are most important for success in your subject area. As you read these skill lists you might be thinking of specific examples and ways of determining whether or not your students can demonstrate the skills. Study Guide 2 of this module includes information on how to construct reading skills tests to measure accomplishment of these reading skills.

Art

Generally, students in art classes must be able to:

1. Develop the specialized vocabulary which includes such words as *acetone, asymmetric, batik, bisque, burnish, engrave, frontage, grog, lithography, vermiculite,* and *abstract expressionism.*
2. Analyze prefixes, suffixes, and stems of technical terms for their specific word meaning.
3. Follow directions exactly as for firing ceramic products.
4. Take notes when listening to lectures or reading about various media or well known artists.
5. Locate and use reference materials with information about art criticism and the history of art.
6. Read critically to note viewpoints and see relationships among various aspects of different cultures.
7. Read diagrams such as an illustration of how to make some leather project requiring a certain type of stitching.
8. Adjust rate of reading to purpose and the nature of the material.

Business Education

Students in business education classes, such as accounting, bookkeeping, business mathematics and typing, must be able to:

1. Recognize symbols quickly, such as in typing or transferring information to different forms.
2. Read in phrases at a rapid rate as is required in typing.

3. Follow written directions accurately as in using different types of typewriters, copy machines, calculators, or in keeping detailed records such as a payroll register.

4. Understand the meaning of technical terms such as *division of labor, synthetic, profit, technology, consignment,* and *proprietorship.*

5. Read graphs, charts, and diagrams such as in a cash receipts journal, eight column worksheet, and balance sheets.

6. Comprehend material which is commonly presented in textbooks. Emphasis is on noticing significant details, major ideas, following specific directions, and applying a study strategy such as SQ3R.

7. Use the different parts of reference books such as handbooks for secretaries or accountants.

8. Rapidly alphabetize materials such as is required in filing or locating records.

9. Critically read application forms, invoices, tax forms, and legal papers.

English Language Arts

Reading is required extensively for success in the English language arts area. In most schools English teachers have the major responsibility for teaching word recognition skills, locational and study skills, as well as the skills necessary to read different types of literature. Specifically, students in English classes must be able to:

1. Understand word meanings and use word pronunciation techniques by using context clues, structural analysis skills, phonics, and the dictionary.

2. Read literature to identify significant details, central ideas, mood, sensory images, sequence of ideas, relationships among ideas, and make inferences about characters, settings, and events.

3. Organize ideas into an outline, summarize, take notes from a book or lecture, and identify the patterns used by the authors.

4. Understand specialized vocabulary such as *adjective, figurative language, infinitive phrase, inside address,* and *collective noun.*

5. Learn how to develop a flexible rate of reading in order to read different types of literature: poetry, drama, fiction, nonfiction, and so forth.

6. Critically evaluate what is read by determining the author's purpose, distinguishing facts from opinion, identifying propaganda techniques, and identifying characteristics of good writing.

7. Use the card catalogue, the *Reader's Guide to Periodical Literature,* and other reference materials to locate different information.

8. Develop scope and depth of vocabulary by studying word origins, slang, idioms, denotations and connotations of words, multiple meanings, and word relationships such as synonyms, antonyms, and homonyms.

9. Read creatively by responding to the author's ideas.

10. Develop skill in using reference materials such as dictionaries, encyclopedias, and a thesaurus.

Foreign Language

Students in foreign language classes must be able to:

1. Read orally using correct pronunciation and appropriate phrasing and expression.

2. Distinguish between sounds which are similar.

3. Memorize vocabulary and associate the foreign words with their English counterparts.

4. Comprehend idiomatic expressions.

5. Recognize differences and likenesses in sentence structure and grammar.

6. Use resource books to learn more about the culture and customs of the foreign country.

7. Develop specialized vocabulary words such as *cognates, tense, stem-changing verbs, present perfect subjunctive,* and *auxiliary verbs.*

8. Learn the etymology of words in different languages.

9. Develop skill in using dictionaries to locate words and phrases, pronounce different words, and determine multiple meanings.

10. Develop skill in using aids which are available in the textbooks such as a glossary, vocabulary list, practice exercises, and suggestions for studying.

Health

To be successful in health, students must be able to:

1. Use a study technique such as SQ3R.
2. Understand the technical vocabulary such as *respiratory, tissue, endocrine, ductless glands, personality,* and *convulsion.*
3. Determine the main ideas and important details in selections.
4. Read graphs such as a graph of life expectancy in the United States.
5. Outline and take notes from required reading and lectures.
6. Read diagrams such as those which show the parts of the body.
7. Read charts such as a chart of the characteristics of commonly used drugs.
8. Use an index, appendices, and other textual aids.
9. Read and follow specific directions as required in using first aid.

Homemaking

Homemaking includes such courses as home economics, clothing, bachelor living, child development, and interior decorating. In these courses, students must be able to:

1. Use appropriate reading rates and study methods to read textbooks, articles, and pamphlets.
2. Read and follow directions such as those that are found in recipes.
3. Read bills and statements accurately using the various codes that are available.
4. Read specialized abbreviations, signs, and symbols such as are found in recipes and labels.
5. Read specialized materials such as a thermometer, meters, invoices, and legal forms.
6. Interpret charts, graphs, diagrams, patterns, drawings, and cutaways.

7. Read carefully to understand the instructions for operating various appliances.
8. Critically read newspapers, catalogue and magazine articles including advertisements.
9. Read labels to note ingredients, directions, and cautions.
10. Learn the specialized vocabulary such as *sauté, marinate, gel, burnet,* and *dice.*
11. Determine main ideas, significant details, sequence of events, and see relationships among this information.

Industrial Arts
Industrial arts requires reading skills. Students must be able to:

1. Use the aids that are available in various manuals: indexes, glossaries, list of manufacturers, and so forth.
2. Read and follow safety rules and instructions for care of equipment.
3. Read detailed instructions to produce or repair particular products such as carburetors.
4. Understand the technical vocabulary such as *abrasive materials, arc welding, chamfer, bevel, compression ratio of engines, cotter pin, pumice stone, ripsaw, tannin,* and *whipstitch.*
5. Read and interpret drawings, cutaways, and patterns.
6. Understand explanations and instructions as found in technical books or journals.
7. Read specialized symbols and abbreviations which are used in many illustrations and directions.
8. Read detailed diagrams such as a cross section of a water faucet, an exploded view of a valve-stem assembly, or blueprint for making a portable classroom.
9. Read tables such as the uses, colors, and strengths of different plastics.

Mathematics
In order to succeed in mathematics students must be able to:

1. Read detailed material slowly to determine the significant and insignificant facts.

2. Read visual materials such as diagrams and geometric forms.
3. Remember the meanings of symbols and abbreviations.
4. Interpret materials used to express relationships: principles, axioms, formulas, and equations.
5. Proofread carefully to locate errors.
6. Locate and read reference materials concerning famous mathematicians such as Galois, Fermat, and Leibniz.
7. Read tables such as a table of squares and square roots or common logarithms of numbers.
8. Read various types of graphs such as a bar graph, line graph, pictograph, and flowcharts.
9. Understand the specialized vocabulary such as *transitive property, integer, vector, quadratic, function* and *tangent.*
10. Follow directions precisely as in detailed explanations of various processes which require step-by-step operations.
11. Understand common stems, prefixes, and suffixes.
12. Use an appropriate study strategy for reading verbal problems.
13. Critically analyze statistical records such as tax data and financial reports.
14. Use an index, table of contents, or other aids to locate information quickly.

Music

It is no surprise that many reading skills are required in music. The students must be able to:

1. Read the words of songs and divide words into syllables.
2. Understand the meanings of specialized music terms such as *adagio, cantata, exposition, impressionism, prelude, recapitulation, vibrato,* and *timbre.*
3. Read about the lives of musicians and the history of music by employing a study strategy such as SQ3R and an appropriate rate of reading.
4. Learn the specialized symbols and notations required to read music.
5. Evaluate critical reviews by noticing the author's bias.

6. Use special reference books such as a dictionary of musical terms, indexes of literature in music and so forth.

7. Use aids in textbooks such as an index of songs, classified indexes, and so forth.

8. Read different types of literature to appreciate the setting in which the music was written.

Physical Education

Even though many physical education teachers do not require textbooks because their classes usually meet on the field, there are several reading skills which are related to physical education. For an example, students must:

1. Read and follow directions accurately as in noticing the rules for playing various games.

2. Remember details such as the measurements of courts, various positions of the body, and ways of scoring.

3. Read diagrams of plays used in different sports.

4. Read books and articles about different sporting events and characters to note major ideas, significant details, sequence of events, and conclusions.

5. Learn the technical vocabulary such as *fault, love, armdrag, hammerlock, dead ball, anchor, seeded,* and *bootleg play.*

6. Read signals as used by referees in the various games.

7. Read illustrations such as diagrams of a squash court, lacrosse field, or a basketball court.

8. Read charts such as records of World Series games, various champions, and so forth.

9. Locate reference materials with information about sports: *World Almanac,* football guides, and so forth.

Science

An efficient reader of science materials must be able to develop the following related reading skills:

1. Understand the special and technical vocabulary of science such as *angle of reflection, cumulus, electrode, fulcrum, inertia, isotope, ion,* and *conduction.*

2. Understand how details support and illustrate the main ideas, such as in scientific laws.

3. Organize ideas from reading and understand relationships by drawing conclusions and making inferences and judgments.

4. Differentiate facts from opinions.

5. Interpret graphic and visual materials such as weather maps or a diagram of how a refrigerator operates.

6. Read and follow directions as required in doing experiments, such as determining how much light is absorbed and reflected by various materials.

7. Use library skills to locate research, various journals, U.S. government publications, and other reference materials.

8. Apply some study techniques such as PQRST or SQ3R.

9. Analyze words through their stem, prefix and suffix.

10. Read symbols, formulas, and abbreviations.

11. Predict outcomes while reading.

12. Use an appropriate reading rate depending upon materials and purpose.

Social Studies

Social studies teachers need to be aware of the many reading skills which are required for reading in their area. Specifically, students must be able to:

1. Apply some study strategy such as SQ3R.

2. Recognize cause and effect relationships.

3. Read maps (population, rainfall, physical, political, soil, etc.), tables, charts, graphs, and cartoons.

4. Take notes in outline form from a book or other assigned reading.

5. Use library skills such as *Reader's Guide to Periodical Literature,* the card catalog, and the various skills which are required to use reference materials such as encyclopedias and almanacs.

6. Read critically to interpret propaganda techniques, compare and contrast situations, and to distinguish fact from opinion.

7. Find the main idea and supporting details in reading selections.

8. Understand time and space relationships.

9. Be able to use the different parts of a book: summaries, chapter introductions, vocabulary lists, glossaries, preface, and footnotes.

10. Learn specialized vocabulary such as *alliance, autonomy, butte, coniferous, equinox, ingot, typhoon,* and *sovereign.*

Speech and Drama

Many of the reading skills mentioned above are also required for students to succeed in speech and drama classes. Specifically, a student must:

1. Learn the specialized vocabulary such as *pitch, tone, power, fluff, accent, affirmative, articulation, connotative words, denasal quality, filibuster, melodrama,* and *proscenium.*

2. Read for specific directions, such as in guides to good listening, guides for making nominations speeches, and ways of organizing materials.

3. Outline and take notes that are required for preparing speeches and debates.

4. Identify the mood and tone of various characters and settings.

5. Read orally with appropriate expression, phrasing, and rate.

6. Locate reference materials that may be needed in preparing speeches or plays.

7. Critically evaluate what is read, and creatively respond to the ideas, such as in debate preparations.

8. Notice the author's organization and purpose for writing.

Enabling Element 2
Constructing Reading Skills Tests

Specific Objective 2

You will construct reading skills tests to determine the reading skill needs of students in your content area classes.

Enabling Activities

*1. Read Study Guide 2, "Constructing Reading Skills Tests." Identify the procedures and suggestions for making reading skills tests for your content area.

*2. Select some reading skills in your content area which were listed in Study Guide 1 and develop some reading skills tests. Use sample selections from your textbooks (tables, charts, maps, diagrams, symbols) or other appropriate materials which you expect students to read. Perhaps some of your old quizzes can be revised to serve as reading skills tests.

3. Look at some of the standardized achievement tests in your content area. Can the tests be scored in such a way that you would learn about the reading skills that different students need? If so, can you use these as supplements to the teacher-made test in order to identify the specific reading skill needs of your students?

4. Many of the newer textbooks include reading skills tests or review tests. As you evaluate textbooks for possible adoption, you may want to use this as one of your criteria. If your present books contain these skills tests, you will not have to spend as much time constructing them.

5. See Enabling Element 2 in Module 8 for a specific example of a word pronunciation test. After completing Module 8, you will be able to add this test to your battery of reading skills tests.

*Indicates core Enabling Activities

Study Guide 2
Constructing Reading Skills Tests

Most content area teachers construct achievement tests as a routine part of the teaching process. Actually, the construction of reading skills tests differs very little from regular achievement tests or quizzes. Read the three directions below and then do Practicum Exercise 1.

Step 1:   Determine the Reading Skills in Your Content Area

As in developing other tests, the teacher's first task is to determine the objectives which must be tested or evaluated. In constructing skills tests in reading, you must consider the reading skills which students should have accomplished or need to develop in order to read your content area material. Refer to the appropriate list in Study Guide 1 of this module to determine what skills you need to test. For example, if reading a graph is a necessary skill in your content area, you may want to construct a skill test to see which students can read and interpret a graph correctly.

Step 2:   Select and Prepare Sample Materials

Now that you have the reading skills clear in mind, it is necessary to select or prepare sample materials which can be used in constructing the test items. Refer to the examples below for some general ideas for selecting and preparing materials.

Reading Skill	Sample Material
1. Specialized vocabulary	Select words from the glossaries of textbooks or supplemental materials that you use.
2. Symbols, abbreviations, and formulas	Survey your most commonly used materials to see what symbols and abbreviations appear frequently. Find formulas which can be used to see if students can determine relationships.
3. Reading graphs, tables, diagrams and other visual or graphic aids	Find examples in your textbooks and then have the students use the textbooks to answer questions you have prepared.

Reading Skill	*Sample Material*
4. Following specific directions	Locate passages in some of your textual material which include specific directions as found in recipes, experiments, and ''how to'' articles.
5. Using reference materials	List the reference materials which are available in your content area and develop questions to see if students know what is in the different reference materials and how to use them.
6. Using textbooks correctly	Notice the different aids in your textbooks such as preface, index, vocabulary lists, appendices, and so forth. Design questions which will help you determine if the students know how to use these aids.
7. Outlining and note taking	Select a passage which can be outlined or from which notes can be taken. Direct the students to outline the material and then evaluate the form they use.
8. Flexible rate of reading	Select different passages from textual materials which you commonly use. Provide the students with a purpose for reading each selection and then ask them to indicate the appropriate rate at which the selection should be read: slow, normal, or rapid.
9. Evaluating critically	Provide a passage and prepare questions which ask students to detect propaganda, judge the author's purpose, or distinguish fact from opinion.
10. Reading creatively	Find a selection to which the students can react. Write a general question to obtain their reactions.

Reading Skill	*Sample Material*
11. Noticing the main idea, significant details, sequence of events	Again you will need to select passages and then write questions to see if the students can give you the gist of the selection, the most important details, and/or the sequence of events.
12. Drawing conclusions and making inferences	Passages which require students to draw conclusions or make inferences are needed for testing this skill. The suggestions which are included in Module 3 on how to write inference questions may be of value to you as you try to design questions for the passages.
13. Analyzing prefixes, suffixes, and stems	Make a list of affixes and stems which are commonly found in your content area and ask the students to define them or give sample words.
14. Recognizing symbols quickly – visual perception	Prepare a list of symbols which can be flashed on an overhead projector and ask the students to write the symbol as quickly as possible.
15. Using an appropriate study strategy	Make an assignment and ask the students to write down the procedures they used in doing the reading assignment. The check list which is provided in this study guide may also be used. See also Module 7.
16. Reading specialized forms	Provide samples of application forms, legal forms, invoices, and design a list of questions to see if students can read and interpret these samples.
17. Reading in phrases	Select passages and ask the students to make slashes between the appropriate phrases. If you have time, listen to the students read orally as this is another effective way to determine if students can read in phrases.

Reading skill	*Sample Material*
18. Word pronunciation	Prepare a list of specialized vocabulary words which are in your content area. Ask the students to read your list of words to determine if they have difficulty in pronouncing words. See Module 8, Enabling Element 2, for a model test.
19. Oral reading	Of course you will be checking oral reading with Informal Suitability Surveys if you administer them individually. If not, provide opportunities for the students to read orally to you and as they do so, check their phrasing, expression, rate, and articulation.

Some content teachers extract materials from the textbooks or actually use the textbooks when administering reading skills tests. For example, if you would like to determine if the students can use an index, it is appropriate to construct a quiz which requires the students to use the index in their textbook. In other words, constructing reading skills tests does not require extensive preparation if you use materials which are commonly available.

Step 3: Plan the Format of the Test

Your final step is to determine what format should be used in constructing the test items. Should you provide multiple choice questions, true-false questions, short answer, matching exercises, or essay questions? Of course your response to this question would depend upon the nature of the skills which you are testing and the time which you have available for scoring papers. Another consideration is how much mastery you expect of the different skills. For example, generally matching exercises do not require as much mastery of knowledge as do short answer items. Keep in mind the advantages and disadvantages of different types of items and then make your decision. After doing so, write the directions for completing the test.

Practicum Exercise

Sample reading skills tests follow. Examine these examples and use them as models for constructing tests for the reading skills needed in your content area. After reviewing these tests, follow the preceding directions to develop some reading skills tests for your content classes.

Sample Skill Test
Using a Textbook

Explanation to the Teacher: The purpose of this skill test is to determine if the students can use the different parts of a textbook. Your students should get 100 percent correct.

Directions to the Student: Use your textbook to answer the following questions.

1. Who is the author? What are her qualifications?
2. When was the book copyrighted?
3. What is the purpose of each part of the book?
4. Is there a list of tables? Figures?
5. Does the book have an index? When will you use this?
6. Are there pictures and diagrams to help you learn?
7. How are the chapters organized?
8. How are definitions of new words presented?
9. What aids are included at the end of each chapter?
10. Are there any appendices? What information is included in the appendices? How can this information help you?

Sample Skill Test
Symbols in Mathematics

Explanation to the Teacher: This skill test is designed to determine if students can match mathematical symbols with their meanings. You may want to construct such a test which includes the most frequently used symbols in your course.

Directions to the Student: Match the definition with the symbol by placing the appropriate letter in the blanks provided.

_____ 1. +   a. since; because
_____ 2. −   b. is greater than

_____ 3. =   c. degrees
_____ 4. <   d. difference between
_____ 5. >   e. plus; positive
_____ 6. ≧   f. pi; equal to 3.14159+
_____ 7. ≠   g. is equal to
_____ 8. ○   h. is less than
_____ 9. ∩   i. minus; negative
_____10. ∴   j. intersection
_____11. π   k. is equal to, or greater than
_____12. − :   l. not equal to

Sample Skill Test
Reading Tables

Explanation to the Teacher: The purpose of this skill test is to determine if students can read different tables and graphs. Find a representative table and graph in the text. Write five to ten questions which require students to interpret the information. Direct them to look at the table/graph on a particular page and answer the questions. Check together. Sample questions for tables are:

1. What is the title of the table?
2. What is the unit of measurement?
3. What are the column (vertical) and row (horizontal) headings?
4. What is the significance of the table?
5. How can you use the information from the table?

In addition, write five questions which require the student to read the table.

Sample questions for graphs are:

1. What type of graph is used?
2. What is the unit of measurement?
3. What information is presented?
4. How is the information arranged?
5. What symbols are used? What do these symbols mean?
6. What is the significance of the information presented in the graph?

Sample Skill Test
Using Reference Books

Explanation to the Teacher: Construct an informal skill test which requires the student to use some commonly used reference such as the *World Almanac, Reader's Guide to Periodical Literature,* encyclopedia, etc. Have the students use the material as they answer the questions.

Explanation to the Student: Answer the following questions using the current *World Almanac.*

1. What kinds of information are presented in an almanac?
2. Why are almanacs valuable?
3. Where is the index in an almanac?
4. On what page would you find information about New Jersey?
5. What kind of information is presented about New Jersey?
6. On what page would you find information about the Catholic religion?
7. What page tells you about telephones in the United States?

Sample Skill Test
Vocabulary

Explanation to the Teacher: This is a sample vocabulary test to see if the students have mastered words that are commonly used in a business education class. By administering this test, you get some idea of the students' concepts of the different words.

Directions to the Student: Define the following terms with concise responses.

1. Assets–
2. Balance sheet–
3. Certified check–
4. Collator–
5. I.T.W.–
6. Excise tax–
7. F.I.C.A.–

8. Liabilities–

9. Net pay–

10. Promissory notes–

11. Voucher–

12. Requisition–

Sample Skill Test
Vocabulary

Explanation to the Teacher: The following test is designed to measure the students' knowledge of vocabulary. Notice this is a matching test which does not require as much mastery of the knowledge as in the short answer test.

Directions to the Students: Match the words with the definitions by writing the letters from the right hand column in front of the words which match in the left hand column.

1. _____ style

2. _____ amino acids

3. _____ mitosis

4. _____ cell

5. _____ anther

6. _____ hormone

7. _____ muscle

8. _____ coccus

9. _____ instinct

10. _____ pistil

a. The pollen-bearing portion of the male reproduction organ of flowering plants

b. A spherically shaped bacterium

c. Automatic, unlearned behavior

d. Organic compounds that are the building blocks of proteins

e. The basic structural unit of life

f. The female portion of a flower, usually consisting of ovary, style and stigma

g. A secretion of the endocrine gland that controls and coordinates cell and organ functions

h. The process by which the nucleus duplicates prior to cell division

i. An organ or tissue that can contract to produce motion

j. The slender stalk of the pistil of a flower

Sample Skill Test
Study Skills Survey

Explanation to the Teacher: No one knows more about the secondary student's study skills than the student herself. This survey is designed as a self-evaluation to be completed by the students. You can also use it as an observation guide as you work with the students.

Explanation to the Student: Place a check mark in the appropriate column (usually, sometimes, never) which describes how often you use the following study skills.

Questions	*My Habits*		
	Never	Sometimes	Usually
1. Do you survey or glance at the selection before reading it?			
2. Do you raise questions before reading?			
3. Do you adjust your rate as you read? For example, slow down for more difficult material?			
4. Do you try to pronounce and define words in italics?			
5. Do you look for the major ideas and supporting details?			
6. Can you outline the major ideas and supporting details?			
7. Do you answer your questions as you read?			
8. Do you review when you are finished reading?			
9. Are you able to concentrate as you study?			
10. Do you schedule time for study?			

Enabling Element 3
Administering, Scoring, and Using the Results of Reading Skills Tests

Specific Objective 3

You will administer, score, and use the results from reading skills tests in your content area.

Enabling Activities

*1. Read Study Guide 3, "Administering, Scoring, and Using the Results from Reading Skills Tests." Note the suggestions concerning when to administer the tests, how to score and record the results, and the implications for using the results.

*2. Administer some reading skills tests to determine if your students have acquired the reading skills necessary for reading your content area materials.

*3. Make a skills chart to record the reading needs of your students in your content area and use this completed record chart to list skill groups. Modules 5, 6, 7, and 8 will provide many valuable suggestions for teaching some of the reading skills.

4. Establish a skill center which includes materials and activities designed to help students develop a specific reading skill. Obtain the cooperation of the librarian and perhaps other teachers in planning a series of skill centers which are located in the library or media center.

5. Form one skill group with students who need to develop a particular reading skill. Plan three or four lessons concerning the skill. As you conduct your lessons make sure you help the students realize the value of the skill as well as how to acquire the skill or knowledge. Evaluate the reactions of these students

*Indicates core Enabling Activities

and ask yourself if skill groups are helpful. We believe the results you obtain over a period of time will motivate you to continue using skill groups as a technique for providing for individual differences.

Study Guide 3
Administering, Scoring, and Using the Results from Reading Skills Tests

Administering Reading Skills Tests

Now that you have constructed reading skills tests which are pertinent to your content area, it is necessary to try them with the students. Some teachers like to administer the tests at the beginning of the course so they can determine their students' reading needs immediately. This information then can be used in helping the students throughout the semester, quarter, or quinmester. Other teachers use the skills tests as pretests before the unit where the skills are most likely to be used.

Remember the purpose of the reading skills tests is to determine if the students have the prerequisite reading skills to get the most out of their textbooks and supplemental materials. The general guideline then should be to administer the tests early in the semester or immediately before the skills are needed so you can provide the necessary instruction. Of course, diagnosis is most useful when it is continuous. Certainly one of your most important diagnostic devices is observation of students as they read different types of material and respond to your questions. The task of diagnosis is never completed—you are continually evaluating students to determine their instructional needs.

When administering the skill tests, simply tell the students you want to see what they have learned in other classes. Indicate that grades will not be given, but rather the results will be used to help you teach the skills which will help them get more out of their reading. After the tests, informally talk with the students to discuss what they have learned about various reading skills.

Scoring Reading Skills Tests

As indicated, grades are not given for diagnostic reading skills tests. The purpose of the tests is to help you become aware of the reading skill needs of the students. Since this is the case, it will be necessary to evaluate the responses to determine the questions, words, and items which were frequently missed. This analysis will help you know exactly what to teach.

You may want to set a *criterion reference* for scoring a test and then divide the responses into two groups: students who were able to meet the criterion and those who were not able to. For example, you may decide students must get eight out of ten items correct in order to demonstrate accomplishment of the skill. If you do use a criterion reference, you are advised to examine the items which are missed frequently to pinpoint the instructional needs of your students.

A word of caution: If many students miss an item, evaluate the item to make sure it is not too difficult to read or understand. Continually improve your skill tests to make them valid and reliable. Also, if you are making your tests criterion referenced, it is better to set the criterion after you have given the test several times to determine what standards are realistic.

Using Results from Reading Skills Tests

One method of recording the results from reading skills tests that is economical in terms of time and yet very valuable for noticing the instructional needs of the students, is a *skills chart*. Skills charts include a list of skills at the top and the names of each student on the left hand column. A check mark can be placed under the skills by the student's name to indicate successful accomplishment of the skill. You can then glance at the skills chart (see Figure 4) to determine the students who need special help in developing the required reading skills.

Now that you have identified the needs of your students, it is time for instruction. If reading skills are needed by most of the students, you might have a total group instruction. For example, if you want your students to know how to read tables, and most of the students were unable to do so on the skills test, you can develop some lessons that will help them learn to read tables through a group presentation.

Perhaps half of the students demonstrated accomplishment of a skill while the other students did not. In this case, you may want to have a *skill group* designed to help students accomplish this skill. Skill groups are temporary groups in that they are dissolved when most of the

Related Reading Skills in Social Studies

Names of Students	Use of SQ3R Study Method	Read and Interpret Tables	Read Rainfall Maps	Use Index	Vocabulary	Detect Propaganda	Use World Almanac
1. Jimmy		✓	✓	✓	✓	✓	✓
2. Alfonso	✓	✓	✓	✓✓			✓✓
3. Joseph	✓	✓		✓✓	✓✓		✓✓
4. Jennifer		✓	✓		✓✓	✓✓	
5. Mykel	✓	✓		✓✓	✓✓	✓✓	✓
6. Mark		✓					✓
7. Carlos	✓✓	✓	✓				
8. Alice	✓✓	✓✓		✓✓	✓		✓✓
9. May		✓✓		✓✓		✓	✓✓
10. Sally	✓	✓	✓	✓	✓		✓
11. Zody	✓✓	✓					
12. Jesus	✓	✓✓			✓		
13. Odelfa		✓✓	✓				
14. Tina	✓	✓		✓✓	✓✓	✓	✓✓
15. Susan				✓✓	✓✓		✓✓
16. Chris	✓	✓✓	✓	✓	✓✓	✓	✓
17. David		✓✓		✓	✓		
18. Grant	✓	✓✓		✓	✓✓	✓	✓
19. Sandy		✓✓		✓✓	✓		
20. Karen	✓	✓		✓✓	✓		
21. Andrea	✓✓	✓✓	✓	✓✓	✓	✓	✓
22. Miguel	✓✓	✓					
23. Tony	✓✓	✓✓		✓	✓✓		
24. Andy	✓			✓✓	✓✓		
25. Lynette	✓		✓	✓✓			✓
26. Beth	✓						
27. Bobby	✓			✓✓	✓✓		
28. Tasha	✓				✓✓		
29. Tonya	✓	✓					✓
30. Liska							

Figure 4

Sample Skills Chart

129

students have accomplished the skill. The scheduling of skill groups is flexible depending upon the other demands for the teacher's time.

Since teaching time is limited, you may want to plan some *skill centers*. A skill center is a place in the classroom, study hall, or library where you store the materials, equipment, and supplies concerning some particular skill. For example, a skill center on how to read tables would include many practice activities and examples designed to help students read tables. Keep in mind that a skill center does not have to be an entire corner of a room or require a special table for display. A skill center might be located in a cardborad box to which the students come and take materials to help them accomplish the skill. The purpose of the skill center is to provide instruction and practice activities to help students develop skills independently. Of course, some students may need additional teacher or peer instruction; however, once you have set up the skill center, many students will be able to use the activities independently.

Skill centers are especially valuable when only a few students need to develop the skill. Providing for all the individual needs of your students is impossible; thus, you need materials to which you can refer students. As you plan skill centers, try to include activities which are self-correcting. Also, provide opportunities for students to help each other. These techniques are valuable since your time is limited.

There are other suggestions in the following modules which can be used to help you meet the needs of your students. Module 8 will provide ideas for helping students pronounce words, and Module 5 suggests many activities to help children develop the specialized vocabulary in your area. Module 6 provides ideas for helping children comprehend what they read, and Module 7 will help you teach some study strategies which will help your students. Even with all of these ideas, you will have students who are so far behind that help is needed. You are not expected to teach beginning skills to your students; simply help them develop the reading skills related to your area. Module 10, ''Identifying and Helping Problem Readers,'' provides suggestions for helping problem readers learn in the content classes. In addition, it suggests the resource persons to whom problem readers should be referred.

Post-test

Directions: The following questions are designed to measure your accomplishment of the objectives in this module. Check your responses with the answers on the following pages to determine if you have met the objectives of the module. You can recycle if necessary after checking your responses.

1. State six major reading skills which are required to read materials in your content area.

2. List the three steps which are involved in constructing reading skills tests in your content area. Give an example from your subject area for each of the steps.

3. Define criterion reference reading skills tests and indicate two ways of using the results from a criterion reference test.

Answers to the Post-test

1. A comprehensive list of skills can be found for thirteen different content areas in Study Guide 1 of this module. If you are able to list six reading skills needed to read materials in your content area, you have accomplished this objective.

2. The three steps in constructing reading skills tests are:
   a. Determine a reading skill required in your content area,
   b. Select or prepare sample materials, and
   c. Plan the format and the directions for the test.

   The examples will vary for different content areas. In general, you should specify some particular skill, describe kinds of materials which the students must read in order to demonstrate the skill, and state whether or not the format should be multiple choice, short answer, true false, or essay. For example, if you are a social studies teacher you may have the following responses:
   a. Determine skills such as reading graphs.
   b. Select or prepare materials such as graphs indicating rainfall, population, or production such as found in a social studies text.
   c. Suggest questions that you might have to determine if students can read and interpret graphs.

3. A criterion reference reading skills test is a test which measures a particular skill and then includes a criterion to determine whether or not students have demonstrated the skill successfully. Two ways of using the results are:
   a. Plan skill groups and skill centers for individuals who have not demonstrated the skills.
   b. Expect students who have demonstrated the skills to read the textual material, and perhaps tutor other students.

Final Note

You now know how to determine the reading needs of students in your content area classes. This skill is not valuable unless you are committed to doing something with the results. Make a commitment to actually meet the individual needs of your students by setting up skill centers, meeting with skill groups, and teaching the reading skills as a part of your normal instructional activities. Is not this what *To Sir, with Love* was all about?

Selected Bibliography

Allington, R. L. "Improving Content Area Instruction in the Middle School." *Journal of Reading*, 1975, *18*, 455–61.

Bechtol, W. M. *Individualizing Instruction and Keeping Your Sanity*. Chicago: Follett, 1973.

Bormuth, J. "The Cloze Readability Procedure." *Elementary English*, 1968, *45*, 429–36.

Carpenter, H. M., ed. *Skill Development in the Social Studies*. Washington, D.C.: National Council for the Social Studies, 1963.

Chance, L. L. "Using A Learning Stations Approach to Vocabulary Practice." *Journal of Reading*, 1974, *18*, 244–46.

Derby, T. L. "Informal Testing in Vo-Ed Reading." *Journal of Reading*, 1975, *18*, 541–43.

Frankel, J. C. "Reading Skills through Social Studies Content and Student Involvement." *Journal of Reading*, 1974, *18*, 23–26.

Harris, L. A., and Smith, C. B. *Reading Instruction Through Diagnostic Teaching*. New York: Holt, Rinehart and Winston, Inc., 1972.

Harrison, L. J. "Teaching Accounting Students How to Read." *Journal of Business Education*, 1960, *35*, 169–70.

Johnston, J. D. "The Reading Teacher in the Vocational Classroom." *Journal of Reading*, 1974, *18*, 27–29.

Maxwell, M. J. "Developing a Learning Center: Plans, Problems and Progress." *Journal of Reading*, 1975, *18*, 462–69.

Palmatier, R., and Bennett, J. M. "Note Taking Habits of College Students." *Journal of Reading*, 1974, *18*, 215–18.

Sanacore, J. "Locating Information: The Process Method." *Journal of Reading*, 1974, *18*, 231–33.

Thomas, J. I. *Learning Centers: Opening Up the Classroom*. Boston: Holbrook Press, 1975.

Viox, R. G. "Evaluating Reading and Study Skills in the Secondary Classroom: A Guide for Content Teachers." *Reading Aids Series*, Newark, Delaware: International Reading Association, 1968.

Module 5

Teaching Word Meanings

CONTENTS

Prospectus

Rationale

No one needs to convince you that teaching word meaning is an important part of your subject area teaching responsibility. You know without the specific technical vocabulary students will not be able to read assignments or understand your lectures.

You know word meaning is important but do you know how important? Do you realize that approximately 60 percent of comprehension is accounted for by vocabulary? In other words, comprehension is 60 percent word meaning. Are you aware that subject area word knowledge correlates highly with overall knowledge, success, and grades in the subject area? As a subject area teacher, you will need to systematically expand the vocabulary of your students. This module will help you effectively teach word meanings.

Objectives

TERMINAL OBJECTIVE: You will be able to introduce and expand word meanings in your subject area.

Specific Objectives:

1. You will list three levels of word meaning and write a definition for the word *barrier* at each of the three levels of word meaning.
2. You will list the six major guidelines for teaching word meaning in your subject area.
3. You will categorize a list of instructional activities into three levels of word meaning, and you will indicate which activities develop the fullest meaning of words in your subject area.

Resources and Time Required

All the resources required are provided to complete the starred core Enabling Activities. For the extension Enabling Activities, you will need to refer to textbooks, workbooks, charts, etc., from your teaching area. The estimated time to complete starred core activities is three to four hours.

Pre-test

Directions: For each question, determine the word that indicates your belief regarding your competency. If you are in doubt, choose NO.

1. Words have many meanings, and each mean-   YES NO
ing has many denotations and connotations.
The more a person knows about a word, the
more he will understand about what he reads.
Can you list three levels of word meaning and
define the word *barrier* at each of the three
levels?

2. Teaching is both a science and an art. To be an   YES NO
effective teacher, you must be aware of what
researchers and practitioners have learned
about teaching your subject area. This must be
combined with your creative ability to develop
the best possible instruction. Can you list six
major guidelines for teaching word meanings
in your subject area?

3. Word meaning is one of the real stumbling   YES NO
blocks to understanding written material. This
stumbling block can be removed by the teacher
who chooses appropriate activities to introduce
and teach word meanings in his subject area.
Can you categorize a list of instructional activities into the three levels of word meaning,
and indicate which activities are best for developing the fullest meaning of words in your
subject area?

Branching Program Alternatives for Pre-test Responses

1. Words can be defined at three different levels of word meaning. If you can list three levels of word meaning, and define the word *barrier* at each level, you are ready for Enabling Element 2. If not, Enabling Element 1 will help you acquire the information needed to do so.

2. As teachers we need to be aware of the guidelines for teaching word meanings suggested by research and experience. If you can list six major guidelines for teaching word meaning, you are ready for Enabling Element 3. If not, Enabling Element 2 will present these guidelines to you.

3. The activities you choose to teach word meaning will dictate the level of understanding acquired by your students. If you can list three activities for introducing new words at each of three levels of word meaning, *and* indicate the three activities which develop the fullest meaning of words in your subject area, you are ready for the Post-test. If not, Enabling Element 3 will help you accomplish this task.

Enabling Element 1
Levels of Word Meaning

Specific Objective 1

You will list three levels of word meaning and write a definition for the word *barrier* at each of the three levels of word meaning.

Enabling Activities

*1. Read Study Guide 1, "Levels of Word Meaning," to identify four types of vocabulary.

*2. Read Study Guide 1, "Levels of Word Meaning." Afterwards, write a statement describing each of the three levels of word meaning. Write a definition of the word *barrier* at all three levels of word meaning.

*3. Identify five words from your subject area and define them at each of the three levels of word meaning.

4. Define the word *democracy* at each of the three levels of word meaning.

5. Write a statement describing how understanding of what a student hears and reads is improved as words move through the three levels of word meaning in the student's vocabulary.

6. Teach the five words from Enabling Activity 3 to students at each of the three levels of word meaning. When you finish teaching, ask the students to describe how this activity increased their understanding of each word.

*Indicates core Enabling Activities

140

Study Guide 1
Levels of Word Meanings

Just about every person has four vocabularies which develop from birth in approximately this order: listening, speaking, reading, and writing. Reading vocabulary is generally the largest for high school students and adults.

There is no precise agreement on the size of vocabularies at various age levels. For example, research findings for twelfth graders vary on their estimates of vocabulary size between 15,000 and 45,000 words. The lack of agreement seems to be due to the manner in which a word is defined. Some educators consider *walk, walking,* and *walked,* as one word; others consider these to be three words. Other educators count each definition of a word as a new instance of a word. In the latter case, the word *run,* which has at least 130 definitions, would be considered as 130 separate words.

High school students, like all of us, are constantly adding new words to their vocabularies. While the period of vocabulary growth is most rapid between 2½ to 7 years of age, growth remains considerable as long as schooling is continued. When schooling is discontinued most adults add only about twenty-five new words a year to their vocabulary. In the middle to latter years of life, there is some evidence of overall decline in vocabulary size.

As a word comes into our vocabulary, it generally passes through at least three distinct stages of specific understanding. At first we have only a very specific understanding or association with the word. This means that the learner has only a single definition, instance, event, or object associated with the word. For example, the word *sofa* at this level is perceived as a specific object of a precise size, shape, or color, probably located in the living room of the learner's home. The learner is not aware that there are other sofas located in other homes, stores, and offices.

At the second stage the learner has more than a specific understanding of the word; he begins to develop a functional understanding. Now he can answer the question, "What is the function of a *sofa?*" At this level *sofa* becomes something we sit or recline upon, and can be used in a sentence to demonstrate understanding.

At the third and most abstract level of understanding, the learner develops a general idea or concept of *sofa.* For our purposes, a concept can be thought of as a cluster of impressions or perceptions for which words are used as labels. At the third level, the learner understands that *sofas* come in a variety of shapes, sizes, and colors, to mention a few things, and that they are part of a larger category called furniture. Sofas are not the only type of furniture; there are many other things, such as tables and chairs, which are also classified as furniture. At this level of understanding the learner has a more complete understanding of the word *sofa*. Since word meanings are constantly changing, it is probably safe to say that the complete understanding of a word is never acquired.

Words, as they come into our vocabularies, do not automatically or naturally rise through the three stages of this hierarchy. Many words are transfixed at the specific or functional levels and never reach the general or conceptual level. Students with vocabularies containing words principally at the specific or functional levels will have serious problems understanding their reading assignments, because authors communicate at the general or conceptual vocabulary level.

It is our responsibility as teachers to encourage and foster vocabulary growth in number of words as well as depth of meaning. Students need to know many words and need to have the fullest meaning possible of the words they know.

Today's secondary school students take a variety of courses during their years in school. The variety of courses contain many new words students must learn in order to master the subject areas. While most subject area teachers are aware of the importance of vocabulary to the understanding of their subject area, many teachers fail to teach for general or conceptual understandings of words. Instead their strategy is to cover as many words as possible briefly defining each as they go along. Research does not demonstrate that mere incidental exposure to large numbers of words expands vocabulary or develops conceptual understandings of words. For the most part, the teacher who is rushing through his vocabulary lessons, briefly and only verbally defining words, is wasting both his time and that of his students.

Words are understood at three levels of understanding. A word becomes transfixed in the hierarchy of understanding at the specific, functional, or general level depending on how it is experienced or learned. Asking students to look up a list of words in a dictionary generally transfixes those words at the specific level in the hierarchy. Asking students to define words as used in sentences, to obtain suitable synonyms, and to write a single sentence using each word, generally transfixes words at the functional level of understanding. Providing direct experiences with new words and asking students to incorporate the new words into their written and oral assignments, as well as their daily discussions, generally transfixes the new words at the general or conceptual level of understanding.

As a general rule, the more direct experiences a student has with a word, the more likely the word will become transfixed at the general or conceptual level of understanding. The more vicarious and incidental the experience, the more likely the word will become transfixed at the specific or functional level.

Defining Words

To be sure you understand the various levels of word meaning, we will take you through the process of defining three words. The following list of words has been chosen since they are common words and known to all of us.

telephone

jump

vote

Now before we define these words, let's review each of the three levels of word meaning. At each level we will give you an explanation as well as a sample sentence using the word *book*.

Specific Level of Word Meaning. At this level the student has a word associated with a single idea, event, definition, or object. If you ask the student to define the word *book*, he might respond, "A book is something found in schools."

Functional Level of Word Meaning. At this level, the student understands one of the major uses or functions of a word. If asked to define the word *book*, he may respond, "A book is something you read." Or he may demonstrate an understanding by using the word in a sentence, "I like to read books."

General or Conceptual Level of Word Meaning. At this level, the student recognizes that a word has more than one meaning or function. The student recognizes that there are many ideas associated with the word and he clusters these ideas by some common element. When he is asked to define the word *book*, he responds, "Since books can be used for storing, obtaining, or transmitting information, they are a way of sharing information or a means of communication.''

You now should have the levels of meaning in mind and a fair understanding of their distinctiveness. A detailed look at the words *telephone, jump,* and *vote* should further clarify these definitions for you.

Telephone. At the specific level of word meaning, a student recognizes that a telephone is a colored object that hangs on a wall, sits on a desk, or the like. At the specific level of word meaning, the student would define *telephone* as, "It hangs on the wall," or "There is one in the office," or a similar statement. At the functional level of word meaning, the student recognizes a major use of a telephone. When asked how to define *telephone,* this student responds with something like "I use it to call my friends," or "You talk on it." At the general or conceptual level of word meaning, the student recognizes that a telephone is one of many different means for communicating with people and there are telephones located in many places throughout his community, nation, or world.

Jump. At the specific level of word meaning, *jump* is what a student does when he moves his body up and down. It is not uncommon at this level of understanding for a student to actually demonstrate by jumping. At the functional level of word meaning, a student defines *jump* as the thing he does when he jumps rope, high jumps, pole vaults, and other similar things. At the functional level he defines *jump* in terms of some accomplishment, "I like to jump up and down." At the general or conceptual level, *jump* is defined as a method of exercise or a method of transportation, to mention just two of the ways in which the word *jump* can be conceptualized.

Vote. At the specific level of word meaning, the most common specific association with the word *vote* is "something done during elections." Remember, at this level a student has only a single association with the word. That association may be an event, a definition , or an instance to mention just three possibilities of associations. At the functional level of word meaning, probably the most common function heard is "a way of getting someone elected." In any event, at this level the student describes the word in terms of its major function or use. At the general or conceptual level, the student realizes that *vote* is just one part of a complex government process called democracy.

It should be clear from these three examples that at the specific level of word meaning, a student has only a single something associated with a word. At the functional level of word meaning, he is able to describe a major use of a word or use the word in a sentence which demonstrates his understanding. At the general level, the student has many facts and ideas associated with the word. He recognizes and uses the word in many different sentences and contexts.

Practicum Exercise

Now let us see if you can define a word at the three levels of word meaning. We will use a word that we are sure everyone knows—the word is *noun*. For each of the following levels of word meaning, formulate an explanation of how the word *noun* would be defined.

Specific Level of Word Meaning

Functional Level of Word Meaning

General or Conceptual Level of Word Meaning

Answers to Practicum Exercise

Compare your explanations with ours.

Specific Level of Word Meaning.   At this level, the word *noun* can be defined as a word, or some specific noun such as *John* or *dog*. Only a single observation or definition need be associated with the word.

Functional Level of Word Meaning.   At this level, the word can be defined in terms of a major use or function, or used in a sentence which demonstrates understanding, i.e., "a word used in talking or writing" or "a sentence containing a noun or pronoun."

General Level of Word Meaning.   At this level, you have many facts and ideas associated with the word. You may see the noun as one of the major form classes or parts of speech denoting person, place, or thing. You can use and recognize the word *noun* in different sentences and you are able to identify nouns in written and oral language. At this level, you have a more complete understanding of the word.

If you feel you can now define words at the three levels of word meaning, you are ready to move to Enabling Element 2. If not, you may want to obtain a dictionary, thesaurus, or a book containing synonyms and get together with someone using these modules to further clarify this concept of vocabulary development.

Enabling Element 2
Guidelines for Teaching Word Meaning

Specific Objective 2

You will list the six major guidelines for teaching word meanings in your content area.

Enabling Activities

*1. Read Study Guide 2, "Guidelines for Teaching Word Meaning," and prepare a written list of generalizations to guide you while teaching word meanings.

*2. From your list of prepared generalizations, prepare a second list of six key phrases.

*3. Examine your list of key phrases and prepare an acronym that will assist you in recalling them as you teach word meanings.

*4. Distribute the list of guidelines to your students. Ask them to comment on the validity of this list for improving their word knowledge.

5. With students and teachers, discuss the list of guidelines for teaching word meaning. Determine if their experiences agree with findings from research and practice.

6. Evaluate some of the popular vocabulary development books on the market using the guidelines presented in this Study Guide. For example, one guideline suggests that the study of Latin stems has questionable value for vocabulary development. Look at some of the popular books to see how much stress is placed upon the study of Latin stems. Which books would you recommend to your students?

---

*Indicates core Enabling Activities

Study Guide 2
Guidelines for Teaching Word Meaning

One of the authors once overheard two teachers discussing whether or not teaching was a science or an art. One teacher maintained that teaching was a science, and therefore required only the application of basic principles and guidelines developed through research. The second teacher maintained that it was really an art, the talents for which were most likely transmitted from one person to another genetically. After considerable discussion, the two teachers concluded that teaching was both a science and an art. As scientists, teachers read research on teaching and examine carefully their own practices to arrive at generalizations and guidelines to become more effective and efficient teachers. As artists, teachers use their creative genius and talents to make the subject of their teaching interesting and relevant to their students' needs.

Manzo and Sherk in "Some Generalizations and Strategies for Guiding Vocabulary Learning" presented an excellent list of guidelines for vocabulary improvement. Their list was developed after a systematic examination of research on vocabulary acquisition. Teachers who follow these guidelines will improve the efficiency and effectiveness of their vocabulary instruction. Selected guidelines taken directly from their list (modified for our purposes) follow:*

1. New words are learned best when taught as labels for direct experiences.
2. Vocabulary development must have the continued and systematic attention of all classroom teachers.
3. Many encounters with a word in like and differing contexts are necessary before it can be learned.
4. The teacher's attitude toward vocabulary improvement and the superiority of her own vocabulary are contagious and vital factors in improving student vocabulary.
5. Study of a limited number of words in-depth is more productive than superficial acquaintance with lists of words.

---

*Reprinted with permission from the *Journal of Reading Behavior,* vol. 4, no. 1, Winter 1971–72, pp. 81–82.

✓ 6. It is possible, but maybe practically foolish, to teach words which are not part of the verbal community in which students live. The lack of opportunity for use must result in eventual atrophy.

✓ 7. Introducing vocabulary consistently with only one or two activities does not encourage word learning.

8. The wide reading method of acquiring vocabulary which stresses little more than wide free reading with no other attention paid to words is usually not very effective for influencing rapid and marked improvement.

9. The study of Latin positively influences knowledge of morphemes, but does not seem to influence knowledge of vocabulary.

A review of these guidelines suggests that word meaning instruction must be intensive, systematic, and regularly provided in an enthusiastic manner by every subject area teacher. Preferably words should be introduced with direct and real experiences in a variety of contexts and gamelike situations. Words should be selected for daily assignments based upon students' needs and the continued use of these words should be stressed in all assignments. Keeping these guidelines in mind as you teach will improve the effectiveness of your vocabulary instruction.

Guidelines 1 through 6 are probably the most important for increasing the effectiveness of your vocabulary instruction. These guidelines suggest things that you must do in order to increase your effectiveness, while Guidelines 7 through 9 deal with questionable practices for improving the vocabulary of your students.

Go back and read Guidelines 1 through 6 again. This time decide which are the key words in each guideline statement. Make notes which will help you remember the guidelines. When you are through, return to and continue reading with the next paragraph.

In Guideline 1, did you choose *direct experiences?* Students develop the fullest understanding of words when they learn them from real experiences rather than vicarious ones. A teacher can create situations which allow words to be taught through direct experiences. In such situations, students must use new words to communicate with each other and with the teacher.

In Guideline 2 the key words are *continued and systematic attention of all classroom teachers*. Vocabulary development cannot be left up to a few teachers—it is every teacher's responsibility. Vocabulary instruction is most effective and efficient when it occurs daily and is systematic in nature.

In Guideline 3 the key words are *many encounters . . . in like and differing contexts*. Numerous encounters with words in varying types of oral discussions, reading materials, and writing assignments are necessary for students to develop the fullest understanding of the words you want them to learn. Many encounters are also needed to provide the necessary *mass* and *distributed* practice students need in order to get the word and its definition from immediate to long-term memory. Unless a word is acquired and stored in long-term memory, it will soon be forgotten and surely not used by the student as a building block for further knowledge.

In Guideline 4 the two most important words are *teacher's attitude*. Most of the research completed on teaching demonstrates that the teacher is the most important school-related variable to students' success or failure. When teachers approach vocabulary instruction with enthusiasm and positive attitudes, the vocabulary growth among students is considerable. On the other hand, when teachers approach vocabulary instruction with a casual or negative attitude, vocabulary growth is minimal.

A limited number of words in-depth is the heart of Guideline 5. Many teachers feel they have too much course content to cover and too little time to cover the material. These teachers do not develop in-depth word meanings. Often many words are assigned to students for study at one time and the burden falls upon the students to develop the in-depth understanding. The best vocabulary instruction focuses upon a few words, their varied meanings, uses, and application in reading, writing, listening, and speaking.

Guideline 6 contains two separate although related important ideas. The first deals with teaching words that . . . *are not part of the verbal community in which the student lives*. The second is *the lack of opportunity for use must result in eventual atrophy*. This guideline is not suggesting teachers teach only those words and meanings which are common to the verbal community in which the students live. It is suggesting, however, that when teachers select words for vocabulary instruction they select those that will help students in their daily communication of information. You should try to avoid teaching words that will not be used either in the verbal community in which the student lives or the education community in which he is educated. Obviously the lack of opportunity to use words will cause the words to be quickly forgotten.

One of the ways to help yourself remember the six major guidelines is by using an acronym. Acronyms are words made up from beginning parts or beginning letters of other words. Sometimes these are real words, and sometimes they are nonsense words. Look over the key words you have selected and see if you can build an acronym to help you remember the six major guidelines for making your vocabulary instruction more effective.

Our acronym is below. If you like your acronym better than ours, we encourage you to remember and use your own.

Guideline	Acronym	Key Words
6	V	Verbal community
3	O	Opportunities for use
2	C	Classroom teacher
4	A	Attitude
1	B	Build meanings through direct experience
5	S	Study in-depth

You now have in your memory six key guidelines for teaching word meaning. You are now ready to look at some activities for teaching word meaning.

Enabling Element 3
Activities for Teaching Word Meaning

Specific Objective 3

You will categorize a list of instructional activities into three levels of word meaning, and you will indicate which activities develop the fullest meaning of words in your subject area.

Enabling Activities

*1. Prepare a list of all the activities you can think of which can be used to teach word meanings to your students. Place a plus (+) in front of those you feel are the best activities for developing the most complete understanding of a word. Place a minus (−) in front of those you feel develop the least complete understanding of a word.

*2. Read Study Guide 3, "Activities for Teaching Word Meanings," to become familiar with a number of activities which can be used to teach word meanings, and to determine with which of the three levels of word meaning each activity is associated.

*3. Compare the list of activities you prepared in Enabling Activity 1 above with those presented in Study Guide 3. Did you learn some new ways to teach word meaning?

*4. Compare your ratings of instructional effectiveness of activities with our ratings. Did you identify the most effective activities?

5. Prepare a written list of activities you will use to teach word meanings as you work with students in your subject area. We hope you will emphasize activities that develop the broadest and most complete understanding of words.

---

*Indicates core Enabling Activities

152

Study Guide 3
Activities for Teaching Word Meaning

In this Study Guide a number of activities are provided which can be used as models for developing instructional activities for word meaning. These activities are arranged according to the three levels of word meaning presented in Study Guide 2. To review, the three levels of word meaning are:

1. **Specific level of understanding.** At this level the student has one object, event, instance, definition, or the like associated with a word. The student usually can only recognize and/or recall the single association. He may have the word *democracy* associated with a type of government or the United States, but he has no further understanding or other associations with the word.

2. **Functional level of understanding.** At this level the student states a major use of the word or can use the word in a sentence that demonstrates his understanding. At this level he not only understands that a democracy is a type of government, but in a democracy people vote to select representatives who pass laws and administer the government. ''In a democracy, people select their representatives.''

3. **General level of understanding.** At this level the student has many facts and ideas associated with the word. He recognizes and can use the word in a variety of sentences or contexts. The student recognizes that a democracy is government by many people. It is based on the beliefs that all people have the same rights, freedoms, and responsibilities. He may further understand that we have a representative democracy in the United States where the people elect public officials who act according to the people's wishes.

Through classifying activities by levels of word meaning, we hope to help you evaluate the activities you have been using for developing word meaning. We also hope to provide you with ideas for selecting future activities. One word of caution before we begin. Activities at the specific level are not inherently bad. When coupled with higher level activities, they sometimes form a learning chain from the simple to the complex. They become undesirable when they are overemphasized and are the only activities used to develop word meanings.

Read each of the following sets of activities for developing word meaning. The activities are classified by level of word meaning. Determine where the activities you listed and rated are classified.

Activities

A. Activities which develop primarily but not exclusively the **specific level of word meaning.** These activities usually lead to a single association between word and object, event, instance, or definition.

1. Locate isolated words in a glossary and write a definition and sentence.

2. Locate isolated words in a dictionary and write a definition and sentence.

3. Memorize Latin or Greek stems and associate them with single meanings.

4. Memorize the common meanings of isolated prefixes and/or suffixes.

5. Match prefixes, suffixes, and stems with their most common meanings.

> pre ⟍ ⟋ to pile up
> struct ⟍✕ before
> ment —— action or resulting state

6. *Scrabble, Probe, Spill and Spell,* and such games are generally useful for word identification. Rarely do such games bring about a discussion of word meaning and when they do usually only one definition or synonym is mentioned.

7. Programmed vocabulary enrichment books introduce a single word at a time, define the word, and then use it in a number of sentences. The programmed teaching technique often works for words related to the student's academic or social needs. What is wrong with most of the programmed texts is that the words are not matched to the student's academic or social needs and therefore atrophy results soon after the lesson is completed.

8. Vocabulary exercise workbooks generally consist of a number of separate lessons. Usually there are 35 or more lessons in a workbook. Each lesson focuses on two or three elements of vocabulary development. For example, it is not uncommon to find a prefix, suffix, and a stem all taught on the same page. In most cases the explanations are so incomplete neither the teacher nor the student can understand the real direction of the lesson and the lessons do not provide the extensive practice material needed to develop more than a vague association with a word or affix. Generally no provision is made for transfer of learning to regular classroom activities.

B. Activities which develop primarily, but not exclusively, the **functional understandings of words.** Examples of directions to the student are included with each sample activity. These activities develop and expand a major use or function of a word.

1. Study word relationships. Words become efficient tools when their relationships are understood. It is helpful for students to classify words under headings, to know synonyms and antonyms, and to understand functional relationships. A sample activity follows:

a. Synonyms. Choose a word from Column A and match it with a word in Column B.

A	*B*
walk	parcel
victory	promenade
package	triumph

b. Antonyms. Read the list of words provided and circle each word as it appears in the story, then write its antonym.

gentle	_____
courteous	_____

c. Classifications. List the foods that should be eaten at mealtimes, and those that would be best at snack time.

candy	doughnuts	bread	soap ?
eggs	peas	hamburger	
soda	popcorn	ice cream	

d. Analogies. Complete each analogy. Then write *O* before analogies which state opposites, and *S* before those which state similarities.

_____ Heart is to human as carburetor is to _____.
(e.g., car)
_____ Chisel is to stone as saw is to _____ (e.g. wood)
_____ January is to summer as July is to _____.
(e.g., winter)

e. Similes and metaphors are analogies which demonstrate the likenesses between words. In similes the words *like* or *as* are used to show the relationship.

It's *like* walking on a cloud.
I'm *as* happy as a lark.

With metaphors the words *like* and *as* are not used but the intent is the same.

All the world's (like) a stage.

f. Homonyms are words that sound alike but have different spellings and meanings. Read each sentence and underline the homonym that fits the sentence meaning.

They sang a (hymn/him) in church.
There wasn't a (berry/bury) left on the bush when the (bear/bare) finished.

2. Prefixes, suffixes, and stems. Research suggests that this method of vocabulary study may be more beneficial for more able students. The major part of this study should occur after the fourth grade.
Example:

a. Prefixes change the meaning of words. Match the correct meaning and modified stems in each of the following:

1. _____ pre heat   a. to pay in advance
2. _____ pre pay   b. to attach before
3. _____ pre fix   c. to heat before needed

b. Suffixes change the function of a word. Change the function of each stem word to complete the sentences.

1. engage   Mary and Bob's _____ party was last night.

2. depend   John was a _____
              employee.

c. Stems. Many English words have been made by adding prefixes and suffixes to Latin or Greek word parts. These word parts are stems. Knowledge of these stems will help unlock the meaning of many English words.

Example: spec or spect means to look. What do these words mean?

inspector _____

spectacle _____

spectator _____

3. Word Origin. This activity requires the use of a college-level or unabridged dictionary and is mainly intended for use with upper level, high ability students. Have students trace the history of common words in specific subject areas or general language use. They may be surprised to learn their original meanings.

4. Crossword puzzles are a good activity for developing multiple meanings of words provided the same words reappear in different puzzles and are associated with different meanings.

5. Explanation, discussion, application technique. Prior to reading new material, the teacher selects words that need explanation. These words are usually presented in phrases or sentences so that context clues are used. Then the teacher explains or checks the students' knowledge of the meaning of these words, shows illustrative material if available, and gives additional examples of their use. Students should also give additional examples of use.

Example: The following words are written on the board. They are read aloud and their meaning is discussed. Then the sentences are written on the board, and the blanks are filled in with the words:

arena	delicatessen	mysterious	urge
hooted	bellowed	glimmer	

a. The _____ was filled with mouth-watering smells of many foods.

6. Pictures, graphs, charts, and other visuals. A single or collection of visuals associated with an object or event a word represents are very useful for developing word meaning.

C. Activities which develop primarily, but not exclusively, the **general or conceptual understandings of words.** These activities develop clusters of information to provide the broadest understanding of a word.

1. Real and direct experiences are the best basis for concept development. A visit to a museum containing Civil War regalia provides a conceptual or idea basis for reading about the Civil War. When such first-hand experiences are not available, audio-visual aids are the next best means for providing experiences.

2. Teach word meaning through a study of context clues provided by authors. It is one of the best techniques for defining words. Examples of some of the more common context clues follow:

   a. Definition clues. The unknown word is defined in the descriptive context.

      Example: To provide continued protection for employees and customers, banks have security guards who stand watch throughout the day and night. A watch is a two-hour period of duty.

   b. Synonym clues. In this type of context clue a known synonym is used to define an unfamiliar word.

      Example: ''Several types of antennae (plural of antenna) have been developed for wireless communication. Sometimes radio waves must be sent in only one direction. One kind of antenna *focuses,* or *beams,* the waves toward one particular place. The antenna sends the waves in a beam similar to a beam of light.''

      (1) Focus and beam (are, are not) the same. (are)

      (2) Focused waves (are, are not) like a beam of light. (are)

   c. Familiar expression clues. This type of clue requires previous knowledge of common expressions. A common expression is used to relay an idea or offer clarity.

   Example: She was as proud as a peacock. It was gone like the wind. She was light as a feather.

   d. Experience clues. Children and adults may rely upon past experience to supply the meaning of a new word. The unknown word is determined from past experience.

   Example: Early detection and treatment of cancer act as a *deterrent* to death.

   deterrent means _____

   (1) We walked *warily* across the ice-covered bridge. warily means _____

   (2) Early treatment of cancer by surgery or radiation can save a life or at least *alleviate* much suffering. alleviate means _____

   e. Comparison or contrast clues. The unknown word may be compared or contrasted with something known.

   Example: John is extravagant, but not his brother. He could almost be called penurious. (miserly)

   f. Summary clues. The new or unknown word may summarize the ideas that precede it.

   Example: The young women used make-up, a wig, outdated clothes, and elderly actions to impersonate an old woman in the play.

   g. Reflection of situation or mood clues. The general tone of the sentence or paragraph provides a clue to the unknown word.

   Example: After Herbert trampled all of the flowers, squirted Althea with his water gun, and pulled the dog's tail, mother punished him for his *devilishness*.

3. Comparison of geographical, historical, social, or the psychological significance of words is a good way to develop higher level word meanings.

Example: Suppose you live in Florida and are writing to someone in another part of the United States, say Minnesota. Which of the following words might *not* have the same meaning to the person you are writing. Write *S* for same and *D* for different.

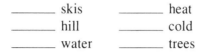

_____ skis   _____ heat
_____ hill   _____ cold
_____ water   _____ trees

4. Audio-visual aids. When first-hand material is not available, audio-visual materials dealing with the topic are useful. Movies, slides, filmstrips, pictures, charts, maps, and recordings may be used.

5. Figures of speech. The English language is rich with expressions in which a combination of words has an idiomatic meaning that cannot be gained directly from its elements. These should be directly taught.

Example: Read the sentence and explain the real meaning.

When he heard the news, he hit the ceiling.

6. Word study through connotations. Connotations are implied emotional meanings attached to words through stress, gesture, or past experience. Connotations may be positive or negative feelings transmitted with words. Our language is replete with them. A discussion of connotative word meanings should start with denotative or dictionary meaning. Start with a word like "yellow." The dictionary will define it as a color but it can be placed in a sentence to imply fear or cowardice.

When he saw the mouse, he turned yellow and ran.

Connotation study is an excellent means of developing multiple meaning of words.

7. Word coining. Take prefixes, suffixes, and stems and combine them in a new way to develop new words. This will help to develop the total meaning of the parts.

Example: de + port = deport   de + auto = deauto
           de + plane = deplane   de + part = depart

de + bus = debus   de + horse =
                                    dehorse
de + rail = derail   de + train =
                                    detrain

8. Changes in word meaning. Studying the changes in word
   meaning over a period of time can develop an interest in
   word study. Most desk dictionaries have a code which will
   tell you the (obs) obsolete word meaning, the (OE) Old
   English word meaning, and the like. Study of word changes
   √ expands students' associations with a word. Expanding
   associations through varied experiences is what moves a
   word to the general level of understanding.

After completing this Study Guide, you should be aware of the
more *and* less effective instructional activities for developing the meaning of a word. You should also be able to classify activities into one of
three levels of word meaning: specific, functional, and general. If you
have acquired these competencies and the competencies for Objectives 1
and 2, you are ready for the Post-test. If you have not acquired these
competencies, reread your material, talk with an associate, or see your
instructor.

Post-test

Directions: Read each of the following statements and complete each
Post-test item.

1. You must strive to develop the broadest meanings of words
   specific to your subject area. List and describe the three levels
   of word meaning and write a definition of the word *barrier* at all
   three levels of word meaning.

2. To be more effective and efficient in the teaching of new words
   and their meanings, you need to follow certain instructional
   guidelines identified through research and practice. List the six
   major guidelines for teaching word meanings to insure the
   effectiveness of vocabulary instruction.

3. You have become familiar with a number of commonly used
   activities for teaching word meanings. You will recall that the
   activities used to introduce the meaning of a word can determine
   the level at which that word is eventually understood. Read over
   the following list of nine instructional activities for teaching
   word meaning. Categorize each activity into one of the three
   levels of word meaning as a way of specifying the level of word
   meaning developed by each activity. Use the letter *S* to indicate
   specific level of word meaning, the letter *F* to indicate functional level of word meaning, and the letter *G* to indicate
   general or conceptual level of word meaning. Then decide
   which of the three activities are considered best for developing
   the fullest meanings of words.

   _G_____ a. Studying word origins.

   _F_____ b. Completing crossword puzzles.

   _G_____ c. Studying figures of speech.

   _S_____ d. Looking up words in a glossary and writing sen-
            tences.

_G_F___ e. Studying the meanings of a word in different written and oral contexts.

_____ f. Memorizing Latin roots.

___S___ g. Playing word identification games.

___F___ h. Studying the meaning of prefixes.

___G___ i. Coining new words by changing prefixes and suffixes.

Answers to the Post-test

1. The three levels of word meaning and a description of each follow:
   a. Specific instance or association level. At this level the student has only one object, event, observation, or definition associated with a word.
   b. Functional level. At this level the student is able to describe a major use of the word and/or use the word in a sentence which demonstrates his understanding.
   c. General level. At this level the student has many facts and ideas associated with the word. He recognizes and uses the word in many different sentences or contexts.
   d. Some possible ways of defining the word *barrier* at three levels of word meaning are:

   Specific Level of Word Meaning (a single association)
   (1) "a fence"
   (2) "mountains out there"
   (3) "the reef in the ocean"

   Functional Level of Word Meaning (describe or use in a sentence)
   (1) "It is like when you put a fence as a barrier in front of a house to keep dogs out."
   (2) "The mountains were a barrier which made it difficult for the early settlers to get to California from the east coast of the United States."
   (3) "A barrier reef separates deep from shallow water or warm from cold water."

   General or Conceptual Level of Word Meaning (Many ideas or facts are associated with the word, which can be used in a variety of sentences.) "There are many types of barriers. Barriers to physical movement, barriers to developing personal relationships, and more. Almost anything can be used as a barrier if it is used to block or inhibit something else.''

2. The six major guidelines for effective teaching of word meaning are:

a. New words are learned best when taught as labels for direct experiences.

b. Vocabulary development must have the continued and systematic attention of all classroom teachers.

c. Many encounters with a word in like and differing contexts are necessary before the fullest meaning of the word can be acquired.

d. The teacher's attitude toward vocabulary improvement and superiority of the teacher's own vocabulary are contagious and vital factors in improving student vocabulary.

e. Study of a limited number of words in depth is more productive than superficial acquaintance with lists of words.

f. It is possible, but perhaps foolish practically, to teach words that are not part of the verbal community in which students live. The lack of opportunity for use must result in eventual atrophy.

3. The nine instructional activities for teaching word meaning have been categorized into the three levels of word meaning. The circled letters designate the three activities which will develop the fullest meaning of words.

> S = specific level of word meaning
> F = functional level of word meaning
> G = general or conceptual level of word meaning

_F_ a. Studying word origins.

_F_ b. Completing crossword puzzles.

_G_ ⓒ Studying figures of speech.

_S_ d. Looking up words in a glossary and writing sentences.

_G_ ⓔ Studying the meanings of a word in different written and oral contexts.

_S_ f. Memorizing Latin roots.

   S   g. Playing word identification games.

   F   h. Studying the meaning of prefixes.

   G (i.) Coining new words by changing prefixes and suffixes.

Final Comment

If you have satisfactorily completed all Post-test items, you are ready for another module. If not, refer to appropriate Enabling Elements and attempt to resolve your difficulty. If you cannot resolve your difficulty, contact the instructor.

Selected Bibliography

Bloom, B. S.; Hastings, J. T.; and Madaus, G. F. *Handbook on Formative and Summative Evaluation of Student Learning*. New York: McGraw-Hill, 1971.

Bruland, R. A. "Learnin' Words: Evaluating Vocabulary Development Efforts." *Journal of Reading*, 1974, *18* (3), 212–14.

Chance, Larry L. "Using a Learning Stations Approach to Vocabulary Practice." *Journal of Reading*, 1974, *18* (3), 244–46.

Dale, E.; O'Rorke, J; and Bamman, H. A. *Techniques of Teaching Vocabulary*. Palo Alto, California: Field Educational Publications, 1971.

Davis, N. B. *Basic Vocabulary Skills*. New York: McGraw-Hill, 1969.

Dawson, M. A., ed. *Teaching Word Recognition Skills*. Newark, Delaware: International Reading Association, 1971.

Deighton, L. C. *Vocabulary Development in the Classroom*. New York: Teachers College Press, Columbia University, 1959.

Goldfield, B. "Semantics: An Aid to Comprehension." *Journal of Reading*, 1973, *16* (4), 310–13.

Hafner, L. E. *Improving Reading in Middle and Secondary Schools, Selected Readings*, 2nd ed. New York: Macmillan, 1974.

Karlin, R. *Teaching Reading in High School*, 2nd ed. Indianapolis: Bobbs-Merrill, 1972.

Kottmeyer, W. *Decoding and Meaning*. New York: McGraw-Hill, 1974.

Manzo, A. V., and Sherk, J. K. "Some Generalizations and Strategies for Guiding Vocabulary Learning." *The Journal of Reading Behavior*, 1971–72, *4* (1), 78–89.

Petty, W. T.; Herold, C. P.; and Stoll, E. *The State of Knowledge About the Teaching of Vocabulary*. Champaign, Illinois: National Council of Teachers of English, 1968.

Robinson, H.A.; and Thomas, E. L., eds. *Fusing Reading Skills and Content*. Newark, Delaware: International Reading Association, 1969.

Thomas, E. L., and Robinson, H. A. *Improving Reading in Every Class: A Sourcebook for Teachers.* Boston, Massachusetts: Allyn and Bacon, 1972.

Thorndike, E. L., and Lorge, I. *The Teacher's Word Book of 30,000 Words.* New York: Teachers College Press, Columbia University, 1944.

Module 6

Helping Students Comprehend

CONTENTS

Prospectus

Rationale

As students progress through the educational system, the reading materials they use become increasingly more technical. Because of the increased technical nature of the writing, increased demands are placed upon the reader's comprehension skills. For many students the demands eventually overtake their comprehension competencies. Unless these students are provided with some assistance in obtaining meaning from the printed material in subject areas, their performance will dwindle and eventually they may fail.

Subject area teachers are generally the most qualified persons on the school faculty to help these students with their comprehension needs in the subject areas. No other teachers are better acquainted with the nature of the reading material, style of writing, and the strategies for content analysis than subject area specialists. Subject area teachers also know the qualifications of subject area writers and the subtleties with which they communicate. Subject area teachers are the most qualified teachers in our secondary schools to teach subject area related reading comprehension skills. In short, subject area teachers are the best readers of the materials in their respective areas! And the best readers should teach students how to read in their subject areas.

To help students improve in their comprehension subject area material, subject area teachers need only to make minor instructional changes. This module deals with four basic competencies subject area teachers need to have in order to improve the comprehension achievement of their students. First, teachers need to know the basic comprehension behaviors. Second, they need to know how to prepare questions to assess the comprehension behaviors. Third, teachers need to know how to analyze questions they ask to obtain the procedure or thinking processes used to obtain answers. Throughout this module we refer to this procedure for obtaining answers as a "question-answering strategy." Fourth, teachers need a plan for developing comprehension behaviors) The purpose of this module is to provide subject area teachers with these four competencies.

Objectives

TERMINAL OBJECTIVE: You will prepare a lesson plan that uses the Introspective Comprehension Strategy to improve the comprehension achievement of students in your subject area.

Specific Objectives:

1. You will list and describe the six major categories of questions in the Classification Scheme for Reading Questions.
2. You will write one question for each of the six categories in the Classification Scheme for Reading Questions.
3. You will write the step-by-step procedure used for answering a question.
4. You will list the instructional steps in the Introspective Comprehension Strategy, and you will prepare a lesson plan designed to teach a strategy for answering a specific type of question on a reading assignment.

Resources and Time Required

In addition to white paper and a writing instrument, the participant will need a copy of her subject area textbook to complete this module. Other materials required for completing this module are provided. The estimated time to complete the starred core Enabling Activities is four to six hours.

Pre-test

Directions: For each question, determine the word that indicates your belief regarding your competency. If you are in doubt, choose NO.

1. It is important for teachers to ask students to read material to answer specific questions. Can you list and describe six major categories of questions in a classification scheme for reading questions?   YES   NO

2. Students must be asked questions by their teachers at various levels in a hierarchy of questions. Can you write one question for each of six categories in a classification scheme of reading questions?   YES   NO

3. Teachers have a responsibility to help students figure out the answers to questions they ask. Can you list the steps you mentally go through to determine the answer to questions you ask?   YES   NO

4. By slightly altering present instructional approaches, subject area teachers can improve their students' comprehension of textual materials. Can you list the instructional steps in a comprehension strategy and prepare a lesson plan designed to teach students how to answer specific types of questions?   YES   NO

Branching Program Alternatives for Pre-test Responses

1. If you can list and describe the six major categories of questions in the Classification Scheme for Reading Questions, you are ready for Enabling Element 2. If not, Enabling Element 1 will provide you with this useful information.

2. Knowing how to write questions at various levels of difficulty is an important prerequisite for teaching comprehension. If you can write questions for each of six categories in a classification scheme for reading questions, you are ready for Enabling Element 3. If not, Enabling Element 2 will help you develop this important competency.

3. If you can write in detail the procedure you follow for answering questions, you are ready for Enabling Element 4. If not, Enabling Element 3 will help you understand your question-answering strategies.

4. The comprehension behaviors of students are most likely to improve when the teacher has a strategy for improving them. If you can list the instructional steps in the Introspective Comprehension Strategy and prepare a lesson plan to teach a reading assignment, you are ready for the Post-test. If you are unfamiliar with this instructional strategy, Enabling Element 4 will be of interest to you.

Enabling Element 1
Comprehending Comprehension

Specific Objective 1

You will list and describe the six major categories of questions in the Classification Scheme for Reading Questions.

Enabling Activities

*1. After completing Study Guide 1, "Comprehending Comprehension," list the six major categories of questions in the Classification Scheme for Reading Questions.

*2. Share the Classification Scheme for Reading Questions with your colleagues. Together determine if there are types of questions pursued in your subject area which are not included in this scheme. If there are, add them to the appropriate list.

*3. Randomly select questions from lesson plans in your subject area textbook. Compare them with the questions in the classification scheme. Are there types of questions proposed by the textbook author(s) that are not listed in the Classification Scheme for Reading Questions? If so, add them to the appropriate list.

4. When you examine the questions asked by your textbook author(s), tally the number that fall into each of the six categories of the classification scheme. You may be surprised at how few questions fall into certain categories. It is not uncommon to find that most questions fall into the Recognition and Recall or Translation categories.

*5. Use the Classification Scheme for Reading Questions to prepare questions to go with a future reading assignment. Duplicate the

questions and distribute them to your students. Direct your
students to use these questions as purposes for reading. Determine if having purposes that require different levels of comprehension make the reading assignment more interesting for
your students.

Study Guide 1
Comprehending Comprehension

Most often students in your subject area will demonstrate their comprehension of printed material by some type of oral or written response.
Generally the response comes as a result of a question you have asked.
Each day as you are working with students you will ask many questions
and receive hundreds of answers.

If an inventory was prepared of all the questions subject area
teachers ask, the inventory could be used to demonstrate the comprehension behaviors required for success in content areas. Once the questions
were inventoried, they could be classified into a few basic types of
questions. These basic types of questions could probably be arranged
into a hierarchy from rather simple recognition and recall questions to
rather difficult and complex evaluation questions. Once such a classification scheme has been developed, it could be used by subject area
teachers for developing reading questions. It could also be used to
illustrate for students the types of reading comprehension behaviors they
must possess in the various subject areas.

A sample classification scheme is included in this Study Guide.
The Classification Scheme for Reading Questions is a collection of
questions classified into six categories. The categories are arranged in
approximate order from the simplest to the more difficult and complex.
The scheme was developed by Nativadad Santos. She developed it after
a thorough examination of taxonomies prepared by Bloom and Sanders.

The Santos Classification Scheme for Reading Questions is included in this Study Guide because it is a valuable tool for both assessment and instruction of comprehension behaviors. It has these specific
advantages:

1. It includes nearly all questions that can be asked.

2. It is divided into six major categories of questions.
3. Each category requires a different comprehension behavior.
4. The categories are arranged in approximate order from simple recognition and recall to the more difficult and complex evaluation.

At this point it is necessary for you to become familiar with the Classification Scheme for Reading Questions which follows. Start by skimming the classification scheme to identify the six major categories of reading questions. Next read the introductory statement which follows each category. As you do so, ask yourself "What type of thinking or comprehension behaviors are required to answer questions that fit this category?" Last, look at the specific types of questions that fit under each category. As you look at these, ask yourself "What mental steps would a student go through to answer these questions?" Now go ahead and examine the classification scheme for the three purposes identified.

Classification Scheme for Reading Questions

1. *Recognition or Recall Questions*
   A reading question falls under this category if it can be answered verbatim with specific information found in the selection read, and if it requires the reader to repeat or locate the information, as in:
   a. responding to direct factual questions in which the fact is given in the selection read;
   b. enumerating or making a list of information presented in the selection read;
   c. quoting the author or character in the selection;
   d. recalling who said a given quotation taken verbatim from the selection read;
   e. reciting a stanza of a poem, an essay, rules, from memory;
   f. reading aloud the part that answers a factual question, or the part called for.

2. *Translation Questions*
   A reading question falls under this category if it requires the reader to restate a specific information in his own words or in another form of communication, while keeping the idea basically unchanged, as in:

a. explaining in his own words the meaning of technical terms, vocabulary words, and stated meanings;

b. restating a problem, generalization, principle, rule, procedure, in his own words;

c. paraphrasing parts of a selection, or summarizing a selection;

d. retelling a selection according to a given set of topics; describing or retelling parts of events of a selection to prove a point; retelling additional stories related to the topic in his own words;

e. following printed directions;

f. changing poetry to prose or vice versa; changing a statement to a question;

g. illustrating or drawing information recorded verbally; describing a picture, poster, sketch, drawing, painting, or object in his own words;

h. presenting information by making a graph, diagram, chart, table, or map.

3. *Application Questions*

A reading question falls under this category if it requires the reader to recall an appropriate and previously learned skill or abstraction (generalization, principle, theory, rule, technique, or procedure) and then use it to explain or solve a problematic situation which is presented in a new context, as in:

a. making use of previous knowledge to make comparisons, observations, and explanations, or to answer a question;

b. applying new information or principles learned from the selection read to explain a phenomena or a problematic situation;

c. using a theory or principle to predict the probable effects of certain factors;

d. applying rules or organizing ideas, as in:
   (1) classifying or grouping
   (2) indexing
   (3) outlining
   (4) rearranging a given set of ideas alphabetically, chronologically, or in proper sequence;

e. applying arithmetical procedures and skills to solve and/or explain arithmetical problems;

f. applying skill in locating information, as in:
    (1) a dictionary
    (2) an encyclopedia
    (3) an atlas
    (4) other general references;
g. identifying and/or giving examples to fit a previously-stated definition or abstraction;
h. identifying elements of style used in the selection read, such as rhyme, free verse, satire;
i. identify propaganda devices used in persuasive material, facts vs. opinions, author's biases or prejudices, and emotive language;
j. identifying literary devices of humor, wit, satire, mood, tone, and figures of speech.

4. *Analysis Questions*

A reading question falls under this category if it requires the reader to identify the component parts of a given communication, and/or to determine relationships among these component parts or among parts of ideas as in:

a. indicating which are the assumptions, conclusions, generalizations, or supporting facts explicit in a given communication;
b. making inferences, conclusions, generalizations, or implications; anticipating or predicting outcomes from evidence presented;
c. identifying in a given communication what information is given, what is not given, and/or what is to be solved in a story problem;
d. identifying clues from which inferences may be drawn, as in:
    (1) connotative expressions
    (2) character's actions, traits, remarks
    (3) the setting
    (4) figurative language
    (5) semantic variations;
e. identifying relationships, as in:
    (1) cause-effect relationships
    (2) sequential relationships
    (3) logical relationships (analogies, antecedents)

       (4) past-present relationship

       (5) main ideas and details

       (6) central theme;

  f. indicating whether ideas are similar, different, contradictory, supportive, related, relevant, irrelevant, essential, extraneous, in proper sequence, true or false, right or wrong, good or bad;

  g. identifying author's purpose and point of view;

  h. identifying parts of a given communication which makes the communication false.

5. *Synthesis Questions*

A reading question falls under this category if it offers a variety of possibilities and allows the reader freedom of expression. At the same time it requires him to compose a unique communication, devise a proposed procedure, or derive new relationships, as in:

  a. using a given word, phrase, or expression in his own words;

  b. rearranging a given set of ideas into unique sentences or paragraphs; substituting words or phrases to make ideas more correct;

  c. writing an original rhyme, poem, essay, or story;

  d. reading aloud the part called for and giving the passage his own expression; dramatic reading; choral reading;

  e. pantomiming; retelling or dramatizing a selection or parts of it using one's own words and expressions; presenting a pageant;

  f. relating a personal experience;

  g. discussing or giving a short talk or extemporaneous speech on a given topic; telling an original story;

  h. submitting a plan for a project needing construction, an experiment, a program, a skit, or a dramatization;

  i. suggesting solutions to a problem; listing possible problems that might sum up a situation;

  j. suggesting different titles to a given communication; suggesting scenes or events pictured from a given communication;

  k. formulating rules to observe in performing or judging a performance or presentation;

  l. giving different endings to a given communication;

   m. relating a general problem to a local situation;

   n. sharing personal experiences; relating one's personal experience to the content of what is read or to the question asked;

   o. pretending;

   p. giving an opinion or making decisions without justifying one's views.

6. *Evaluation Questions*

A reading question falls under this category if it requires the reader to determine whether a given communication meets standards set up by the student herself or presented to her. It also requires her to make decisions and to support her views in her own words, as in:

   a. judging agreement between ideas or sources of information, and justifying one's views;

   b. forming an opinion or taking a stand on an issue, and justifying one's views;

   c. indicating whether a conclusion, generalization, main theme, or thesis logically follows the facts presented; selecting the best conclusion from a set of suggested conclusions, and justifying one's views;

   d. indicating whether ideas are similar, different, contradictory, supportive, related, relevant, essential, or in proper sequence, and justifying one's views.

   e. judging or criticizing a given communication, and justifying one's views for:

accuracy	completeness
authenticity	practicability
relevancy	reasonableness
adequacy	authoritativeness
value	logical consistency
imagination	etc.;

   f. judging the relative merits of information from different sources, or sources of information, and justifying one's views;

   g. judging characters in a story, and justifying one's views;

   h. evaluating suggested endings to a story, summaries, a performance, a declamation, an oration, a speech, etc., and justifying one's views and/or suggesting ways of improvement;

i. evaluating pictures for accuracy, appropriateness, suitability, richness of imagination, and justifying one's views;

j. evaluating statements for ambiguities, over-specificity, omissions, distortions, inconsistencies, inaccuracies, overstatements, and justifying one's views;

k. judging and proving the truth or falsity of statements by pointing out supportive statements or evidence, and justifying one's views.

The Classification Scheme in Review

As you read the Classification Scheme for Reading Questions, you noticed there were six major categories of questions each requiring its own comprehension behaviors, or, if you wish, "thinking strategies." You noticed that each level of the strategy tends to be built upon the preceding level, suggesting a true hierarchy. You may have also noticed that the first four levels require the reader to converge upon the answer to the question using the information available. In the last two levels the reader uses the information that is available as well as looking outside of the material she is reading for additional information. This additional information is combined with the facts and the reading selection to arrive at an answer to the question. This section contains a review of some of the main ideas you should have obtained from your examination and study of the Classification Scheme of Reading Questions.

Recognition or Recall questions was the first category presented in this classification scheme. Questions of this type require the reader to identify or recall from the reading passage exact statements in order to provide verbatim answers. Since the comprehension behaviors required at this level are rather simple, the question-answering strategy is not very elaborate.

Translation questions are closely related to Recognition and Recall questions. The chief difference is that the translation questions require that the reader answer the questions in his own words and not verbatim. Translation questions require a higher level question-answering strategy than Recognition or Recall questions because they require the reader to translate the answer in his own words.

Application questions require that the learner use in some new situation the information obtained through reading. This information can be used in any way as long as a change takes place in something as a result of the use of the information. The information can be used to make comparisons, to outline, or to locate information to mention just a few of the ways specified under this section of the classification scheme. Application questions require a still higher level question-answering strategy because they require that the reader use the information in some way to alter some situation or product.

Analysis questions require that the learner analyze what he has read to identify the organization of the material, the basic components of the communication, and the relationships between those components. Basic components are such things as assumptions, inferences, and connotative expressions to mention a few. Analysis questions require a still more complex question-answering strategy because they require the reader to separate the communication into parts, which are then analyzed.

Synthesis questions form the fifth category. Synthesis questions require that the learner obtain information from what he has read and combine it with information from other sources (background of experience, discussions, books, magazines, lectures, and the like) to form a new or different idea or product. The idea or product must be new or different and be greater than its parts. The synthesis question-answering strategy builds upon but is different and more complex than the preceding strategies because it requires the reader to combine information from various sources to form something new.

Evaluation questions form the sixth and final category in the classification scheme. Evaluation questions require the learner to make a decision. The decision is made after reading for information relative to the question and reading to obtain criteria for evaluating the information. The decision, information gathered, and evaluation criteria must be justified by the reader. The evaluation question-answering strategy is the most complex and difficult one for students to master. It requires the reader to identify important information, to evaluate the information in terms of specified criteria, and to make a decision which he must defend.

Figure 5 provides a graphic summary of factors in the Classification Scheme for Reading Questions. This Summary Form demonstrates the interrelatedness and increased complexity of comprehension behaviors as questions move from Recognition and Recall to Evaluation.

If you will reflect for a minute, you will probably realize that the Classification Scheme for Reading Questions is a rather complete model of the reading comprehension requirements of your subject area. The classification scheme probably contains most of the questions you ask,

Figure 5

Summary Form
Classification Scheme for Reading Questions

Question Categories	Type of response required					
	Recognize or recall answer verbatim	Change verbatim answer to own words	Use information to alter some situation or product	Separate communication into parts for analysis	Combine information for various sources to form something new	Evaluate and justify the decision
Recognition or Recall	X					
Translation	X	X				
Application	X	X	X			
Analysis	X	X	X	X		
Synthesis	X	X	X	X	X	
Evaluation	X	X	X	X	X	X

This form demonstrates the interrelated nature and hierarchy in the Classification Scheme for Reading Questions

answer, or ask your students to answer in your subject area. Because of its comprehensiveness, the classification scheme should be invaluable to you for preparing questions which stimulate thinking among your students.

If you can now name and briefly describe the six major categories for classifying reading questions from the Classification Scheme for Reading Questions, you are ready for Enabling Element 2. If not, complete the task before moving on. If you are having difficulty, reexamine this Enabling Element or see your instructor.

Enabling Element 2
Preparing Reading Questions

Specific Objective 2

You will write one question for each of the six categories in the Classification Scheme for Reading Questions.

Enabling Activities

*1. Read Study Guide 2, "Preparing Reading Questions." Prepare one question for each of the six categories on the reading selection, "Comprehension is the Cornerstone of Education."

*2. Identify some reading selections from your subject area textbook. Prepare two or three questions for each of the six categories of reading questions. Use these questions for establishing purposes for reading the assignment.

3. Make copies of the Classification Scheme for Reading Questions available for your students. Familiarize them with the various kinds of reading questions that can be constructed. Have your students construct questions for each of the six categories that can be used for establishing purposes for reading.

4. Exchange copies of questions with other staff members who have prepared, from common reading assignments, questions on each of the six categories. You may find that some teachers are better than others at writing certain types of questions.

*5. Get together with a group of colleagues in your subject area, and using the classification scheme, identify the more important types of questions for your subject area. Arrange the questions

*Indicates core Enabling Activities

in a hierarchy from the least difficult to the most difficult. This activity will leave you with a classification scheme for reading questions specific to your subject area. Use this scheme for developing questions when you are planning future reading assignments.

Study Guide 2
Preparing Reading Questions

Your first step toward improving the comprehension achievement of your students is to write a variety of questions. Not only is a variety of questions necessary, but the questions should be on a hierarchy from Recognition and Recall to Evaluation. The Classification Scheme for Reading Questions contains the desired hierarchy. It was introduced in Enabling Element 1 and will be used for preparing questions in this Enabling Element.

It is now time to begin writing questions using the Classification Scheme for Reading Questions. At this point, it would be valuable for you to reacquaint yourself with the classification scheme, particularly the variety of questions that can be prepared under each classification. When you have completed this task, read the following selection, "Comprehension is the Cornerstone of Education." When you are finished reading this selection, we will discuss the preparation of questions and ask that you prepare one question for each of the six levels in the classification scheme.

Comprehension Is the Cornerstone of Education

Comprehension of subject matter materials is one of the major objectives of public and private education. As a major objective of education, it becomes one of the chief responsibilities of every teacher. Many teachers, however, teach as if they believe comprehension to be an innate ability which students have or have not. Their teaching behavior leads an observer to conclude that developing comprehension abilities is the objective of the student and not of the teacher. Teachers such as these make no attempt to explain the processes involved in obtaining information from textual material. They merely make assignments and leave it to the student to discover the intricate processes which lead to understanding. Given that human beings are our most important natural resource, we can no longer allow miseducation such as this to take place. In the future, subject area teachers will have to assume their rightful responsibility for developing the comprehension skills indigenous to their specific subject areas.

You will recall that the classification scheme contains six basic categories for questions. Under each category are descriptions of questions that can be classified in the category. If you look at each category closely, you will notice that it is highly unlikely that all the questions provided in the category could be applied to one reading selection. As the nature and intent of an author differs, so will the type of questions which can be prepared over the reading selection.

Following this paragraph is a series of questions prepared over the selection, "Comprehension is the Cornerstone of Education." You will notice there are questions for each of the six categories but that the number which could be prepared for each category is not the same. The reason for this is that some questions are appropriate for this passage and some are not. Next to each question is a code number and letter that corresponds to a category on the Classification Scheme for Reading Questions. For example, question 1a corresponds to 1a on the scheme, "responding to direct factual questions in which the fact is given in the selection read." Compare each of our questions with its appropriate classification. From this comparison you should recognize the ease with which questions can be prepared using the scheme.

Also notice that we have provided some code numbers for additional questions which could be prepared under each category. At this time we are not providing the additional questions but you may want to look at the categories designated for additional questions. By doing so, you will learn which additional categories lend themselves to questions that you could prepare.

Outline for Preparing Questions, Form A
"Comprehension Is the Cornerstone of Education"

1. Recognition or Recall
    1 a. According to this author, what is one of the major objectives of public and private education?

1 c.

1 f.

2. Translation
   2 a. In your own words, define ''comprehension.''

   2 d.

3. Application
   3 c. Does this selection offer an explanation for the observation that comprehension scores on standardized tests do not continue to improve as students matriculate through high school?

   3 g.

4. Analysis
   4 a. What are the major assumptions made by this author that underlie his conclusion regarding future responsibilities of subject area teachers?

4 b.

4 g.

5. Synthesis
   5 c. Prepare a one-act play containing two actors who assume
        the roles of the two types of teachers described in this
        selection. What are their chief differences?

   5 j.

6. Evaluation
   6 b. How would you defend the author's conclusions?

   6 h.

Practicum Exercise

Now it is your turn to write some questions. On the Outline for
Preparing Questions, Form A, we provide code numbers and letters for
questions under each classification. Following some of the code numbers and letters are questions, following others there are no questions.
Your assignment is to formulate questions for the categories where
questions do not presently exist. Using the selection, "Comprehension
is the Cornerstone of Education," and the Classification Scheme for
Reading Questions, decide on at least one question for each of the six
categories. We are sure you will find the task sufficiently easy to be

encouraged to design additional questions under the Recognition and Recall classification and the Analysis classification. You may want to examine the classification scheme provided to determine if still additional questions could be prepared. When you have completed your task, begin reading with the following paragraph.

Answers to Practicum Exercise

Now that you have completed your task, we are sure you will agree that the classification scheme makes it easy to prepare the questions. It is now time for you to compare your questions with those we prepared. Look at the six categories of questions in the Outline for Preparing Questions, Form B, which follows. Compare your questions with the questions we prepared. A comparison should demonstrate to you the adequacy of your questions as well as reinforce our point that the classification scheme makes writing questions an effortless task.

Outline for Preparing Questions Form B
"Comprehension is the Cornerstone of Education"

1. Recognition or Recall
   1 a. According to this author, what is one of the major objectives of public and private education?
   1 c. What did the author say teacher's behavior leads an observer to conclude?
   1 f. Read aloud the sentence in which the author states the future responsibilities of subject area teachers.
2. Translation
   2 a. In your own words, define "comprehension."
   2 d. List in order the major points made by the author.
3. Application
   3 c. Does this selection offer an explanation for the observation that comprehension scores on standardized tests do not continue to improve as students matriculate through high school?
   3 g. If you were to observe teachers such as those the author spoke of, what would you expect to see?

4. Analysis

    4 a. What are the major assumptions made by this author that underlie his conclusion regarding future responsibilities of subject area teachers?

    4 b. From your examination of this selection, what inferences can you draw about the author?

    4 g. What was the author's purpose or motivation for preparing this selection?

5. Synthesis

    5 c. Prepare a one-act play containing two actors who play parts and assume the roles of the two types of teachers described in this selection. What are their chief differences?

    5 j. What is another title for this selection?

6. Evaluation

    6 b. How would you defend the author's conclusion?

    6 h. What supportive or contradictory facts do you have or can you think of that substantiate or refute the author's conclusion? What additional facts are needed to strengthen the author's conclusion?

Now that you are familiar with the Classification Scheme for Reading Questions and can use this scheme to prepare questions in each of the six categories, it is time to look at strategies for answering questions.

Enabling Element 3
Strategies for Obtaining Improved Answers to Questions

Specific Objective 3

You will write the step-by-step procedure used for answering a question.

Enabling Activities

*1. Read Study Guide 3, "Strategies for Obtaining Improved Answers to Questions," and list the steps in your question-answering strategy for an inference question.

*2. For a passage of your choosing, write six questions at the various levels identified in the Classification Scheme for Reading Questions. When you have finished, list the step-by-step procedure you went through to answer each question.

*3. Arrange a meeting with a group of colleagues to discuss and refine strategies for answering questions. Share the sample strategies from this Study Guide to initiate the discussion. Group discussions are probably the best way to refine thinking on question-answering strategies.

4. Reproduce the sample question-answering strategies provided and distribute them to your students. Use the various strategies as a basis for discussing comprehension improvement in your subject area.

5. Discuss with other colleagues in your subject area the various types of strategies used by students for answering questions. How well students answer certain types of questions should provide some insight into the types of questions which should be stressed in future reading assignments.

*Indicates core Enabling Activities

191

Study Guide 3
Strategies for Obtaining
Improved Answers to Questions

Each question you prepared for the reading selection in Enabling Element 2 has its own unique answer. Likewise, each question requires a different procedure or thinking process to obtain this answer. We call this procedure or thinking process for obtaining answers to questions a strategy. Specifically we refer to it as the question-answering strategy.

As a teacher it is your responsibility to improve the question-answering strategies of students in your subject area. You are the most appropriate teacher to improve these strategies since your strategies have become highly refined as a result of years of reading and studying in your specialty.

However, before you can help your students improve their question-answering strategies, it is necessary for you to become more familiar with your own strategies for answering questions. This will take some time since your strategies are likely to be automatically executed when you are confronted with a question. It is unlikely that you typically think in the detail that will be required of you to improve the comprehension of your students. Since there is no time better than now to begin developing your awareness of your question-answering strategy, let's begin. The following Practicum Exercise will help you develop an awareness of your question-answering strategies.

Practicum Exercise 1

Directions: (1) Read the question which establishes a purpose for reading the selection. (2) Read the essay. (3) Determine your answer to the question. (4) List the step-by-step procedure you followed to arrive at your answer.

Essay
Purpose for reading: Why did the author write this essay?

A Civil Air Patrol Cadet

Hello! My name is Robbie DuBois and I am a cadet Major in Civil Air Patrol. Civil Air Patrol is a volunteer civilian auxiliary of the United States Air Force. I am the cadet unit leader of the Riverside, Florida, Squadron of

Civil Air Patrol. Civil Air Patrol is open to boys and girls, ages fifteen–twenty. In Civil Air Patrol we learn search and rescue procedures so we can assist in locating lost military and civilian aircraft. We go on flight practice missions. We also learn how to get along with others and to be good citizens. I think every high school boy or girl should learn these things. That is why I enjoy my volunteer job and serve as a member of Civil Air Patrol.

Answer to purpose setting question.

Procedure for answering the question.

Answers to Practicum Exercise 1

Did you write your answer? Did you list the step-by-step procedure to arrive at your answer? If you did, compare your question-answering strategy and answer with ours.

1. We surveyed the question and the passage to be sure they contained no unfamiliar words, expressions, or ideas. Many questions are misunderstood or answered incorrectly because the reader does not take time to clarify an unfamiliar word, expression, idea, or the like.
2. Next we read the question to be sure the intent was clear. Many questions are answered incorrectly because they are misunderstood. Sometimes restating the question in another form helps. In this case, "Why did the author write this story?" can be changed to "What was the writer's purpose for writing this story?"
3. Then we examined the passage for all the facts relevant to the question and disregarded those facts not relevant to the question under investigation. The relevant and verifiable facts are:

   a. The writer is a member of Civil Air Patrol.
   b. The writer is a cadet Major and unit leader.
   c. Civil Air Patrol is a volunteer organization for boys and
      girls.

4. Next we studied the facts to determine if all or some of the facts
   needed to answer the question had been identified. All the facts
   necessary to answer the question posed at the beginning of this
   story are not stated in this story. At this point we had a hunch
   about the answer to the story.

5. If our examination of the facts had suggested that all the facts
   necessary to answer the question were available, we would have
   reached a conclusion and answered the question accordingly.
   When all the facts are present, the reader reaches a conclusion.
   Conclusions are final statements or decisions reached when all
   the facts are present. In a conclusion all the facts are identifiable. Since all the facts were not identified, a conclusion could
   not be drawn.

6. In our examination of the facts we determined that all the facts
   necessary to answer the question were not available. It was then
   necessary to determine which facts were missing. What is
   missing is a statement asking others to join or explaining that a
   membership drive is now open. After all, this could be merely
   an information blurb on Civil Air Patrol.

7. Background of experience, discussion with others, additional
   reading, hunches, and the like were used to supply the missing
   facts. These missing facts are really hypothesized facts that are
   not verifiable in the selection. Background of experience suggests that this style of writing is often used in recruitment cam-
   paigns. Reading other personal appeal recruitment reports led
   us to believe that the real intent was recruitment. This was further substantiated by the fact that this is a volunteer organization
   and volunteer organizations always seem to be looking for more
   members.

8. The verifiable facts and hypothesized facts were combined to
   answer the question. Since all the facts are not present in the
   selection, a conclusion cannot be reached and an inference has
   to be drawn. The question, ''Why did the author write this

story?'' requires that the reader analyze the component parts of the communication to make an inference. (See the Classification Scheme for Reading Questions, Analysis 4 b). Inferences are final statements requiring the reader to combine verifiable facts from her reading with hypothesized facts from other sources. The answer we inferrred was ''to entice boys and girls ages fifteen to twenty to join Civil Air Patrol.'' Since all the facts are not present in the selection, our answer is an inference and not a conclusion.

Does your strategy agree with the strategy listed here? If it did not, how did it differ? It is quite possible that although you have a different strategy your answer agrees with ours. It is always wise to remember that strategies may differ even though the answers may not. We do not know enough about the way in which people think to conclude that only one strategy exists for answering a particular type of question. When the answers are in agreement, it makes little difference that the strategies differ. The fact that question-answering strategies differ is only important when the answers differ; for that is when the teacher provides the student with a new strategy to assist her in answering a question. You will learn more about using your strategy to help students develop question-answering strategies in the next Enabling Element.

Occasionally, equal support can be found and arguments can be made for two or more answers to the same question. When this impass is reached, both answers should be accepted as possibilities of equal merit. Remember, however, that your goal is to develop whenever possible sufficient evidence to identify the one best answer. Emphasizing the need to identify the best answer encourages precise thinking among our students.

You have now had an opportunity to read our question-answering strategy. By now you have had ample opportunity to compare your strategy with ours. If you feel yours is incomplete, now is an excellent time to refine your strategy so that it will be useful to you when you teach.

Practicum Exercise 2

At this point you are familiar with the process for writing questions and the process for examining your step-by-step procedure for answering these questions. Using the following selection, formulate one question for each category in the Classification Scheme for Reading Questions. Then examine the following Sample Question-Answering Strategies. Using the sample strategies as guides, create the specific question-answering strategies for each of the questions you prepared. This activity will further develop your insight into your question-answering strategies; and, as a result will enhance your effectiveness in working with the comprehension problems of your students.

Fish Propulsion

Fish, like humans, do not use the same method for propelling or moving through the water. Some fish move through the water with snake like motions. These snake like motions are caused by muscle contractions throughout the body. Other fish propel through the water using a combination of muscle contraction and the side motion of their caudal or tail fin. The third type of swimmer uses his caudal fin almost exclusively. This swimmer keeps his body almost rigid as he moves through the water. One category of fish has a unique way of propelling through the water. The flying fish emerges from the water and spreads his large pectoral fin and glides over the water for hundreds of feet. The method used for propulsion seems to be related to the size of the fish and the speed at which the fish swims.

Directions:

Using the preceding selection, create one question for each category in the Classification Scheme for Reading Questions.

Recognition or Recall question: *List the four ways mentioned in the paragraph that fish use to propel themselves through water.*

Translation question: *In your own words, describe how the flying fish propels itself through water.*

Application question: *Describe the Caudal and pectoral fins on fish).*

Analysis question: *What system of propulsion would appear to be the most common type?*

Synthesis question: *With your knowledge of fish in the northern Indiana lakes we have studied, classify them as to their methods of propulsion through the water.*

Evaluation question: *To what use could you put this information*

When you are finished preparing questions, read the following Sample Question-Answering Strategies. Follow the directions which appear after the sample strategies.

Sample Question-Answering Strategies

Included in this section are sample question-answering strategies for the six categories of reading questions. These are *general* strategies for each category. Question-answering strategies for specific questions within each major category will differ slightly from the sample strategies which follow. They differ, as all strategies will, with the intent of the question. These strategies are provided as samples for your examination and study, and as models for creating your own question-answering strategies.

Recognition or Recall Strategy

1. Check the question and passage to be sure that it does not contain unfamiliar words, expressions, or ideas. If an unfamiliarity is detected, clarify it before proceeding.

2. Be sure the intent of the question is clear. Rephrasing the question sometimes serves as a check on understanding.

3. Read the selection and identify the precise statement(s) which answer the question.

4. Reread the selection to verify that you have identified all the information necessary to answer the question.

5. Answer the question in the precise words from the passage.

Translation Strategy

1. Survey the question and passage to see if it contains any unfamiliar words, expressions, or ideas. If an unfamiliarity is detected, clarify it before proceeding.

2. Be sure the intent of the question is clear. Rephrasing the question sometimes helps insure clarity.

3. Read the selection and identify the precise statement(s) which answer(s) the question.

4. Check the passage to be sure that you have identified everything necessary for answering the question.

5. Answer the question in the precise words from the passage.

*6. Restate the answer in your own words.

*7. Compare your restated answer with the precise answer to be sure it contains all of the facts or ideas.

Application Strategy

1. Determine if the question or passage contains unfamiliar words, expressions, or ideas. If it does, clarify before going further.

2. Obtain a clear understanding of the specific problem or situation contained in the question. Be sure to understand how the infor-

---

*Indicates new step(s) not contained in preceding strategy

mation to be obtained from the reading will be applied to the specific problem or situation. Identify and state the problem or situation. Restate the question so it specifies what information must be obtained to solve the problem or change the situation.

3. Read and locate the precise information required by your question.

4. Reread the selection to be sure all available information has been obtained.

5. Examine the obtained information to be sure it does not contain new or inaccurate information.

*6. Using the information obtained from reading the selection, solve the problem or change the situation as directed by the question.

*7. Check the answer to be sure the problem or situation has been solved or changed appropriately.

Analysis Strategy

1. Examine the question and passage to identify any unfamiliar words, expressions, or ideas. Clarify before proceeding.

2. Be sure the intent of the question is understood. Restate the question if necessary to clarify the intent.

*3. Read the selection to identify how the material is organized, the basic components of the material, and the relationship between the component parts.

*4. Read and locate information required by your question.

*5. If necessary, gather additional information from various sources.

*6. Look for the relationships between information from various sources.

7. When the reader has obtained all the necessary information, an answer should be prepared.

8. Test the answer for accuracy against the selection and other sources of information.

---

*Indicates new step(s) not contained in preceding strategy

Synthesis Strategy

1. Check the question and passage for unfamiliar words, expressions, or ideas. These should be clarified before going further.
2. Be sure the intent of the question is clear. Restate the question if necessary.
3. Identify all relevant information available from the passage.
4. Supply information from other sources as needed.
*5. Synthesize the information from various sources and compose an answer to the question. The answer should be new, different, and broader than the sum total of its parts.
*6. Test the answer to be sure it is sufficient to cover the information gathered.

Evaluation Strategy

1. Check the question and passage to be sure that it does not contain any unfamiliar words, expressions, or ideas. Clarify as necessary.
2. Be sure the intent of the question is understood. Rephrase the question if necessary to substantiate that you understand the intent of the question.
3. Identify important information from the passage.
*4. Establish the evaluation criteria.
*5. Evaluate each basic unit of information in terms of the appropriate criteria.
*6. Examine all evaluations and prepare a final decision.
*7. Justify the information gathered, evaluation criteria, and your final decision.

Practicum Exercise 2

Directions: As previously directed, formulate the answer to each of your questions and list the steps in your question-answering strategy.

---

*Indicates new step(s) not contained in preceding strategy

Recognition or Recall answer and strategy.

Translation answer and strategy.

Application answer and strategy.

Pectoral — the two small fins on the
lower front part of the fish used
for direction.
Caudal — tail fin of a fish used for
propulsion.

Caudal — used context clues
pectoral — looked in dictionary

Analysis answer and strategy.

Synthesis answer and strategy.

Evaluation answer and strategy.

Answers to Practicum Exercise 2

We could not anticipate the questions you wrote so it was not possible for us to provide you with strategies for each of your questions. However, we feel by now you should be able to evaluate your own strategies. To do this, compare your strategies with the sample strategies we provided. Since your strategies are specific to questions within each category, and ours are *general strategies* for each category, your strategies will probably contain steps in addition to those we have listed. If you are having difficulty listing the steps in your strategy, or feel uncomfortable with the strategy you have developed, we suggest you reread appropriate components of this Study Guide, complete additional Enabling Elements, examine reference sources by Bloom or Sanders in the selected bibliography, or see your instructor.

You should now be able to prepare questions and develop question-answering strategies. You are now ready to discuss improving the reading comprehension of your students in your subject area. Using the Introspective Comprehension Strategy is one way of improving comprehension achievement. Enabling Element 4 addresses itself to this topic.

Enabling Element 4
The Introspective Comprehension Strategy

Specific Objective 4

You will list the instructional steps in the Introspective Comprehension Strategy, and you will prepare a lesson plan designed to teach a strategy for answering a specific type of question on a reading assignment.

Enabling Activities

*1. Read Study Guide 4, "The Introspective Comprehension Strategy." When you finish reading, list the steps to be followed when teaching such a strategy.

*2. After completing Study Guide 4, prepare a lesson plan designed to teach a strategy for answering a specific question.

*3. Prepare a number of questions at each of the six levels in the classification scheme using reading material you will soon be assigning to your students. From this assignment, identify students who have difficulty answering specific types of questions and group them according to difficulty. Prepare and teach a question-answering strategy using The Introspective Comprehension Strategy.

4. Organize open discussion groups where students can meet informally and discuss their reading habits and strategies.

5. Teach The Introspective Comprehension Strategy to aides or the more capable students. Have them work along with students who need additional assistance.

6. Share your lesson plans and materials with your colleagues. By so doing, each of you will gather an excellent collection of lesson plans.

---

*Indicates core Enabling Activities

Study Guide 4
The Introspective Comprehension Strategy

Now that you are familiar with the classification scheme, can prepare questions at different levels in a hierarchy, and have examined your own processes for answering questions, you are ready to teach. Teaching your students to comprehend your subject area material by studying strategies for answering different types of questions is not a long or involved process. Nor does it detract from the study of your subject area. In fact, teaching students to comprehend reading assignments for different purposes will enhance their understanding and appreciation of your subject area.

This Study Guide introduces the Introspective Comprehension Strategy. It is a simple strategy which draws heavily upon the background and reading style of the subject area teacher. The strategy is based upon the assumption that subject area specialists are the best readers of their own subject area materials. The word *introspective* denotes *looking into one's self* for the question-answering strategies of comprehension.

The Introspective Comprehension Strategy consists of six steps. These six steps are:

1. Setting the purpose for learning. This step is designed to substantiate for your students their need for instruction.

2. Assessing the comprehension strategy. This step is designed to determine the precise steps in the learner's strategy for answering a specific type of question.

3. Teaching the comprehension strategy. This step is designed to teach a strategy to obtain the best answer to a question.

4. Testing the comprehension strategy. This step is designed to determine if the strategy you taught is understood by the learner.

5. Generalizing the comprehension strategy. This step is designed to enable the learner to use the strategy to answer a specific type of question in a variety of subject area materials.

6. Applying the comprehension strategy. This step is designed to give the learner daily practice with the strategy in order to raise performance to the automatic response level.

The procedure for using the Introspective Comprehension Strategy follows, along with a more substantial discussion of its components and its application. The format is the same one you would follow when teaching students how to comprehend subject area material. The instructional plan is set into motion when a student *incorrectly* answers a number of questions of the same type: Recognition and Recall, Translation, Application, Analysis, Synthesis, or Evaluation. Your study of the instructional plan should begin by surveying the six-step outline to identify the six major steps in the instructional plan. Then read the material under each step to determine precisely what you must do to improve the comprehension of your students using the Introspective Comprehension Strategy.

**Procedures for Using the Introspective
Comprehension Lesson Plan**

A. Setting the Purpose for Learning: The purpose of this step is to substantiate the need for instruction. It is assumed if a lesson is to be taught, it is because a group of students had difficulty answering two or more questions of the same type—probably in similar material. The material the students had difficulty comprehending would be the material used for teaching this lesson. Point out to the student that their difficulty in answering a particular type of question is the reason for this lesson. Further explain that with some instruction the students will be able to answer such questions and as a result will improve their comprehension achievement.

B. Assessing the Comprehension Strategy: The purpose of this step is to determine the step-by-step procedure followed by the students when they answered the question incorrectly.

   1. The teacher starts by restating one or two questions and supplying the answers provided earlier by students. As an alternative, the teacher may ask students to state their own answers. It is advisable to write the answers on a surface for continued reference by all students.

   2. Ask one of your students for a step-by-step explanation of how he arrived at his answer. You may wish to repeat this procedure with another student.

3. As the students reveal their question-answering strategies, list the steps in these strategies on a common surface such as a chalkboard.

4. Do not accept "I don't know" answers. Continue to question the students to obtain the specific steps they followed which led them to their incorrect answers.

C. Teaching the Comprehension Strategy: The purpose of this step is to teach the necessary components in a strategy designed to identify the best answer to a question.

1. Using the passage where the students demonstrated their original difficulty, direct the students to observe while you read the passage aloud.

2. As you read the passage aloud, describe and demonstrate how you are determining the most preferred answer to the question that your students answered incorrectly.

3. As you describe and demonstrate your strategy, write the steps on a chalkboard.

4. When you are through reading, describing, and demonstrating your strategy, review the steps with your students. After your review, cover or remove the steps from your students' view.

5. Ask selected students to list and explain the steps in the procedure you described to be sure they understand the question-answering strategy you just taught them.

6. Next, have the students compare their original strategies with the teacher's strategy to identify like and different steps, and explanations.

7. Discuss with your students how they must modify their strategies in order to obtain the most desired answer to questions of the type being studied.

8. Have your students explain how they would apply the new strategy to similar questions.

9. The students must *understand* and be able to explain the strategy before the teacher goes to the next step.

SPECIAL NOTE: A student may arrive at the preferred answer using an equally acceptable but different strategy than the teacher. If this is the case, the teacher should not attempt to change the student's strategy. It does us all well to remember that cognitive styles differ and desired answers can be obtained in a number of different ways.

D. Testing the Comprehension Strategy: The purpose of this step is to determine if the students understand and have acquired the strategy presented by the teacher.

1. Provide the students with a reading assignment similar in reading level and content to the initial assignment.

2. Have a number of questions prepared of the same type as those with which the students experienced difficulty.

3. Direct the students to read the passage silently to find the answer to one of the questions.

4. When they have finished reading, have the students explain what they did as they looked for the answer to the question.

5. The students should eventually arrive at or near the preferred answer. In some cases, students fail to provide an improved answer. If this is the case, the teacher should return to the teaching step and reteach the strategy through additional demonstrations. Reteaching is most effective when it is done with new material; but when new material is not available, it is permissible to use the same material.

6. When the students can apply the strategy and obtain the preferred or best answer, go to step E, Generalizing the Comprehension Strategy.

SPECIAL NOTE: Students should be taught at the onset that often there exists a range of acceptable answers; but in any range, one preferred answer usually exists. Striving for the best possible answer is what refines the process of critical thinking.

E. Generalizing the Comprehension Strategy: The purpose of this step is to provide students with opportunities to use the strategy with different subject area materials.

1. Provide students with newspapers, magazines, and monographs used in your subject area. Assist your students in applying their strategies to the different types of subject area materials.

2. The students should be led to realize that in general the question-answering strategy remains the same even though the material may differ.

F. Applying the Comprehension Strategy: The purpose of this step is to point out the need for daily practice to raise application skill to the automatic response level. This is the final step. The teacher provides her students with opportunities to answer similar questions in everyday classroom activities and assignments. Strategies are soon forgotten unless opportunities are provided for continuous application.

You should now understand the design and procedures for implementing The Introspective Comprehension Strategy. To make the concept even clearer, in the next section we will provide an example of how a lesson may be taught using this plan.

The following Demonstration Introspective Comprehension Lesson Plan will explain how comprehension is improved through the study of an Analysis (4 b—inference) question. This instructional plan was developed using the selection, "A Civil Air Patrol Cadet" which follows. You may want to refer to this selection as you read the instructional plan.

Question: Why did the author write this essay?

A Civil Air Patrol Cadet

Hello! My name is Robbie DuBois and I am a cadet Major in Civil Air Patrol. Civil Air Patrol is a volunteer civilian auxiliary of the United States Air Force. I am the cadet unit leader of the Riverside, Florida, Squadron of Civil Air Patrol. Civil Air Patrol is open to boys and girls, ages fifteen–twenty. In Civil Air Patrol we learn search and rescue procedures so we can assist in locating lost military and civilian aircraft. We go on flight practice missions. We also learn how to get along with others and to be good citizens. I think every high school boy or girl should learn these things. That is why I enjoy my volunteer job and serve as a member of Civil Air Patrol.

Demonstration Introspective Comprehension Lesson Plan

A. Setting the Purpose for Learning
Let us assume that a student answered the following question:

Question: "Why did the author write this story?"
Answer: "He wanted to tell us what Civil Air Patrol cadets do."
Since this answer is not the best answer to the question, the teacher points out the obvious need for instruction. She also indicates that the instruction should improve the student's comprehension of the passage and help him answer other questions of this type.

B. Assessing the Comprehension Strategy
If you do not have the student's answer to the question recorded, ask him to repeat his answer and record on chalkboard, paper, etc. Ask the student to explain how he arrived at this answer. Record each step. Probe to obtain specific steps.

A recorded strategy elicited from a student may appear as follows:

1. "I read the passage."
2. "I found statements that say what cadets do."
3. "I concluded that he wanted to share these things."

C. Teaching the Comprehension Strategy
1. Give the student a copy of the essay, "A Civil Air Patrol Cadet." Direct him to read silently as you read aloud.
2. As you read, describe and demonstrate each step in *your* strategy.
    a. Be sure there are no unfamiliar words, expressions, or ideas and that the intent is clear.
    b. Gather the relevant and verifiable facts.
    c. Decide if all the facts needed are supplied. If not, a conclusion cannot be drawn. Instead, an inference will have to be drawn.
    d. Determine what facts are missing.
    e. Use your experience, conversations with others, outside reading, and best hunches to supply the missing facts.
    f. Combine verifiable and hypothesized facts that are relevant and formulate your inference.
3. Write each step on the chalkboard, etc., as you proceed.
4. When you are through, review your strategy to provide a total overview. Remove or cover the strategy.

    5. Ask the student to list and explain each step to check on his understanding.

    6. Compare strategies and point out likenesses and differences.

    7. Have the student explain how his strategy needs to be modified.

    8. Have the student explain how he would handle a similar question in another passage.

D. Testing the Comprehension Strategy

    1. Prepare two questions of similar type dealing with one passage from similar reading material. If necessary, the same material may be used.

    2. Direct the student to read the material silently to answer one question.

    3. When he is ready, ask him for his answer. Also ask him to explain what he did to answer the question. He should list the strategy you taught him.

    4. Repeat step 3 with a second question to provide additional practice.

E. Generalizing the Comprehension Strategy
Assist students in applying the question-answering strategies to all the different types of reading materials used in your subject area, ie., magazines, newspapers, another textbook, to mention just a few.

F. Applying the Comprehension Strategy
Provide daily practice opportunities to answer similar questions in classroom activities and assignments. Such opportunities should be provided until the skill is at the automatic performance level.

Now it is your turn. *First* use the Classification Scheme for Reading Questions, and prepare a number of questions over a reading assignment that you will soon assign your students. Prepare some questions for each of the six major levels of the classification scheme.

Second, provide your students with these questions and the reading assignment. After they have completed the assignment, ask them to write their answers to the questions. If you wish, you may use a group question-answer discussion technique but it is easier for students to mislead you with this technique. Analyze the students' answers to the questions. Students with fuzzy, incomplete, or incorrect answers can be placed in small groups for instruction.

Third, select one group of students having difficulty with a specific type of question and prepare a lesson following the guidelines provided. An outline form for developing an introspective comprehension lesson follows.

Fourth and finally, provide instruction following the steps provided in the earlier discussion.

We hope your lesson goes well. If not, refer to the discussions to determine why you had difficulty or see your assigned instructor.

If you are familiar with the Introspective Comprehension Strategy and can prepare a lesson plan for teaching a question-answer strategy, you are ready for the Post-test. If not, refer to the appropriate Enabling Elements or see your instructor.

Introspective Comprehension Lesson Plan

A. Setting the purpose for learning

B. Assessing the comprehension strategy

C. Teaching the comprehension strategy

D. Testing the comprehension strategy

E. Generalizing of the comprehension strategy

F. Applying the comprehension strategy

Post-test

Directions: Read each of the following statements and complete each Post-test item.

1. As part of this module, you were introduced to the Classification Scheme for Reading Questions. List and describe each of the six major categories of questions in this classification scheme.

2. The Classification Scheme for Reading Questions is a useful tool for writing questions. Write one question for each of the six categories using the following selection.

Sleep

Sleep is an unconscious state from which a person can quickly be aroused. During sleep the function of most vital organs is reduced. This reduction causes a person to become cool and require covers for comfortable sleeping. When a person sleeps, he goes through periods of light and heavy sleep. He also goes through periods when he does and does not dream. Dreaming seems to have an effect upon the quality of sleep. While the range of hours of sleep a person needs varies, most adults sleep approximately six to eight hours a day. Sleep cannot be stored in a body like energy in a flashlight battery and therefore most people need to sleep sometime during each twenty-four hour period.

3. Before you can help students understand their question–answering strategies, you must understand your own. Write the step-by-step procedure for answering the evaluation question that you prepared for the preceding selection.

4. The Introspective Comprehension Strategy is an instructional plan for helping students refine their question–answering strategies. First, list the steps in this instructional plan. Second, prepare a brief statement describing what takes place at each step during the instructional process.

Answers to the Post-test

1. The six categories and their descriptions follow:
    a. Recognition and Recall questions. Questions in this category require a verbatim answer.
    b. Translation questions. Questions in this category require the learner to locate the exact answer and then translate the answer into his own words.
    c. Application questions. Questions in this category require the learner to apply what he has read to solve a problem or change a situation.
    d. Analysis questions. Questions in this category require the learner to separate what he has read into parts and analyze each part.
    e. Synthesis questions. Questions in this category require the learner to combine information from what he has read with information from other sources to form a new idea or product.
    f. Evaluation questions. Questions in this category require the learner to evaluate what has been read and then make a decision using a specified set of criteria. The learner must also justify her information, decision, and the evaluation criteria.
2. Compare each question you wrote with the Classification Scheme for Reading Questions. If you have prepared at least one question for each of the six categories, you have demonstrated the required competency.
3. Compare your question-answering strategy with the following evaluation strategy taken from the Sample Question-Answering Strategies from Enabling Element 3. If your strategy contains the same steps, you have demonstrated the required competency.

Evaluation Question–Answering Strategy

1. Check the question and passage to be sure that it does not contain any unfamiliar words, expressions, or ideas. Clarify as necessary.
2. Be sure the intent of the question is understood. Rephrase the question if necessary.
3. Identify important information from the passage.
4. Establish the evaluation criteria.
5. Evaluate each basic unit of information in terms of the appropriate criterion or criteria.
6. Examine all evaluations and prepare a final decision.
7. Justify the information gathered, evaluation criteria, and your final decision.

4. Introspective Comprehension Lesson Plan
   a. Setting the purpose for learning.
      At this step, the teacher establishes the need for instruction.
   b. Assessing the comprehension strategy.
      Here the teacher asks the students to explain how they answered a question. The purpose of this step is to assess the adequacy of the learners' strategy for answering a specific type of question.
   c. Teaching the comprehension strategy.
      This step contains the procedures for teaching the question–answering strategy.
   d. Testing the comprehension strategy.
      This step is designed to determine if the strategy taught is understood by the learners.
   e. Generalizing the comprehension strategy.
      At this step, the teacher teaches the students how to use the strategy with various kinds of subject area materials.
   f. Applying the comprehension strategy.
      At this step the learner is provided with daily practice sessions to raise his performance in the application of this strategy to the automatic response level.

Final Comment

You have now acquired a competency which will help you improve substantially the comprehension achievement in your subject area. Using this competency requires only minor instructional effort by most subject area teachers. We hope you will make this minor adjustment.

If you have satisfactorily completed all Post-test items, you are ready to move to another module. If not, refer to appropriate Enabling Elements, see your instructor, or refer to the Selected Bibliography.

Selected Bibliography

Altick, R. D. *Preface to Critical Reading,* 4th ed. New York: Holt, Rinehart, and Winston, 1967.

Axelrod, J. "Some Flaws in Commercial Reading Comprehension Materials." *Journal of Reading,* 1974, *17* (6), 474–79.

Bloom, B. S., Hastings, J. T., and Madaus, G. F. *Handbook on Formative and Summative Evaluation of Student Learning.* New York: McGraw-Hill, 1971.

Bloom, B. S. et al. *Taxonomy of Educational Objectives: Handbook I, Cognitive Domain.* New York: David McKay, 1956.

Burmeister, L. E. *Reading Strategies for Secondary School Teachers.* Reading, Massachusetts: Addison-Wesley, 1974.

Carin, A. A., and Sund, R. B. *Developing Questioning Techniques: A Self-Concept Approach.* Columbus, Ohio: Charles E. Merrill, 1971.

Galloway, P. "How Secondary Students and Teachers Read Textbooks." *Journal of Reading,* 1973, *17* (3), 216–19.

Hafner, L. E., ed. *Improving Reading in Middle and Secondary Schools.* New York: Macmillan, 1974.

Herber, H. *Teaching Reading in Content Areas.* Englewood Cliffs, New Jersey: Prentice-Hall, 1970.

Karlin, R. *Teaching Reading in the High School,* 2d ed. Indianapolis, Indiana: Bobbs-Merrill, 1972.

Manzo, A. V. "Guided Reading Procedure." *Journal of Reading,* 1975, *18* (4), 287–91.

Moore, W. E. *Creative and Critical Thinking.* Boston: Houghton Mifflin, 1967.

Putnan, L. R. "Don't Tell Them To Do It, Show Them How." *Journal of Reading,* 1974, *18* (1), 41–43.

Raths, L. E. et al. *Teaching for Thinking: Theory and Application.* Columbus, Ohio: Charles E. Merrill, 1967.

Robinson, H. A. *Teaching Reading and Study Strategies: The Content Areas.* Boston: Allyn and Bacon, 1975.

Robinson, H. A., and Thomas E. L., eds. *Fusing Reading Skills and Content.* Newark, Delaware: International Reading Association, 1969.

Sanders, N. M. *Classroom Questions: What Kinds?* New York: Harper and Row, 1966.

Module 7

Helping Students Use Study Strategies

CONTENTS

Prospectus

Rationale

Reading for most students is too often a passive activity. Passive reading may be justified when the purpose is to relax or escape from daily routines. When, however, the purpose is to acquire and retain information with maximum efficiency, reading must be an active process.

As teachers we need a plan to insure the active participation of our students with their reading assignments. Francis Robinson (1974) and others have developed study strategies for actively involving the learner in the reading process. If you teach these strategies to your students and plan your reading assignments so they can be applied, your students will improve in general subject material awareness, general comprehension, retention, and reading rate.

Objectives

TERMINAL OBJECTIVE: You will become acquainted with three study strategies; you will describe and apply the SQ3R Study Strategy.

Specific Objectives:

1. You will write the key words for the SQ3R Study Strategy and a paragraph describing each step in the process of using SQ3R.
2. You will write the five major steps in preparing an instructional plan to teach the SQ3R Study Strategy.
3. You will write two alternative study strategies and specify for which subject area each is appropriate.

Resources and Time Required

To complete the core Enabling Activities in this module, you will need blank paper, a writing instrument, and one of your subject area textbooks. The estimated time required to complete the core Enabling Activities is three to four hours.

Directions: For each question, determine the word which indicates your belief regarding your competency. If you are in doubt, choose NO.

1. Students who do poorly on follow-up tests based upon reading assignments can improve their performance if they use the SQ3R Study Strategy. Can you name the key words for the SQ3R Study Strategy and write a paragraph describing each step in the process of using SQ3R?

   YES   NO

2. Once familiar with SQ3R, you will want to teach this study strategy to your students. Can you write the five major steps in preparing an instructional plan to teach the SQ3R Study Strategy?

   YES   NO

3. Although SQ3R can be applied to any subject area, alternative study strategies are introduced in this module for certain subject areas. Can you write two alternative study strategies and specify for which subject area each is appropriate?

   YES   NO

Branching Program Alternatives for Pre-test Responses

1. Every students needs a study strategy for reading. If you can name a study strategy and write a paragraph description of each step in the strategy, you are ready for Enabling Element 2. If not, you will find Enabling Element 1 helpful.

2. If you can write the five steps in an instructional plan for teaching SQ3R, you are ready for Enabling Element 3. If not, Enabling Element 2 will provide you with an instructional plan for teaching the study strategy.

3. A number of alternative study strategies are available. If you know two additional study strategies and can associate them with specific subject areas, you are ready for the Post-test. If you feel you need additional information, Enabling Element 3 will be helpful.

Enabling Element 1
The SQ3R Study Strategy
(What is the SQ3R Study Strategy?)

Specific Objective 1

You will write the key words for the SQ3R Study Strategy and a paragraph describing each step in the process of using SQ3R.

Enabling Activities

*1. Read Study Guide 1, "The SQ3R Study Strategy," to identify the five key words associated with this strategy.

*2. After reading Study Guide 1, write a sentence describing each step in the procedure for using SQ3R with a reading assignment.

*3. Practice using the SQ3R Study Strategy with reading assignments containing few or no side headings.

4. Compare the reading rate and comprehension scores after reading two similar assignments, one using SQ3R and the other using your present reading strategy. What do your findings suggest?

*5. Reproduce the section entitled, "The Components of SQ3R," and distribute it to your colleagues. Discuss the possibilities for using this study strategy with materials in a number of subject areas.

*6. Select a reading assignment from a student textbook in your subject area. The reading assignment should be approximately six to ten pages in length *or* require approximately twenty to thirty minutes of sustained silent reading by your students. Following the recommended procedure in "Using the SQ3R Strategy," read the assignment. You will use this to demonstrate the procedure to your students.

*Indicates core Enabling Activities

Study Guide 1
The SQ3R Study Strategy
(What is the SQ3R Study Strategy?)

An educator by the name of Francis Robinson was concerned about the reading comprehension level of high school students. He found that the typical reader remembers only about half of what he is asked for on a quiz immediately following the reading assignment. He found this to be true for both average and superior high school students.

Recognizing this problem, Francis Robinson devised the SQ3R Study Strategy as a technique for increasing immediate understanding and prolonging the retention. The SQ3R Study Strategy he devised is well supported by results obtained from studies investigating the learning process.

SQ3R represents the five steps in the study strategy. The five steps are *Survey, Question, Read, Recite, and Review.* The first three steps evolved from research which demonstrated (1) the value of skimming over and summarizing headings prior to reading and (2) the value of knowing the comprehension questions prior to reading an assignment. Skimming to obtain an overview of the textual material provides an orientation to the material and clues to what information will be presented. Questions provide specific purposes for reading and directions on how to read. Furthermore, the questions are generally connected by a thread of logic that make them easier to remember. Because questions reveal to us the specific information we are looking for, they are valuable in assisting us in remembering the information.

When the first three steps, Survey, Question, and Read, were applied to reading assignments, Robinson found the result was a higher level of immediate understanding. This, however, did not totally satisfy Robinson for he knew that approximately 80 percent of what was read would be forgotten within two weeks. He also knew retention could be improved by test-type reviews after the reading assignment. When test-type review sessions were used following reading, forgetting was reduced from 80 to 20 percent after a two-week period. Because of this substantial change in retention, Robinson added the final two components to his study strategy: Recite and Review.

The SQ3R Study Strategy introduced thirty years ago by Francis Robinson has withstood the test of time. It has been widely accepted because the study strategy is designed to serve as an advanced organizer, provide specific purposes for reading, provide self-comprehension checks, and fix information in memory. The SQ3R Study Strategy does not require additional reading time; in fact, it generally requires less reading time when the technique is mastered.

The Components of SQ3R
(What are the Components of SQ3R?)

There are five basic components or steps in the SQ3R Study Strategy. The student follows the steps in the same order as they occur in the formula statement SQ3R: Survey, Question, Read, Recite, and Review. Here is an overview of the five components:

SURVEY

When the reading material includes side headings, the Survey consists of reading all side headings and the final or summary paragraph. If the reading material does not have side headings, the Survey consists of skimming paragraphs for topic sentences until a transition point is located. When a transition point is located, the reader is advised to stop and reflect on the ideas in the last set of paragraphs read. A question is then formulated about those ideas. This process is continued until the end of the assignment is reached.

QUESTION

Now the headings or major points are changed into questions. A question is used because of all sentence forms it probably provides the reader with the most specific direction. The questions serve as an advanced organizer for the total assignment and each specific question provides immediate and specific direction for reading. *Notice* that all the titles and subtitles in this module have been changed to questions to illustrate the ease with which this can be accomplished.

READ

Taking each question in turn, read to locate the answer. The reader may skim, skip, or reread material as he so chooses. The style of reading should vary with the purpose for reading.

RECITE

Recitation is used to check on clarity of ideas and to fix ideas in memory. After an answer to a question has been located or reasoned out, the reader should pause and recite the answer. Most students should recite their answers aloud. Students, like most of us, are less accepting of their ideas when they are spoken aloud.

REVIEW

A review is used to fix the overall organization as well as the specific ideas in memory. Generally, one review should occur immediately following the completion of the reading assignment. A second review should take place within the next twenty-four hours. For students with memory difficulties, periodic or spaced reviews are advised throughout the reading assignment.

Now that you are aware of how SQ3R was developed and are familiar with the five components of the study strategy, it is time for you to use the study strategy.

Using the SQ3R Strategy
(How Do I Use SQ3R With a Reading Assignment?)

Before you can teach SQ3R to others, it is important that you understand how to use this study strategy. To insure that you will have no difficulty when teaching this strategy to your students, follow our suggestions for using the strategy on a reading assignment in one of the student textbooks in your subject area. As soon as you get the textbook, we can get started.

Practicum Exercise

Identify a six to ten page selection in the textbook. The reading assignment should take approximately twenty to thirty minutes for your average reader to complete. Choose a selection you would like your students to read because later we will ask you to use this passage with your students.

1. *Survey.* Begin by surveying the headings, charts, graphs, pictures, and then reading the final paragraph or summary. Surveying consists of a rapid reading of side headings or topic sentences. This provides the reader with an overview of the content and the thread of organization. Stop reading and complete this step. When complete, begin reading with step 2.

2. *Question.* When the survey has been completed, use the information you have obtained from headings and topic sentences to

formulate questions. For most of us, questions provide a clearer focus than other types of sentence construction. A well formulated question cuts down considerably on the amount of time it takes to locate information. Stop reading and complete this step; then begin reading with step 3.

3. *Read.* Now read to locate the answers to your questions. Reading is not defined here as looking at every word on every line of every page. It is perfectly legitimate to skim material, to skip material, and to reread material. You must remember that the objective is to obtain the information necessary to answer your questions. Your style of reading should vary dramatically as the nature of your questions change. Just as there is more than one type of question, there is also more than one style of reading. Stop reading and complete this step. When completed, begin reading with step 4.

4. *Recite.* After you have located the answer to each question, look away from the textbook and recite the answer in your own words. It is important to recite the answer in your own words to be sure you understand what you have read and avoid parroting. Depending on how important the information is, you may want to write a brief phrase to assist you with the future recall of the information. Stop reading and complete this step. When completed, begin reading with step 5.

5. *Review.* When you finish the assignment, review the ideas obtained from your reading. Remember, immediate recitation followed by periodic reviews is what reduces memory loss from 80 to 20 percent at the end of a two-week period. Stop reading and complete this step. When completed, begin reading the next paragraph.

How was it? If you are like most teachers, you found it very easy to apply this study strategy. You also found you remembered more of what you read. If you timed yourself, you probably found it took you less time than you expected to complete this assignment. You surely noticed that your reading style varied with the nature of the question you asked—and it should! Remember, effective and efficient readers vary their reading style with their purpose for reading.

You are now familiar with the SQ3R Study Strategy and have applied it to a textbook in your teaching area. Now it is time to move on to a discussion on teaching the SQ3R Study Strategy.

Enabling Element 2
Recommended Steps for Teaching SQ3R
(How Do I Teach SQ3R?)

Specific Objective 2

You will write the five major steps in preparing an instructional plan to teach the SQ3R Study Strategy.

Enabling Activities

*1. Read Study Guide 2, "Recommended Steps for Teaching SQ3R," to identify the major steps in an instructional plan to teach the SQ3R Study Strategy.

*2. Apply the SQ3R study strategy to a 6–10 page reading assignment from a textbook available to all your students.

*3. Demonstrate the use of the SQ3R Study Strategy to a small group of students. This will provide you with an opportunity to practice teaching the SQ3R Study Strategy in a controlled environment.

4. Teach a group of students how to use the SQ3R Study Strategy in their reading assignment.

5. Maintain a record of the amount of time spent in actual classroom instruction of SQ3R. Ask the students to maintain records on the estimated amount of time they have saved in reading assignments. After a reasonable amount of time, compare the two to determine if you have gained or lost in learning time as a result of teaching SQ3R.

*6. Demonstrate for your students the application of the SQ3R Study Strategy in newspapers, magazines, and other materials.

7. Select two reading assignments of equivalent difficulty in length. Assign students to read the first using their traditional

---

*Indicates core Enabling Activities

reading approach and the second using the SQ3R Study Strategy. After each assignment has been completed, ask each student to record the amount of time it took to complete each assignment. Then have each student answer some written questions over the assignment. Compare percentage of comprehension and reading time using the two techniques. This experiment should demonstrate the value of the SQ3R Study Strategy.

Study Guide 2
Recommended Steps for Teaching SQ3R
(How Do I Teach SQ3R?)

Now it is time to prepare yourself to teach the SQ3R Study Strategy. The instructional procedures are divided into five steps, each of which is explained in detail.

Selecting Materials

1. Select a reading assignment six to ten pages in length or one requiring twenty to thirty minutes of sustained silent reading by your students. Select reading assignments from suitable textbooks for your students. Actually for your first lesson you may use the practice lesson from the Practicum Exercise in Study Guide 1 if the selection is suitable.
2. Duplicate copies of "The Components of SQ3R" found in Study Guide 1. You will need a copy for each student.
3. Collect copies of non-textbook materials without side headings. You will need one copy for each student in your group. Preferably all students should have a copy of the same material if the material is suitable.

Apply SQ3R

1. Read the six to ten page textbook selection using the SQ3R Study Strategy.
   a. *Survey* the selection
   b. *Question* the material

c. *Read* and answer the questions

d. *Recite* answers

e. *Review* questions and answers

2. If you are using the selection from Study Guide 1, you have already done this.

Schedule Instruction

Schedule three fifty-minute periods for teaching the study strategy to your students. Preferably the three lessons should be taught within the same week.

Instruction

1. During the first fifty-minute period:

   a. Explain to your students that you are going to introduce them to the SQ3R study strategy that is to be used when reading assignments in your class. Tell them the SQ3R strategy will raise their level of understanding, extend retention, and save study time. You may want to share other facts on how Francis Robinson developed the strategy.

   b. Distribute copies of "The Components of SQ3R" to each student. Discuss each component so your students understand its function.

   c. Demonstrate the application of SQ3R using the selection you prepared. Answer any questions your students have.

   d. Assign the same selection to your students. Direct them to apply SQ3R as they read the assignment.

   e. When your students have finished reading the assignment, record their reading time and check comprehension. Use this information in the following discussion.

   f. Begin a group discussion in which SQ3R is compared with prior reading strategies. Point out the advantages of study strategies such as SQ3R.

2. During the second fifty-minute period:

   a. Review the SQ3R components.

   b. Demonstrate the application of SQ3R with another textbook selection.

c. Assign a different selection to be read than you used for demonstration purposes. Direct the students to apply SQ3R as they read.

d. When the assignment is completed, record their reading time and check comprehension. Review the advantages of SQ3R.

e. Assign another shorter selection to provide additional practice using SQ3R.

3. During the third fifty-minute period:

a. Discuss the application of SQ3R to materials without side headings.

b. Demonstrate the application of SQ3R to materials without side headings.

c. Assist students in using SQ3R with a reading assignment in a material that does not contain side headings.

d. When the assignment is completed, record reading time and check comprehension. Discuss advantages of SQ3R with this type of material.

Practice

Schedule ten to fifteen-minute class periods for additional demonstrations and student practice sessions. At least twenty teacher-directed practice sessions will be needed to raise this study strategy to the automatic performance level. This is the level where it is just as easy to apply SQ3R as it is to do anything else. It is probably worth mentioning, that in stress situations, students have a tendency to resort to their most secure and automatic behavior patterns. This means that your students may apply SQ3R in practice activities but not in "reading" assignments unless you provide sufficient practice to raise the skill to the automatic level of behavior. May we also suggest that you encourage the use of SQ3R Study Strategy in every assignment. Do so by providing time for surveying and suggesting questions which can be used to guide reading. Whenever a new type of instructional reading material is used, demonstrate how you apply the strategy to this new material. Always stress and reward improved comprehension and extended memory as a result of using SQ3R.

You are now familiar with the major steps in a lesson plan designed to teach the SQ3R Study Strategy. Before we go on, review the five steps.

Recommended Steps for Teaching SQ3R

1. _____
2. _____
3. _____
4. _____
5. _____

We hope you now know how to use and teach the SQ3R Study Strategy. Take the next step and teach the strategy to someone. All the directions are provided and you have already prepared the material.

Final Comment

We hope that you do not feel that considerable classtime will be lost through the teaching of SQ3R. Actually, you will save time just as your students will save time as a result of increased comprehension, prolonged retention, and decreased reading time.

Enabling Element 3
Alternative Study Strategies
(What Study Strategies are Alternatives to SQ3R?)

Specific Objective 3

You will write two alternative study strategies and specify for which subject area each is appropriate.

Enabling Activities

*1. Read Study Guide 3, "Alternative Study Strategies," to identify two formulas associated with study strategies. Print the two strategies vertically on a piece of white paper.

*2. After reading Study Guide 3, write the appropriate word next to each letter in the two formulas. These formulas were recorded by you earlier on a piece of white paper.

*3. Preceding each list of letters for the two formulas, print the name of the subject area for which each study strategy was designed.

4. Locate a mathematics or science textbook and practice applying the two strategies.

5. Duplicate and distribute to your students copies of the PQRST and SQRQCQ Study Strategies found at the end of this Study Guide. Discuss and demonstrate the application of these study strategies as appropriate.

6. Provide students with daily practice sessions using both strategies until the application of these strategies becomes automatic.

---

*Indicates core Enabling Activities

Study Guide 3
Alternative Study Strategies
(What are the Alternative Study Strategies?)

As you know by now, SQ3R is a study strategy designed to insure the active participation of the learner in the reading process. While this study strategy is in a general way applicable to the reading of textual material in any content area, other strategies have been developed which appear to be more appropriate for mathematics and science.

SQRQCQ—Mathematics (Fay, 1965)

Leo Fay developed a strategy applicable to mathematics. His strategy follows the letter formula, SQRQCQ. The words and a brief description associated with each of the letters in the formula follows:

Survey: Read rapidly to determine intent.
Question: Determine what is being asked.
Read: Read for facts.
Question: Decide upon the processes to be used.
Compute: Do computation.
Question: Ask yourself, "Does the answer appear correct?" Check answer against problem and arithemetic facts.

You can see how effective the SQRQCQ study strategy is by following its application to the following two word problems.

Problem 1

John has been earning $55 a week working for Mr. Tomilson. With the money he earns, John wants to purchase a new motorcycle which costs $349. How many weeks will John have to work to earn enough money to purchase the motorcycle on a cash sale?

Now follow the application of the SQRQCQ study strategy to the solution of this problem.

Survey: Read the complete problem rapidly but carefully to determine the intent or outcome. From a survey of this problem, we learn that John wishes to purchase a motorcycle with his weekly earnings and he would like to know how long it is going to be before he can obtain the motorcycle.

Question: Now that the intent or outcome is clear, put it into a question form. Remember a question is used because of all sentence forms, it probably provides the most specific directions to the reader. Questions also serve as an advance organizer for sifting and locating key information. The question being raised by this problem is, ''At John's present weekly earnings, how long will it take him to purchase the motorcycle he wishes to own?''

Read: Now it is time to look through the problem and identify the pertinent facts. The pertinent facts are: (1) John earns $55 a week, and (2) the motorcycle John wishes to purchase costs $349. While there are no other substantiated facts which are needed, there are some implied facts. First there is an assumption that there will be no weekly deductions from John's $55 salary. Second, it is assumed that his weekly earnings will continue at $55 a week as long as it takes him to accumulate sufficient money to purchase the motorcycle. Third, it is assumed that the motorcycle cannot be purchased for a discount nor will it increase in cost during the time John is acquiring his money.

Question: Now it is time to ask oneself, ''What mathematical process must be followed to obtain the correct answer to the question?'' If the total cost of the motorcycle which is $349 is divided by the weekly earnings of $55, we will obtain the number of weeks John has to work to accomplish his goal.

Compute: The computation is now carried out and when this is through, an answer of seven weeks is obtained.

Question: At this point one should ask, ''Does the answer appear to be correct?'' A simple check can be made to determine the correctness of the answer. Realizing that division is verified through multiplication, the participant multiplies seven weeks times a weekly earning of $55 and obtains a total earnings for the seven weeks of $385. Since $385 is more than the needed $349, one realizes that seven weeks surely is long enough to work to acquire the money. The question arises, however; ''Could sufficient money have been earned in six weeks?'' The answer to this question is obtained by multiplying six weeks times the $55 weekly earnings to obtain a total figure of $330. Now one can see that at the end of six weeks, John does not have enough money to purchase the motorcycle but at the end of seven weeks, he has more

than enough. Since the question raised at the beginning of
this process asks for a number of weeks, seven weeks is the
correct answer.

Practicum Exercise 1

Now it is your turn to apply the SQRQCQ study strategy to a
mathematics problem. By applying the strategy to the following problem, you will experience the power of this strategy.

Problem 2

Peter borrowed $95 from his father at an 8 percent yearly interest rate. He
agreed to pay the loan at the end of three months along with the interest.
How much must he repay?

Describe the procedure you followed to solve this problem.

Survey:

Question:

Read:

Question:

Compute:

Question:

We are sure you found the letter formula very helpful for organizing your attack on this problem. You probably proceeded in the following manner:

Answer to Practicum 1

Survey: Your quick but careful survey of the problem revealed to you that Peter borrowed money which he would have to pay back at a specific time along with a certain amount of interest for its use.

Question: The question being raised in this problem is, "What is the total principle and interest to be paid at the end of three months on a $95 loan at an 8 percent yearly interest?"

Read: The facts are: (1) the total amount borrowed was $95, (2) the loan is to be repaid in three months, (3) the 8 percent interest is a yearly interest rate and Peter only has to pay interest on his loan for the three month period of time he used his father's money. An assumed fact is that all the conditions of the loan will remain constant.

Question: Next you ask yourself, "What mathematical processes must be carried out to solve this problem?" First, what is the yearly interest at 8 percent? This is a multiplication task. Second, what fraction is three months of one year? This is a process of reducing fractions. Third, how much is the interest for three months? This is a division process. Fourth, how much is the total principle and interest for three months? This is an addition process.

Compute: The yearly interest at 8 percent is $7.60. Three months is
equal to one quarter of a year. (¼ of $7.60 = $1.90) ($95 +
$1.90 = $96.90)

Question: At this step, ask yourself "Is the answer reasonable?" Next,
check each step of your answer to see if it is correct. Your
verification revealed that the total principle plus interest
payment of $96.90 is correct.

We hope your answers and explanations agreed in kind with those
presented here. If they did, find two written problems in a mathematics
textbook and solve these problems using the SQRQCQ study strategy.
Prepare a written explanation of your solution, duplicate, and distribute
it to your students. Now you are ready to teach your students how to use
the SQRQCQ strategy.

PQRST—Science

George Spache (1963) developed a study strategy which according
to Fay (1965) is applicable to science. His strategy follows the letter
formula PQRST. The words and a brief description associated with each
of the letters in the formula follows:

Preview: Skim selection to obtain an overall impression.

Question: Develop questions to be used as purposes for reading.

Read: Using the questions as guides, read the selection.

Summarize: Organize information and summarize, preferably in
written form.

Test: Compare your summary with the facts in the selection.

Before we look at some passages characteristic of science writing,
a few points need to be made. First, scientific materials are written in a
different style than most of the materials students are accustomed to
reading. Science textbooks for the most part are not designed with the
expressed purpose of imparting information. They do contain a considerable amount of information, but the emphasis is upon developing a
way of thinking often referred to as the *inquiry* or *scientific method.*
Second, in science textbooks the reader is generally required to accumulate numerous details which are being formulated by the author into a
generalization, theory, or concept. Once the generalization, theory, or
concept has been formed, the student is required to test it through a series

of experiments. With these points in mind, let us see how the PQRST study strategy is applied to the following selection. The science selections in this module are typical of, but shorter than most selections found in science books.

Your Nervous System

In your body the nervous system regulates all other systems. The nervous system can be divided into three separate but related systems. First is the *central nervous system* which includes the brain and the spinal cord. Second, is the *peripheral nervous system* which includes the outward extention of nerves from the spinal cord to the base of the brain. Third, is the *autonomic nervous system* which controls both the central and peripheral systems through conscious activity and sensations. When we think of these three systems, it is best not to think of them as discrete systems; but rather as interrelated systems, the interrelationship of which is necessary to sustain good health and life.

Read to learn how PQRST was applied to this passage.

Preview: Skim the title and the selection to gain an overall impression. You notice that the selection deals with the central nervous system. There are some important points that the author has highlighted for your attention. Anything that appears in capital letters or italics should be given special attention during the previewing. The previewing suggests that there are at least four important areas of information discussed in this selection. The general topic is the nervous system; specific topics are the central nervous system, peripheral nervous system, and autonomic nervous system.

Question: There are at least four questions that would be developed over this selection. What is a nervous system? How do each of these parts relate to the nervous system: the central nervous system? peripheral system? autonomic system?

Read: Using the questions as guides, read the selection slowly. Carefully pay particular attention to the facts which cluster around your questions. Remember that in scientific writing, facts are very important. While many facts are needed to substantiate the theory, only a single fact is needed to refute it.

Summarize: Take the facts that you have gathered and organize them into clusters around the four questions. First, summarize the facts around the three questions which relate to the central nervous system, peripheral nervous system, and autonomic nervous system. Second, summarize all the facts for the major question on the nervous system.

Test: Examine the passage to be sure that you have included all the facts necessary for each summary statement. Check your summaries to be sure they contain only facts that can be found in the passage.

Practicum Exercise 2

Now it is your turn to apply the PQRST study strategy.

Weather Symbols

The weather map used by meteorologists contains a variety of information. The quantity of information and ease of reading require that the information be codified. Three major classes of weather symbols are codified under (1) precipitation, (2) cloud cover, and (3) barometric change.

The precipitation code includes an asterisk for snow, a dot for rain, and an inverted triangle for showers. The symbols may be combined. For example, a dot over an inverted triangle means rain showers. An asterisk over an inverted triangle means snow showers.

The cloud cover code is a simple one. It uses only a circle. A clear circle indicates clearness or no clouds. A half shaded circle indicates partly cloudy weather. A fully shaded circle means cloudy.

The barometric code is also simple. A horizontal line means steady. A line rising to the right indicates rising barometric pressure. A line falling to the right indicates falling barometric pressure.

Your knowledge of these signs will enhance your understanding of weather reporting. It will also improve your map reading ability.

For each of the following key words in the PQRST study strategy, describe the procedure you used as you read "Weather Symbols."

Preview:

Question:

Read:

Summarize:

Test:

Answer to Practicum Exercise 2

The PQRST letter formula is a helpful device for remembering key words that will assist you in understanding scientific writing. You should have found these key words helpful as you read "Weather Symbols." You probably read this passage in the following manner.

Preview: You skimmed the title and the selection to gain an overall
            impression. As you were skimming, you noticed that there

was a sequence of three numbers used in the selection. The numbers should have alerted you to something important. If you stopped and read the sentence containing those numbers, you learned a great deal about the selection. You learned that the selection was probably a discussion of three different types of codes. A quick glance at each of the succeeding paragraphs should have verified that observation.

Question: At least two major and three minor questions should come to mind. While yours may not have been exactly like ours, they were probably somewhat similar. What are weather symbols? What are weather symbols used for? What are the weather symbols for precipitation? for cloud cover? for barometric change?

Read: Using the questions as guides, you read the selection slowly and carefully clustered your facts around your questions.

Summarize: You took the facts that you had gathered and organized them into clusters around the questions you raised. First you summarized the minor questions and second the major questions.

Test: At this step you examined the passage to be sure that you had included all the necessary facts in your answer. You checked your summaries to be sure they contained only facts that could be found in the passage. Having done this, you are satisfied with your answers.

If your answers and explanations agreed with those presented here, you are ready to try PQRST on scientific material of your own choosing, after which we hope you will share this study strategy with your students.

Some Cautions

One word of caution before we leave our discussion of study strategies. Both the SQRQCQ and the PQRST study strategies are effective study tools when students are familiar with vocabulary and mathematical operations in mathematics and vocabulary and scientific method in science. Furthermore, these study strategies can only be effectively applied when they are built upon a sound foundation in basic comprehension skills. Any study strategy must have as its foundation the core reading skills of word pronunciation, vocabulary, and comprehension. No study strategy should ever be thought of or used as a substitute for these core skills. When students lack the core reading skills, knowledge of subject area vocabulary or knowledge of mathematical operations or scientific method, instruction in these fundamentals should precede instruction in study strategies.

Upon completion of this study guide, you should be aware of two alternative study strategies, their letter formulas, and the subject areas for which they are appropriate. If you have acquired these competencies and the competencies for Specific Objectives 1 and 2, you are ready for the Post-test. If you have not acquired these competencies, do so before going on the the Post-test. If you are confused about a point, reread your material, talk with a colleague, or see your instructor.

Summary of SQRQCQ and PQRST Study Strategies

SQRQCQ—Mathematics

Survey:	Read rapidly to determine intent.
Question:	Determine what is being asked.
Read:	Read for facts.
Question:	Decide upon the process to be used.
Compute:	Do computation.
Question:	Ask yourself, does the answer appear correct? Check your answer against problem and arithmetic facts.

PQRST—Science

Preview:	Skim selection to obtain an overall impression.
Question:	Develop questions to be used as purposes for reading.
Read:	Using the questions as guides, read the selection slowly and carefully to obtain appropriate information.
Summarize:	Organize information and prepare a written summary.
Test:	Compare information with summary. Test for completeness and accuracy.

Post-test

Directions: Read each of the following statements and complete each Post-test item as directed.

1. SQ3R is the first study strategy discussed in this module. This strategy was introduced by Francis Robinson and has been used successfully for over thirty years. Write the key words associated with each letter in the SQ3R formula statement. Also write a paragraph describing each step in the process of using SQ3R.

2. Your students will enjoy applying SQ3R to their reading assignments. But before they can apply it, you must teach it to them. Write the five major steps in an instructional plan for teaching the SQ3R strategy.

3. SQ3R may not be an appropriate study strategy for all subject areas. Write two alternative study strategies and specify for which subject area each is appropriate.

1. The key words associated with the SQ3R formula statement are:
   *S*urvey
   *Q*uestion
   *R*ead
   *R*ecite
   *R*eview

   The following are the recommended procedures for applying SQ3R to reading assignments:

   Survey. Begin by making a quick survey of the reading assignment to obtain a general idea of the selection. Refer to side headings and/or topic sentences as appropriate.

   Question. Turn each heading into a question. If headings are not available, key topics should be turned into questions.

   Read. Read to answer each question. Questions are answered in the order in which they occur.

   Recite. Recite the answer to the question with the eyes averted from the passage. It is often beneficial to write key phrases in outline form.

   Review. Review your questions and answers immediately following the reading assignment. Periodic reviews are advised to enhance retention.

2. The five major steps for preparing an instructional plan to teach the SQ3R Study Strategy are:

   Selecting materials
   Apply SQ3R
   Schedule
   Instruction
   Practice

3. The two alternative study strategies and the subject areas for which each is appropriate follow:

Mathematics
S Survey
Q Question
R Read
Q Question
C Compute
Q Question

Science
P Preview
Q Question
R Read
S Summarize
T Test

Selected Bibliography

Burmeister, L. E. *Reading Strategies for Secondary School Teachers*. Reading, Massachusetts: Addison-Wesley, 1974.

Fay, L. "Reading Study Skills: Math and Science." In Figurel, J. A., ed. *Reading and Inquiry*. Newark, Delaware: International Reading Association, 1965.

Harris, A. J. "Research on Some Aspects of Comprehension: Rate, Flexibility, and Study Skills." *Journal of Reading*, 1968, *12* (3), 205–10, 258–60.

Herber, H. L., ed. "Developing Study Skills in Secondary School." *Perspectives in Reading*. Newark, Delaware: International Reading Association, 1965, *2*.

Herber, H. L. *Teaching Reading in Content Areas*. Englewood Cliffs, New Jersey: Prentice-Hall, 1970.

Karlin, R. *Teaching Reading in High School*. 2d ed. Indianpolis: Bobbs-Merrill, 1972.

Kline, L. W., ed. *Journal of Reading*, 1973, *16* (7).

Marksheffel, N. D. *Better Reading in Secondary School*. New York: Ronald, 1966.

Olson, A. V., and Ames, W. S., eds. *Teaching Reading Skills in Secondary Schools: Readings*. Scranton, Pennsylvania: Intex Publishing Company, 1970.

Robinson, F. P. "Study Skills for Superior Students in Secondary School." In Hafner, L. E., ed. *Improving Reading in Middle and Secondary Schools*, 2d ed. New York: Macmillan, 1974.

Robinson, H. A. *Teaching Reading and Study Strategies: The Content Areas*. Boston: Allyn and Bacon, 1975.

Robinson, H. A., and Thomas, E. L., eds. *Fusing Reading Skills and Content*. Newark, Delaware: International Reading Association, 1969.

Shepherd, D. L. *Comprehensive High School Reading Methods*. Columbus, Ohio: Charles E. Merrill, 1973.

Spache, G. D. *Toward Better Reading*. Champaign, Illinois: Garrard, 1963.

Viox, R. "Evaluating Reading and Study Skills in Secondary Classroom." *Reading Aids Series*. Newark, Delaware: International Reading Association, 1968.

Module 8

Helping Students Pronounce Multisyllable Words

CONTENTS

Prospectus

Rationale

One characteristic of subject area textual material is its unique vocabulary. Generally speaking, this vocabulary consists of hundreds if not thousands of long or multisyllable words. Your students will have to learn to pronounce these words as well as acquire their meanings.

Most middle and secondary students will have acquired the necessary word pronunciation skills to pronounce the many new multisyllable words. However, there is very likely to be a group of students who have not acquired these abilities. These students will rely upon you to provide them with the necessary word pronunciation strategy to read the textual material in your subject area.

It is not the purpose of this module to acquaint you with the word pronunciation skills taught in the primary grades. If you have students who need the primary grade reading skills, Module 10 provides suggestions for handling these problem readers. For the most part, this latter group of students needs the help of trained reading specialists.

The purpose of this module is to provide subject area teachers with a brief but useful strategy for helping students pronounce multisyllable words. You will teach this strategy to students who for various reasons did not acquire this strategy in the upper elementary grades. Soon you will be able to assign them reading materials that would have been difficult prior to possession of this strategy.

Objectives

✓ TERMINAL OBJECTIVE: You will determine the word pronunciation strategies used by students and help them use a strategy for pronouncing multisyllable words.

Specific Objectives

✓ 1. You will prepare a written list of steps which comprises the

253

word pronunciation strategy presented in this module.

√ 2. You will construct, administer, record, and use the results of tests for assessing word pronunciation skills and strategies.

√ 3. You will list each of the major organizational steps and their purpose in lesson plans designed to teach word pronunciation skills and strategy.

Resources and Time Required

Most of the materials required for completing the starred core Enabling Activities are provided. The teacher will need to supply eleven three by five inch white index cards, a single sheet of two by three foot newsprint, and a few sheets of white paper. The estimated time to complete the starred core Enabling Activities is three to five hours.

Pre-test

Directions: For each question, determine the word that indicates your belief regarding your competency. If you are in doubt, choose NO.

1. During reading assignments, many students   YES (NO)
are confronted with multisyllable words they
cannot pronounce even though these words are
often in their listening vocabulary. Can you list
the steps in a word pronunciation strategy
which can be taught to students to assist them
in pronouncing subject area words they have
heard but not seen?

2. Students who are having difficulty pronounc-   YES   NO
ing multisyllable words are not always readily
identifiable. Do you know how to construct,
administer, record, and use the results of tests
for assessing word pronunciation skills and
strategies?

3. To enable students with word pronunciation   YES   NO
difficulties to achieve optimally in your subject
area, you may need to teach them certain word
pronunciation skills and a word pronunciation
strategy. Can you list each of the major organizational steps and their purpose in lesson plans
designed to teach the word pronunciation skills
and strategies?

Branching Program Alternatives for Pre-test Responses

1. Some of your students will be confronted in your subject area textual material with multisyllable words they cannot pronounce. If you can list the steps in a word pronunciation strategy which can be taught to these students, you are ready for Enbling Element 2. If you cannot, Enabling Element 1 presents a word pronunciation strategy you will find valuable.

2. Since all of your students will not need to be taught word pronunciation skills and a word pronunciation strategy, you will need to identify those who need this instruction. If you know how to construct, administer, record, and use the results of tests for assessing these skills and strategies, you are ready for Enabling Element 3. If you do not, Enabling Element 2 will help you achieve the objective.

3. Once you have identified students who need to acquire word pronunciation skills and strategy, you will need to plan for their instruction. Can you list each of the major organizational steps and their purpose in lesson plans designed to teach this skill and strategy? If you can, you are ready for the Post-test. If not, Enabling Element 3 will provide you with this information.

Enabling Element 1
A Word Pronunciation Strategy

Specific Objective 1

You will prepare a written list of steps which comprises the word pronunciation strategy presented in this module.

Enabling Activities

*1. Read Study Guide 1, "A Word Pronunciation Strategy for Subject Area Students," and prepare a list of the seven steps in the strategy.

*2. Obtain a sheet of two-by-three foot newsprint or similar material and record the word pronunciation strategy. Display the strategy in a permanent location in your classroom. As students have difficulty pronouncing words, refer them to the strategy. Your students will find your chart a valuable aid to word pronunciation. Look at the "Strategy Chart" provided at the end of this Study Guide for suggestions.

3. Students who are struggling in their attempts to pronounce longer words may benefit from a discussion and examination of the more common prefixes and suffixes. Lists of common prefixes and suffixes are provided at the end of this Study Guide.

4. You may wish to do a content analysis of your subject area material to identify the many prefixes and suffixes used in your subject area. A form, entitled Subject Area Inventory, is provided at the end of this Study Guide to assist you with this task. Also, Appendix C of Burmeister's book (1974, pp. 298–308) includes an extensive list of prefixes and suffixes used in

---

*Indicates core Enabling Activities

specific content fields. Exposure to the isolated prefixes and suffixes will help your students identify them in unrecognized words.

5. Provide small group practice sessions one or two minutes daily for pronouncing multisyllable words from textual material. You will increase pronunciation effectiveness and efficiency.
6. Duplicate the word pronunciation strategy on book markers and distribute to every student in your class. Give the extras to the librarian or other teachers.

Study Guide 1
A Word Pronunciation Strategy for Subject Area Students

By the end of the sixth grade, some students will not have acquired all the necessary skills to identify some of the longer, specialized words found in the various subject areas. If you wish to assign your subject area reading material to this latter group of students, it will be necessary for you to provide them with some word pronunciation instruction. If you provide this instruction, you will find that your students will complete more reading assignments.

You undoubtedly have some students in your classes who struggle with their reading assignments because they cannot pronounce all the words. If you analyze the words the students have difficulty pronouncing, you will discover the following:

1. Many of the words begin with a prefix and/or end with a suffix.
2. Many of the words contain stems that are composed of two or more syllables. A stem is a base word or unit to which a prefix and/or suffix is affixed such as *pay* in pre*pay*ment.
3. If you observe students who have difficulty pronouncing words, you will notice they approach unrecognized words in a haphazard way rather than with a definite strategy.
4. Furthermore, your observation of these struggling word pronouncers will reveal that many of the students have the elementary phonics skills to pronounce the one- and two-syllable common words.

Using what we know about the kinds of difficulties struggling word pronouncers have, we can develop a strategy that will help many of them pronounce the longer and more complex words. The components of such a strategy follow and are in the appropriate order.

Word Pronunciation Strategy
1. Look for a prefix.
2. Look for a suffix.
3. Locate the stem.
4. Divide the stem into syllables.
5. Try the word in context.
6. Look in the glossary or dictionary.
7. Ask someone how to pronounce the word.

Since this word pronunciation strategy may be new to you, a comment or two about each component seems warranted.

Prefixes are language units which occur before a stem and change its meaning. For example, *un* in *unkind,* and *pre* in *preheat.* Many of the longer words that perplex struggling readers contain prefixes. Since prefixes are easy to spot, occur frequently in words which present pronunciation problems, and have a highly reliable pronunciation, it seems this is the likely place to begin a strategy.

Suffixes are also language units but they occur after the stem to change the function of a word. For example, *able* in *mailable, ly* in *lovely,* and *tion* in *education.* Many of the longer and more perplexing words also contain suffixes. Since suffixes are also easy to spot, occur frequently, and have highly reliable pronunciations, they are placed second in the strategy.

What remains when the prefix and suffix have been removed from a word is the *stem*. The stem is the next component of the word that must be identified. It is a base word to which a prefix and/or suffix may be added; it is the underlying language unit. Some examples are *dance* in *dancer, fair* in *unfairly,* and *skill* in *unskillful.* However, a stem may not always be recognized as a word. Some examples of this fact are *ten* in *pretension, trac* in *subtraction* and *halt* in *exhalt.*

Once the stem has been isolated, the reader must determine if the stem has more than one syllable. If the stem is only a single syllable, chances are the student can pronounce the syllable so this step can be skipped. Stems containing more than one syllable have more than one vowel which is usually separated by one or more consonants. Some examples are con-*sist*, re-*fur-bish*, and di-*vide*. When the stem is two or more syllables, it is necessary to divide it into separate syllables before being pronounced. Two guiding rules that are helpful for dividing stems follow:

1. Stems following the consonant-vowel-consonant / consonant-vowel - consonant (CVC/CVC) pattern are usually divided between the double consonants. Some examples are *but*/*ton*, *can*/*cel*, and *nor*/*mal*. This rule works very well as long as the middle two consonants are not consonant clusters like *ch*, *ph*, *th*, *bl*, *st*, *cr*. Such natural clusters are usually not divided.

2. Stems following the consonant-vowel/consonant-vowel (CV-CV) pattern are usually divided after the first vowel. Some examples are *la*/*bor*, *fla*/*grant*, and *fi*/*nite*. Once the stem has been divided into syllables, the student can pronounce each syllable using those reading skills acquired in the earlier grades.

When the prefix, suffix, and stem have been identified and pronounced, the word should be returned to the sentence and read. *Sentence sense,* or *context clues,* is one of the most useful and reliable word pronunciation clues as long as the word is in the student's listening vocabulary.

Occasionally the steps discussed thus far in the word pronunciation strategy do not help a student pronounce a word. In this case the student should be directed to use a subject area textbook glossary or a dictionary to obtain the pronunciation. If this fails, he should be directed to ask someone for the correct pronunciation of the word.

Now you have the components of the word pronunciation strategy. If you have students in your classes who are struggling with this problem, now you know what to teach them. A number of instructional aids are provided at the end of this Study Guide to assist you as you teach this strategy. They are:

1. The *Strategy Chart.* This is a useful abbreviated list of key components of the word pronunciation strategy. If you wish, you may duplicate the strategy and distribute to students or use it to construct a larger chart for display on a bulletin board.

2. *List of Most Common Prefixes.* This is a helpful list you can bring to the attention of your students to insure that none of these are causing word pronunciation difficulties.

3. *List of Most Common Suffixes.* This list also can be introduced to students to insure none are causing word pronunciation difficulties. Pronunciation difficulties occur more often with suffixes than with prefixes.

4. *Subject Area Inventory.* This is a useful form for examining subject area materials to inventory prefixes and suffixes. Once identified, these prefixes and suffixes can be used to familiarize students with additional causes of word pronunciation difficulties.

Practicum Exercise

Now it is time for you to go to work. As you read this Study Guide, you should have prepared a list of the seven steps in the word pronunciation strategy. List the seven steps.

Answers to the Practicum Exercise

Your list should contain the following steps:

1. Look for a prefix.
2. Look for a suffix.
3. Locate the stem.
4. Divide the stem into syllables. CVC/CVC or CV/CV

5. Try it in context.
6. Look in glossary or dictionary.
7. Ask someone.

Strategy Chart

Key Terms to Remember
1. Prefix
2. Suffix
3. Stem
4. Syllables
   a. CVC/CVC
   b. CV/CV
5. Context
6. Glossary or Dictionary
7. Ask

List of the Most Common Prefixes

ab	dis
ad	en
be	ex
com	in
de	pre
pro	sub
re	un

List of the Most Common Suffixes

ness	ant	ing	ed (d)
er	ment	ful	ly
tion	est	able	ed (ed)
ily	al	ed (t)	ent
y	ive	ance	ous

If you know and have listed the steps in the word pronunciation strategy, you are ready for Enabling Element 2. Enabling Element 2 will help you identify those students who need to develop further their strategy. If not, return through the elements as necessary or talk with your instructor.

Subject Area Inventory

Source: Prefixes	Suffixes	Source: Prefixes	Suffixes

Enabling Element 2
Assessing Word Pronunciation

Specific Objective 2

You will construct, administer, record, and use the results of tests for assessing word pronunciation skills and strategies.

Enabling Activities

*1. Read Study Guide 2, "Assessing Word Pronunciation." Prepare a test for assessing word pronunciation skills and strategies, and two Class Record forms.

2. Prepare an alternative test form for assessing word pronunciation. The test items are included at the end of the Study Guide.

3. Identify two students from your subject area and administer the *Quick Test of Word Pronunciation* and the *Word Pronunciation Strategy Test.* Fill out the Class Record Form appropriately for these two students.

4. Construct and use tests of word pronunciation with different prefixes, and suffixes, and syllabication generalizations.

5. You may discover that a number of your students lack the basic word pronunciation skills taught in the primary grades. You may want to refer to *Phonics in Proper Perspective* by Arthur Heilman and obtain suggestions for teaching these skills. This reference is listed in the Selected Bibliography.

Study Guide 2
Assessing Word Pronunciation

One of the characteristics of subject area material is the introduction of specialized vocabulary. These are words used to label the concepts in

---

*Indicates core Enabling Activity.

each subject area. Specialized vocabulary is one of the components that differentiates one subject area from another.

Generally, specialized vocabularies consist of multisyllable words formed through the use of prefixes, suffixes, and compound stems. Prefixes are useful for altering the meaning of words, suffixes for changing the function of words, and compound stems for forming new words.

Often, students learn to pronounce new subject area words by listening to their teachers. If there are only a few new words to learn, it is not difficult for a student to memorize these words. When, however, there are numerous new words to learn, memorization is an inappropriate technique for most students. Students then must have another method or strategy to help them pronounce words, the pronunciation of which they have forgotten.

Many students during their elementary school years acquire adequate methods or strategies for pronouncing unfamiliar words. These students quite likely will not need additional instruction. Those students who have not acquired a strategy will need your assistance to acquire a workable word pronunciation strategy. If you will take the time to identify these students and teach them the strategy presented in this module, your students will be better able to accomplish your course objectives.

This Study Guide will familiarize you with a simple test you can use to identify students who need to be taught word pronunciation skills and strategy. Enabling Element 3 contains detailed lesson plans for teaching word pronunciation skills and strategy.

Preparing Tests and Record Keeping Materials

1. *Quick Test of Word Pronunciation,* Form A
   Print or type each of the following nonsense words on the unlined side of a three by five inch white index card. Print or type the dictionary respelling on the back of each card.

Front of Card	*Back of Card*
pronabment	pro/năb/ment
abstraimance	ab/strāĭm/ance
comteationly	com/tēą/tion/ly
subsumptarant	sub/sŭmp/tär/ant
demomenence	de/mō/mĕn/ence

Form B of the *Quick Test of Word Pronunciation* is provided at the end of this Study Guide. You may want to use this form for students who were absent or to evaluate achievement after you provide instruction.

2. *Word Pronunciation Strategy Test*

Take one three by five white index card and print or type the following question on one side.

When you come to a word in a sentence that you do not immediately recognize, how do you go about pronouncing that word? (What do you do first, second, third, etc., may be asked if further elaboration is necessary.)

3. *Class Record Form*

Prepare a Class Record Form such as Figure 6 for recording the word pronunciation difficulties of your students. You will need one record form for each class.

Figure 6
Quick Test of Word Pronunciation
Class Record Form

Names of Students	Skills Unknown						Strategy Not Known
	Prefix	Suffix	Single Syllable Stems	Multiple CVC/CVC Stems	Multiple CV/CV Stems	Context Clues	

Test Administration, Interpretation, and Record Keeping

1. Take one of the Class Record forms you prepared. Record on the form the name of every student in the class you have decided to test.

2. Arrange your class schedule to provide approximately three minutes for testing each student.

3. Each student must be tested separately. You will need a place where other students cannot hear what is said. It is not necessary to be out of the sight of other students.

4. When each student arrives at the testing center, explain that you would like to determine if she has the necessary word pronunciation skills and a strategy for pronouncing the longer words which appear in your textual material.

5. Begin by exposing, one at a time, the cards containing the multisyllable nonsense words. Explain that these are nonsense words and you would like the student to pronounce them as if they were real words.

6. As the student pronounces each nonsense word, look for the following difficulties. As a difficulty is identified, place a check after the student's name under the appropriate category on the Class Record Form. Do this for all five nonsense words.

Nonsense Word	Sources of Difficulty
pronabment	pro–prefix
	nab–stem
	ment–suffix
abstraimance	ab–prefix
	straim–stem
	ance–suffix
comteationly	com–prefix
	tea–stem
	tion–suffix
	ly–suffix
subsumptarant	sub–prefix
	sumptar–stem (CVC/CVC)
	ant–suffix
demomenence	de–prefix
	momen–stem (CV/CV)
	ence–suffix

What follows are the nonsense words as pronounced by a student. Look at the errors and then see how they are classified in the Class Record which follows.

Nonsense Word	*Pronounced by Student*	*Errors*
pronabment	pro/nab/ent	1 suffix
abstraimance	ab/strum/ent	1 stem; 1 suffix
comteationly	com/tea/tal/ty	2 suffixes
subsumptarant	sub/sumpt/ent	1 cvc/cvc; 1 suffix
demomenence	de/mome/nence	1 cv/cv; 1 suffix

The recorded errors in the Class Record Form are as follows:

Figure 7
Quick Test of Word Pronunciation
Class Record Form

Names of Students	Skills Unknown						Strategy Not Known
	Prefix	Suffix	Single Syllable Stems	Multiple CVC/CVC Stems	Multiple CV/CV Stems	Context Clues	
Jack		✓✓✓ ✓✓✓	✓	✓	✓		✓

7. Next, take the single three-by-five card containing the Word Pronunciation Strategy Test and place it in front of the student. Ask the student to read aloud and answer the question on this card. It is acceptable to read the question to the student. (It may be necessary to query the student to obtain his most complete answer.) Compare the student's answer with the strategy presented in this module:

   a. Look for a prefix.
   b. Look for a suffix.
   c. Locate the stem.
   d. Divide the stem into syllables.
   e. Try the word in context.

f. Look in the glossary or dictionary
g. Ask someone who knows.

It is not necessary for the student's answer to contain the same precise words, the same number of steps, or have them in the same order. There are many acceptable ways of stating this strategy and you will have to use your own best professional judgment to determine if the expressed strategy is adequate. You will become better at this as you practice. If the student should omit mention of any one of the steps, place a check (✔) after his name under the column Strategy Not Known. For example, when we asked Jack, "When you come to a word in a sentence that you do not immediately recognize, how do you go about pronouncing that word?" He responded, "Look for a beginning and ending that I know and divide the word into syllables." When Jack was asked to tell more about how he pronounced words, he said "That's all I know." In this case, Jack appears to be aware of prefixes, suffixes, and syllabication. Since he does not demonstrate an awareness of context clues, glossary or dictionary, and his responsibility to ask for the pronunciatiation of an unknown word, a (✔) should be placed under Strategy Not Known.

Now it is time for you to identify word pronunciation skill and strategy errors and to classify them appropriately in the Class Record Form (see Figure 8).

Practicum Exercise

Mary pronounced the following words as indicated. Her strategy is also presented. Classify her errors in the Class Record Form provided.

Nonsense Word	Pronounced by Student	Summary of Errors
pronabment	pro/na/bent	_____
abstraimance	ab/strum/any	_____
comteationly	com/toe/ton/ty	_____
subsumptarant	sub/sumt/ance	_____
demomence	de/mon/en/ed	_____

Mary's strategy is "I look for a beginning that I know and guess."

Figure 8
Quick Test of Word Pronunciation
Class Record Form

Names of Students	Skills Unknown						Strategy Not Known
	Prefix	Suffix	Single Syllable Stems	Multiple CVC/CVC Stems	Multiple CV/CV Stems	Context Clues	
Jack		✓✓✓ ✓✓✓	✓	✓	✓		✓
Mary							

Answer to Practicum Exercise

An examination of Mary's errors revealed the following. Checks (✔) should appear in the appropriate columns on the Class Record.

Nonsense Word	Pronounced by Student	Summary of Errors
pronabment	pro/na/bant	1 stem; 1 suffix
abstraimance	ab/staim/any	1 stem; 1 suffix
comteationly	com/tea/ton/ty	2 suffixes
subsumptarant	sub/sumt/ance	1 cvc/cvc; 1 suffix
demomence	de/mon/en/ed	1 cv/cv; 1 suffix

Mary's strategy is inadequate. Her strategy is limited to looking for prefixes and guessing. A check (✔) should be placed in the Class Record Form (see Figure 9) under Strategy Not Known.

If you classified the errors correctly, you are ready for Enabling Element 3, which will provide you with directions and lesson plans for teaching word pronunciation skills and strategy. If not, re-examine appropriate Enabling Elements or see your instructor.

Figure 9
Quick Test of Word Pronunciation
Class Record Form

Names of Students	Skills Unknown						Strategy Not Known
	Prefix	Suffix	Single Syllable Stems	Multiple CVC/CVC Stems	Multiple CV/CV Stems	Context Clues	
Jack		✓✓✓ ✓✓✓	✓	✓	✓		✓
Mary		✓✓✓✓ ✓✓	✓✓	✓	✓		✓

Final Comment

If you will try administering the tests to your students, you will be amazed at the number who can profit from the lessons and strategy found in Enabling Element 3. Go ahead and try!

Quick Test of Word Pronunciation, Form B

Directions: Prepare and administer Form B following the directions provided for Form A.

Front of Card	*Back of Card*	*Sources of Difficulty*
premeply	pre/mĕp/ly	pre–prefix mep–stem ly–suffix
exscreemest	ex/scrēę́m/est	ex–prefix screem–stem est–suffix
subpeedtionous	sub/pēę́d/tion/ous	sub–prefix peed–stem tion–suffix ous–suffix

unpetsuming   un/pĕt/sum/ing   un–prefix
                                         petsum–stem (CVC/CVC)
                                         ing–suffix

besimenable   be/sī/mĕn/able   be–prefix
                                         simen–stem(CV/CV)
                                         able–suffix

Enabling Element 3
Teaching Word Pronunciation Skills

Specific Objective 3

You will list each of the major organizational steps and their purpose in lesson plans designed to teach word pronunciation skills and strategy.

Enabling Activities

*1. Read Study Guide 3, "Teaching Word Pronunciation Skills," to learn the major organizational steps in seven lesson plans designed to develop a precise strategy for pronouncing multi-syllable words.

2. Teach the seven plans to one or two students needing this instruction.

*3. Look through your textual material and locate prefixes and suffixes not included in the lesson plans contained in this Study Guide. Modify the plans to include these prefixes and suffixes.

4. If you have an aide or school volunteer, familiarize her with the instructional procedure in this Enabling Element. Have her teach students who need to acquire the word pronunciation strategy.

5. You may want to use some of your better students as tutors. Peer teaching has been found to be very effective in many situations.

Study Guide 3
Teaching Word Pronunciation Skills

The Word Pronunciation Strategy

The lessons in this Study Guide are designed to develop a precise word pronunciation strategy. The strategy is designed to be applied to

---

*Indicates core Enabling Activities

longer, multisyllable words that often perplex subject area students. These are words in students' listening vocabularies but *not* in their reading vocabularies. If a word is missing from students' listening vocabularies, the problem is word meaning, not word pronunciation. If this is the case, refer to Module 5, "Teaching Word Meanings," for ideas on developing word meaning. If the problem is word pronunciation, the lesson plans in this Study Guide will help you assist selected students in improving word pronunciation.

The lesson plans are designed to develop an understanding of specific word pronunciation skills and the steps in a word pronunciation strategy. When all the lessons have been presented to students, the following skills and strategy will have been developed:

Word Pronunciation Strategy

1. Look for prefix.
2. Look for suffix.
3. Locate the stem.
4. Divide stem into syllables. (CVC/CVC or CV/CV)
5. Try it in context.
6. Refer to glossary or dictionary.
7. Ask someone.

There are seven lessons in the instructional set. Each lesson requires between twenty and thirty minutes to teach. The time varies according to the amount of teacher direction and discussion provided. The lessons should be taught in the same sequence they are presented in this instructional set. Each lesson contains complete directions for instruction.

There are three major organizational steps in each lesson plan. *First* is the motivational step. Here information is provided you can use to substantiate the need or purpose for this skill. *Second* is the instructional step. This contains directions and information for developing word pronunciation skills and strategy. *Third* is the generalization step. At this step the student is led to conclude that the word pronunciation skill he has just acquired is one of a number of skills that form the strategy. The student will soon learn that with each succeeding lesson the generalization gets longer until it consists of all seven steps in the strategy.

Choosing Your Lessons

Not every student will need to be taught every lesson in this set. For example in Study Guide 2, the Class Record reveals that Mary needs instruction in identifying single syllables, identifying suffixes, and syllabication. She also needs to be familiarized with the steps in the word pronunciation strategy. Mary does appear to recognize prefixes and use context clues so she does not need instruction in these word recognition skills. Since Mary does not know the word pronunciation strategy, her first instructional lesson should consist of a review of the prefix generalization, and instruction in suffix recognition using the suffix lesson provided. Beginning with the suffix lesson plan, each plan in succeeding order would be used until Mary is familiar with the skills and strategy she needs.

When students are not familiar with all the steps in the word pronunciation strategy but are familiar with a number of word pronunciation skills, always start your instruction with a review of the prefix generalization. Follow this with a review of each succeeding generalization until you reach the point at which they need the skills instruction. This is necessary to insure students become aware of and use all seven steps in the strategy. When students are fully familiar with the word pronunciation strategy and have only specific skill difficulties, only the specific skill lessons that correspond to their difficulty need to be taught.

Now complete Practicum Exercise 1 to demonstrate that you understand these last guidelines for planning instruction (see Figure 10).

Practicum Exercise 1

If Marty demonstrates the following needs, where and how should you begin instruction?

Answer to Practicum Exercise 1

Since Marty does not know the word recognition strategy, you will need to review the prefix, suffix, and stem generalizations. Then begin teaching with the CVC/CVC Syllabication Lesson Plan and continue through Lesson 7. If Marty knew the word pronunciation strategy, it would only be necessary to teach the two syllabication word pronunciation skills lessons.

Figure 10
Quick Test of Word Pronunciation
Class Record Form

Names of Students	Skills Unknown						Strategy Not Known
	Prefix	Suffix	Single Syllable Stems	Multiple CVC/CVC Stems	Multiple CV/CV Stems	Context Clues	
Jack		✓✓✓ ✓✓✓	✓	✓	✓		✓
Mary		✓✓✓✓ ✓✓	✓✓	✓	✓		✓
Marty				✓	✓		✓
Bob				✓			

Practicum Exercise 2

Now look at the information recorded in the Class Record Form (see Figure 10) for Bob. In Bob's case, where and how would you begin instruction?

Answers to Practicum Exercise 2

Bob is aware of all the steps in the word pronunciation strategy. He is having difficulty only with one word pronunciation skill. He needs instruction in the generalization of CV/CV syllabication.

Now you are familiar with how the Class Record is used to differentiate instruction for students. You are also aware that some students will need to be taught all the lessons in succeeding order. Others will need to have the generalizations reviewed from certain lessons and instruction in certain skills. Still others will need only to be taught specific skills. You are now ready to read the seven lesson plans in the instructional set. Read each lesson, giving your full attention to the three organizational steps, and to the directions and information found under each step.

Word Pronunciation Lessons

Presentation: *Prefix*   *LESSON 1*

A. Purpose:

Being able to detect a common prefix often enables a student to unlock a previously unknown word. This lesson is designed to: (1) acquaint students with a number of commonly reoccurring prefixes, and (2) build recognition of prefixes as word pronunciation units.

B. Instruction:

The following instructional procedure is recommended:

1. Write the following stems on the chalkboard. Have your students read them. Afterwards discuss the meaning of *stem* as a base word to which a prefix and/or suffix is added. You may wish to have your students locate additional examples in the dictionary (Thorndike, 1941).

sent	come	verb	press	grace
fine	done	side	forest	fix
noun	ability	act	camp	

2. Here are some prefixes which are commonly found in reading material. Write each prefix on the chalkboard. Direct your students' attention to each prefix as you pronounce it for them. You may wish to discuss the meaning of the prefix, but this is not necessary since the primary purpose of this lesson is prefix identification and pronunciation (Stauffer, 1942).

ab	ad	be	com	de	pro	re
dis	en	ex	in	pre	sub	un

3. Attach the common prefixes to the known root words presented in Step 1. Now have your students pronounce the new words.

absent	become	adverb	compress	disgrace
define	undone	subside	reforest	prefix
pronoun	inability	exact	encamp	

4. Now that your students are familiar with the common prefixes and had an opportunity to see them in words, a practice activity should be useful. Place the following words on the chalkboard. As you do so, direct your students for each word to (1) identify and pronounce the prefix, (2) identify and pronounce the stem, and (3) blend the two to pronounce the affixed word.

abnormal	defame	prorate	adjoin	degrade
adjust	prewar	export	beside	bespeak
commit	unwed	disarm	input	submit

5. Tell your students many words begin with patterns that look exactly like the prefixes studied. In some cases the beginning patterns are not prefixes but nevertheless some of these words can be pronounced in the same way as the prefixed words. (Example: *pr*each, *per*k, *de*al, *de*an.)

6. Locate words in your subject area materials which contain other prefixes. Teach these prefixes in the same manner as was done in this lesson.

C. Generalization: Through discussion lead your students to conclude that looking for prefixes is the first step in a word pronunciation strategy. You may wish to record this step on a chart or chalkboard for reference prior to introducing the second lesson. You may wish to have your students record this step on a sheet of notebook paper they are reserving for the word pronunciation strategy. It should be recorded as follows:

1. Look for a prefix.

Presentation: *Suffix*   *LESSON 2*

A. Purpose:

Being able to detect one of the common suffixes often enables a student to unlock a previously unknown word. This lesson is designed to: (1) acquaint students with a number of commonly reoccurring suffixes, and (2) build recognition of suffixes as word pronunciation units.

B. Instruction:

The following instructional procedure is recommended:

1. Write the following stems on the chalkboard. Have your students read them. If there are students who are still unclear about the

meaning of *stem,* clarify the meaning at this point. If necessary you may wish to have your students locate examples in a dictionary.

hope	happy	move	educate	walk
mail	high	skill	arm	act
love	talk	nerve	want	

2. Here are some suffixes which are commonly found in reading material. Write each suffix on the chalkboard. Direct your students' attention to each suffix as you pronounce it for them. You may wish to discuss the meaning of the suffix, but this is not necessary since the primary purpose of this lesson is suffix identification and pronunciation (Thorndike, 1941).

ness	ily	est	y	tion
ly	ous	er	ant	ent
able	ance	ed (ed)	ed (d)	ive
al	ing	ed (t)	ful	ment

3. Attach the common suffixes to the known stems presented in Step 1. As you do so, ask selected students to pronounce the new words.

hopeful	higher	active	happily
mailable	talked (t)	nervous	happiness
lovely	movement	education	wanted (ed)
walking	army	happiest	skilled (d)

4. Now that your students are familiar with the common prefixes and suffixes and used them to build words, a practice activity designed to build their recognition of prefixes and suffixes to the automatic recognition level is necessary. Write the following words on the chalkboard. As you do so, ask your students to: (1) identify and pronounce the prefix, (2) identify and pronounce the suffix, (3) identify and pronounce the stem, and (4) blend and pronounce the affixed word.

reloading	prepayment	inactive	department
refreshment	enjoyment	preheated	unfairly
preschooler	abnormally	unskillful	prolonged

5. Locate words in your subject area materials which contain other suffixes. Teach these suffixes in the same manner as in this lesson.

C. Generalization: Through discussion lead your students to conclude that looking for suffixes is the second step in a word pronunciation strategy. You may wish to record this step on a chart or chalkboard for reference prior to introducing the third lesson. You may wish to have your students record this step on a sheet of notebook paper that they are reserving for the strategy. Show your students that at this point they have developed a two-step strategy and it should be recorded as follows:

1. Look for a prefix.
2. Look for a suffix.

Presentation: *Stems*   *LESSON 3*

A. Purpose:

Identification of stems precedes their pronunciation. This lesson is designed to: (1) acquaint students with one- and two-syllable stems and (2) build recognition of stems as pronunciation units.

B. Instruction:

The following instructional procedure is recommended:

1. Place the following words on the chalkboard. Point out to your students that these words contain prefixes and/or suffixes. Identify the stems through analysis of each word, first for the prefix and second for the suffix. Point out to your students that once these elements have been identified, the word or syllable remaining is the stem.

camping	mainly	installment	entrenchment
discovering	enrichment	predisposition	undesirable
reboarding	unsinkable	removed	unknowingly

2. Point out to your students the procedure for pronouncing the above words. First, pronounce the prefix; second, pronounce the suffix; third, pronounce the stem; and fourth, blend and pronounce the word. Now direct your students to pronounce the above words using this strategy.

3. Either the teacher or students may locate words in subject area materials which contain other prefixes and/or suffixes. These words can be analyzed using the strategy detailed in this lesson.

C. Generalization: Through discussion lead your students to conclude that the following strategy should be used when they encounter an unknown word in their reading. You may wish to record this third step on the strategy chart or chalkboard for reference prior to introducing the fourth lesson. Or you may wish to have your students record this step on a sheet of notebook paper that they are reserving for the strategy. Their strategy should now contain these three steps:

1. Look for a prefix.
2. Look for a suffix.
3. Look for a stem.

Presentation: *Syllabication* CVC/CVC *LESSON 4*

A. Purpose:

Often after a prefix and/or suffix has been identified, students find that they are faced with a multi-syllable stem to pronounce. Having a few general guidelines for dividing such stems into syllables will be helpful in these situations. This lesson is designed to: (1) acquaint students with one of two commonly used techniques for dividing stems into syllables, and (2) provide some practice in using this technique as an aid to word pronunciation.

B. Instructions:

The following instructional procedure is recommended:

1. Ask your students to listen closely as you pronounce some words. Tell them that you will be pronouncing two syllable words and you want them to identify the separate syllables after you have pronounced each word. Elongate each syllable as you pronounce the following words:

   cargo   cattle   pencil
   person   summer   circus

2. After you have pronounced the words and the students have identified the separate syllables in each word, write the words on the chalkboard. Then review pronunciation and re-identify the separate syllables. Draw a slash mark (/) between the two syllables in each word.

   car/go   cat/tle   pen/cil
   per/son   sum/mer   cir/cus

3. Bring to your students' attention the fact that each word is divided between two consonants. Furthermore, each word follows the consonant-vowel-consonant / consonant-vowel-consonant pattern (CVC/CVC). Have your students draw from this observation a generalization that they can apply to similar words.

4. A generalization such as the following should be drawn: In multisyllable stems following the CVC/CVC pattern, the separate syllables are usually divided between the two consonants. These exact words need not be used.

5. Now that your students are familiar with the first syllabication technique, a practice activity is necessary to improve their skill in applying the technique. The following words are useful practice words for applying this technique.

carrot	center	donkey	picnic	valley
corner	settle	barrel	follow	grammar
napkin	silver	garden	suggest	bottle

6. Have your students skim over the pages in their most recent reading assignment to locate multi-syllable words following the CVC/CVC pattern. You may wish to locate words in your subject area materials that contain this pattern for additional practice for your students.

C. Generalization: Through discussion lead your students to conclude that the CVC/CVC pattern is useful for dividing multi-syllable stems into their separate syllables. Record this step on a chart or a chalkboard, or have the students record this step in their notebooks. Point out to your students that the strategy is now one step longer.

   1. Locate the prefix.
   2. Locate the suffix.
   3. Identify the stem.
   4. Divide into syllables using CVC/CVC pattern.

Presentation: *Syllabication* CV/CV   *LESSON 5*

A. Purpose:
   Even though a prefix and/or a suffix has been identified, the stem still can be difficult for a student to pronounce. This is generally true

when it is two or more syllables in length. Three syllable stems are unusual but two syllable stems are quite common. A syllabication technique has already been introduced. The purpose of this lesson is to: (1) familiarize students with a second syllabication technique, and (2) provide students with some practice in applying the technique.

B. Instructions:

The following instructional procedure is recommended:

1. Ask your students for their complete attention. Pronounce each of the following words, elongating and stressing each syllable as you do so. After you pronounce each word, have a student pronounce each syllable separately and indicate where the syllable division takes place.

famous   station   silent
hotel   direct   solo

2. Now write the same list of words on the chalkboard. Then pronounce each word as you would in normal speech. Next, have a student pronounce the word and divide it into separate syllables on the basis of their auditory experience. Draw a slash mark between the separate syllables as in the following:

fa/mous   sta/tion   si/lent
ho/tel   di/rect   so/lo

3. Help your students determine that each word is divided after the first vowel and follows the consonant-vowel / consonant-vowel pattern (CV/CV). Have the students draw a generalization from this observation which they can apply to similar words.

4. A generalization containing the following information is appropriate: Multisyllable words following the CV/CV pattern are usually divided between the first vowel and second consonant. These exact words need not be used.

5. Now that your students are familiar with the CV/CV pattern for syllable division, some practice to improve their skill is necessary. The following words lend themselves to division using this technique.

pupil   locate   moment   final
spider   cement   pirate   radar
tiger   vacant   frozen   blatant

6. You may wish to locate other words which follow this pattern in your subject area material.

C. Generalization: Lead your students to conclude that the syllabication technique using the CV/CV pattern should be helpful as a second technique to apply when attempting to pronounce multisyllable stems. Record this step on a chart or a chalkboard or direct your students to record it in their notebooks.

    1. Locate the prefix.

    2. Locate the suffix.

    3. Identify the stem.

    4. Divide into syllables using CVC/CVC or CV/CV patterns.

Presentation: *Context Clues*   *LESSON 6*

A. Purpose:

Sometimes a reader obtains a clue to the pronunciation of a word from the context surrounding that word. Context clues are phrases, sentences, or paragraphs which provide clues to an unknown word. This lesson is designed to acquaint students with such clues as a valuable aid to word pronunciation.

B. Instruction:

1. Place on the chalkboard the following two sentences, each of which contains a missing word. Point out to your students a word is missing for a reason which will be revealed to them in a moment.

    (a) In order to pronounce an unknown word, all learners at all levels must learn how to _____ approach the unknown word. (systematically)

    (b) The word _____ *strategy* being taught through these lessons is a systematic approach for identifying unknown words. (*pronunciation*)

2. Have each student silently read the sentences. Direct each student afterwards to write what he feels is the missing word.

3. Discuss the various word choices for each sentence. Use discussion to build a logical and meaningful basis for selecting words to fill the blanks.

4. After some words have been chosen and all agree they are reasonable insertions, point out to your students that they have proven the value of using context or surrounding sentences and/or paragraphs as an aid in word pronunciation.

5. Obtain a 500-word selection from your latest reading assignment. Delete one word from each sentence, duplicate, distribute, and then lead your students through the process of using sentence and/or paragraph sense to hypothesize and justify choices for the unknown words.

C. Generalization: Through discussion lead your students to conclude that context clues are a valuable aid to word pronunciation. You may record such context clues on the evolving word pronunciation strategy chart, or on the chalkboard for future reference. You may wish to direct your students to record this step in their notebooks under the section they are reserving for this strategy. Point out to your students that their strategy now has five steps.

1. Look for a prefix.
2. Look for a suffix.
3. Locate the stem.
4. Divide into syllables using CVC/CVC or CV/CV pattern.
5. Try it in context.

Presentation: *Glossary, Dictionary, and*   *LESSON 7*
Knowledgeable Reader

A. Purpose:

This lesson is merely a set of comments which need to be made to your students. Surely your students will want to know what they should do if the strategy does not work. This lesson is designed to answer that question.

B. Instructions:

The following instructional procedure is recommended:

1. Point out to your students that the five-step word pronunciation strategy is not infallible. Upon a number of occasions the strategy will not lead them to the correct pronunciation of an unknown word. Point out that there is not a perfect correspondence be-

tween sounds and letters in English and as a result all such strategies that stop at the fifth step fail sooner or later.

2. Tell your students in order to have a near infallible strategy, they need two additional steps. Number 6 is the use of a glossary or dictionary. Number 7 is merely to ask someone who is familiar with the word how the word should be pronounced.

3. Caution your students against skipping the last two steps, for these are as important as the first five. Words that are left unpronounced return to produce the same frustration on following pages. Generally the frustration is heightened as a result of still more new unrecognized words.

C. Generalization: At this point the following generalizations should be recorded on a chart, chalkboard, or in your students' notebooks.

    1. Look for a prefix.

    2. Look for a suffix.

    3. Locate the stem.

    4. Divide into syllables using CVC/CVC or CV/CV pattern.

    5. Try it in context.

    6. Look it up in the glossary or dictionary.

    7. Ask someone.

Practicum Exercise 3

You have now completed reading the seven lesson plans. You were asked to identify the three step organization for every lesson plan. List each step and describe what takes place at that step.

1.

2.

3.

Answers to Practicum Exercise 3

1. The first step is purpose. Contained in this step is the information teachers need to establish a purpose for the instruction. At this step you tell the student what she will be able to do as a result of acquiring this new learning.
2. The second step is instruction. This step contains the necessary directions and information to teach the specific skills.
3. The third step is generalization. This step contains the information and procedure you need to follow to incorporate the new skill into the larger word pronunciation strategy. This step shows the relationship of the individual skill to the overall strategy.

Final Comment

If your students will use the strategy, they will find it a valuable tool for pronuncing words. Insuring that they apply the strategy is your responsibility. If you do not insist upon use of the strategy, your students will soon forget the strategy and all your instructional efforts will have been wasted. In order to reach the automatic application level, students need instruction, practice, and application opportunities under your direction.

If you have accomplished each of the three specific objectives in this module, you are ready for the Post-test. If not, complete them as directed. If you are having difficulty, return through appropriate Enabling Elements or see your instructor.

Post-test

Directions: Read each of the following statements and complete each Post-test item as directed.

1. You should now be completely familiar with a word-pronunciation strategy which can be taught to needful students. List in order of use the steps in such a strategy designed to help students pronounce multisyllable words.

2. Identification of students who need to pronounce multisyllable words should take place at the beginning of the school term. To get ready for this assessment, describe how you will do the following:

   a. Construct word pronunciation tests for skills and strategy.

   b. Administer these tests for skills and strategy.

   c. Record and use the information obtained from the tests.

3. List and explain the three organizational steps in the word pronunciation lesson plans.

Answers to the Post-test

1. The word recognition strategy presented in this module follows. Each skill is listed in the order it should be used or taught.

    Word Pronunciation Strategy

    a. Look for a prefix.

    b. Look for a suffix.

    c. Locate the stem.

    d. Divide the stem into syllables (CVC/CVC) (CV/CV).

    e. Try the word in context.

    f. Look in the glossary or dictionary.

    g. Ask someone who knows how to pronounce the word.

    Your answer need not be stated in the exact words, nor do you need to have this precise number of steps. Your answer, however, should contain all the information presented in this strategy.

2. To identify students who have skill or strategy difficulties, you will need to do the following:

    a. Construct a word pronunciation skills and strategy test. To do this use the words provided for Form A or Form B of the Quick Test of Word Pronunciation. Print each nonsense word on a three-by-five inch white index card with a dictionary respelling on the back of the card. For the Word Pronunciation Strategy Test, print the test question on the three-by-five inch white index card.

    b. The procedures you will follow for administering the tests are:

    (1) On the Class Record Form, list the names of the students you have decided to test.

    (2) Arrange approximately three minutes for testing each student.

    (3) Test each student separately in a quiet area.

    (4) Explain to each student the purpose of your testing.

    (5) Expose one card at a time to test word pronunciation skills with the Quick Test of Word Pronunciation.

    (6) As the student reads the words, record his errors.

    (7) Place the single three-by-five card containing the Word Pronunciation Strategy Test in front of the student. Ask the student to read aloud and answer the question. It is acceptable to read the question to the student if he cannot read it himself.

  c. The Class Record Form should be used to record information regarding the student's skills and strategy. The information on the Class Record is to be used for planning the instructional program for students.

3. The major organizational steps for lesson plans designed to teach skills and strategy are as follows:

  a. Establish a purpose for learning. Tell the student why it is that he needs this instruction and what he will be able to do as a result of learning the skill you are about to teach him.

  b. Provide instruction. This step contains the directions and information necessary to develop competency with a specific skill.

  c. Build a generalization. At this step, the student incorporates his new skill into a word pronunciation strategy which he will use in his attempt to pronounce multisyllable words.

Selected Bibliography

Burmeister, L. E. "Selected Word Analysis Generalizations for a Group Approach to Corrective Reading in the Secondary School." *Reading Research Quarterly,* 1968, *4* (1), 71–95.

Burmeister, L. E. "The Usefulness of Phonic Generalizations." *The Reading Teacher,* 1968, *21* (4), 349–64+.

Burmeister, L. E. *Words–From Print to Meaning.* Reading, Massachusetts: Addison-Wesley, 1975.

Dawson, M. A., ed. *Teaching Word Recognition Skills.* Newark, Delaware: International Reading Association, 1971.

Durkin, D. *Phonics, Linguistics, and Reading.* New York: Teachers College, 1972.

Hafner, L. E., ed. *Improving Reading in Middle and Secondary Schools.* New York: Macmillan, 1974.

Heilman, A. W. *Phonics in Proper Perspective,* 3rd ed. Columbus, Ohio: Charles E. Merrill, 1976.

Johnson, J. H., and Parades, E. "The Longest Tome Begins With a Single Phoneme." *Journal of Reading,* 1975, *16* (5), 376–79.

Karlin, R. *Teaching Reading in High School,* 2nd ed. Indianapolis: Bobbs-Merrill, 1972.

Karlin, R., ed. *Teaching Reading in High School: Selected Articles.* Indianapolis: Bobbs-Merrill, 1969.

Kottmeyer, W. *Decoding and Meaning.* New York: McGraw-Hill, 1974.

Shepherd, D. L. *Comprehensive High School Reading Methods.* Columbus, Ohio: Charles E. Merrill, 1973.

Thorndike, E. L. *The Teaching of English Suffixes.* New York: Bureau of Publications, Teachers College, Columbia University, 1941.

Thomas, E. L., and Robinson, H. A. *Improving Reading in Every Class: A Sourcebook for Teachers.* Boston: Allyn and Bacon, 1972.

Stauffer, R. G. "A Study of Prefixes in the Thorndike List to Establish a List of Prefixes That Should Be Taught in the Elementary School." *Journal of Education Research,* February 1942, *35,* 453–58.

Wallen, C. J. *Word Attack Skills in Reading.* Columbus, Ohio: Charles E. Merrill, 1969.

Wolf, H. S. "A Structured Approach to Pronouncing Unfamiliar Words." *Journal of Reading,* 1974, *17* (5), 356–62.

Module 9

Motivating Reluctant Readers

CONTENTS

Prospectus

Rationale

How often have you heard your fellow teachers say, "How do I get Alfonso and Marian to read their assignments?" This is a question all teachers have about students at one time or another. Students like Alfonso and Marian who have some reading ability but lack the motivation to complete their reading assignments are reluctant readers.

As teachers we have a responsibility to motivate reluctant readers. Motivation, from a teaching point of view, means manipulating variables in such a way as to entice your students to read their assignments.

The ideas presented in this module are designed to help you accomplish this task. The suggestions provided for motivation can be implemented as part of a daily routine in any content area course. They require minimal changes in teacher attitude or instructional technique and initiate considerable student motivation. Ultimately they lead to completed reading assignments.

Objectives

TERMINAL OBJECTIVE: You will acquire and use the provided strategy for motivating reluctant readers.

Specific Objectives:

1. You will write a one-word synonym for motivation and list two sources of motivation.
2. You will list the eight major affective and cognitive factors which influence motivation.
3. You will list the core factors in a motivation strategy and prepare a mnemonic device to be used for retaining the core factors in memory.

294

4. You will incorporate a motivation strategy into a subject area reading assignment.

Resources and Time Required

In addition to the module, the only other materials required are your subject area textbook, paper, and a writing instrument. The estimated time to complete the starred core Enabling Activities is three to four hours.

Pre-test

Directions: For each question, determine the word that indicates your belief regarding your competency. If you are in doubt or know only part of the information for which you are asked, choose NO.

1. Many reluctant readers are merely unmotivated readers waiting for a spark. Can you state a one-word synonym for motivation and list the two principal sources of motivation? YES NO

2. How a student feels and what he thinks are important teacher concerns. Can you list the eight major affective and cognitive factors which influence motivation? YES NO

3. Every teacher needs a strategy for motivating students. Can you list the core factors in a motivation strategy and prepare a mnemonic memory device to aid you in their retention? YES NO

4. Knowing something about motivation does not guarantee application. Can you modify a subject area reading assignment to incorporate the motivation strategy presented in this module? YES NO

Branching Program Alternatives for Pre-test Responses

1. If you can supply a one-word suitable synonym for motivation and identify the two major sources of motivation, you are ready for Enabling Element 2. If you are not sure about the correctness of your synonym or of the two sources of motivation, Enabling Element 1 was prepared for you.

2. You are in good standing if you can list eight factors which bring about a motivated state in a learner; you may go to Enabling Element 2. If your list is incomplete, Enabling Element 2 will help you complete the list.

3. If you can list the core factors in a motivation strategy and have a mnemonic memory device to aid you in their retention, you are ready for Enabling Element 4. If not, you will find Enabling Element 3 valuable for formulating and helping you remember a motivation strategy.

4. Once you have a motivation strategy, incorporating the strategy into a reading assignment is the next thing you must do. If you have a strategy and can incorporate it into a reading assignment, you are ready for the Post-test. If you are unsure of just how this should be done, Enabling Element 4 will explain and demonstrate the procedure.

Enabling Element 1
Motivation

Specific Objective 1

You will write a one-word synonym for motivation and list two sources of motivation.

Enabling Activities

*1. Read Study Guide 1, "Motivation," to identify a one-word synonym for motivation and to discover two sources of motivation.

*2. Using the form "Sources of Motivation" provided at the end of Study Guide 1, see if you can separate the intrinsic from the extrinsic students in one of your classes. Ask yourself what factors influence the motivation of students in the extrinsic group. You may find that you have discovered the very factors which are the subject of Enabling Element 2.

3. Discuss the extrinsically motivated students in your classes with other subject area teachers and determine if they classify these students in the same way. Could it be some subject areas *spark* students more than others?

4. Interview five of the highest achieving students on your intrinsic list. Ask them to tell you what motivates them to achieve. You may compare their answers to see if high achievers achieve for similar reasons. Compare their answers with the factors listed in Enabling Element 2.

*5. Distribute to your students the Incomplete Sentences form provided at the end of Study Guide 1. Ask your students to complete each item to make a sentence which states how they feel about reading assignments. Compile their answers. Do your

*Indicates core Enabling Activities

students' perceptions of your reading assignments agree with yours?

Study Guide 1
Motivation

Motivation is often the explanation for why Angela completes her reading assignments but Ralph does not. Intelligence, language facility, cultural background, and many such factors may be insignificantly different for the two students. Motivational differences may be the significant factor.

Motivation, at one level of understanding, may be considered as *need*. It is an individual need that causes a student to do something that will result in a satisfaction. Need comes from within the learner's environment; thus, teachers manipulate factors in an attempt to create needs.

All of us have had students like Angela who complete their assignments seemingly regardless of what we do. No matter how casual we are in making an assignment or how unclear we are about the purpose of the assignment, Angela always gets the job done. Students like Angela are motivated from within. Psychologists call them *intrinsically* motivated. Students like Angela have such a high need to succeed academically that they always complete their assignments. Teachers need to change the environment very little for students like Angela.

Teachers also have students like Ralph who occasionally complete their reading assignments. Ralph sometimes gets started but too often he fails to reach completion. Many times Ralph does not even seem to be concerned by the fact that he has not completed his reading assignment. Students like Ralph are demonstrating low level or nonexistent academic needs. They are not intrinsically motivated like Angela. Occasionally, however, Ralph does complete his assignment. He completes them when he has a need to do so and the need is created by someone other than himself. Students like Ralph are either extrinsically motivated or motivated by something in their environment. For these students, teachers need to be aware of the factors that influence or bring about motivation. Awareness of these factors followed by planned manipulation is likely to yield more completed reading assignments from reluctant students.

If you would like to identify the *intrinsically* and *extrinsically* motivated students in your class, the following form "Sources of Motivation" should be helpful. The form contains a definition of intrinsic motivation and extrinsic motivation and two columns for the names of your students. When you have your students divided by source of motivation, you may want to examine each group of students to see if you can identify specific motivation factors associated with either intrinsically or extrinsically motivated students.

If you wish to obtain some insight into the ways your students perceive your reading assignments, use the form entitled "Incomplete Sentences." A compilation of your students' perceptions may provide you with additional clues to their sources of motivation.

You now have a definition of motivation and are aware of two sources of motivation. If you can list the motivational factors classroom teachers must manipulate to turn on the extrinsically motivated students, go to Enabling Element 3. If you are unsure of the factors, Enabling Element 2 will identify and discuss them.

Sources of Motivation

Intrinsic motivation: self-starter; started from within; moved to complete a task by innate need.

Extrinsic motivation: externally started; start comes from outside the learner; moved to complete a task by outside influences which develop need.

Names	Names
1.	1.
2.	2.
3.	3.
4.	4.
5.	5.
6.	6.
7.	7.
8.	8.
9.	9.
10.	10.
11.	11.
12.	12.
13.	13.
14.	14.
15.	15.

Incomplete Sentences

Name _____ Class_____ Date_____

Directions: Complete each item to express how you feel about the many
reading assignments you get in school each week. Try to
make complete sentences from each of the following.

1. I complete my reading assignment _____
   _____.

2. Long reading assignments _____
   _____.

3. Teachers who assign only page numbers for reading assignments
   _____.

4. What annoys me most about my reading assignments _____
   _____.

5. Reading _____
   _____.

6. Reading to find the answer to a question _____
   _____.

7. People walking around the classroom when I am reading _____
   _____.

8. Reading at home _____
   _____.

9. Hard books _____
   _____.

10. Answering the teacher's questions correctly after completing my
    reading assignment _____
    _____.

11. Reading about something which interests me _____
    _____.

12. Reading textbooks _____
    _____.

13. When I use the information from my reading _____
    _____.

14. Teachers make reading assignments _____
    _____.

15. Easy books _____
_____.

16. When the teacher tells me I am wrong _____
_____.

17. Being right _____
_____.

18. I would like to help my teacher _____
_____.

19. Reading newspapers and magazines _____
_____.

20. Reading is fun when _____
_____.

Enabling Element 2
Factors Influencing Motivation

Specific Objective 2

You will list the eight major affective and cognitive factors which influence motivation.

Enabling Activities

*1. Read Study Guide 2, "Factors Influencing Motivation," and compile a list of factors which influence motivation.

*2. In *one* of your classes distribute the form "What Motivates Me" included at the end of Study Guide 2. Ask the students to complete the form and turn it in for your future planning needs; or distribute the form and have the students use it as a basis for a discussion on motivational factors and learning.

3. In another of your classes discuss motivation individually with a few high and a few low achieving students. Ask them to list factors which motivate them to achieve in your classes. Did you acquire any new insight into the motives of your students?

4. Think of one of your most reluctant readers. Write a one-paragraph description of this student using the motivational factors presented in Study Guide 2. This activity should provide you with factors you can change or manipulate to increase the work product of this student.

*5. Talk with other teachers who have the same student in class and compare your description. Are there differences in perceptions among teachers? Could it be that some teachers have the *motivational keys* to some students while others do not? Were any of

*Indicates core Enabling Activities

the keys identified? Much can be learned about reluctant readers from talking with other teachers.

*6. Want to learn something about yourself as a teacher? Distribute the form "My Teacher" found at the end of Study Guide 2. Ask your students to complete the form and return it to you. No names are necessary. Tally and analyze the answers to the questions to see how you are perceived by your students.

Study Guide 2
Factors Influencing Motivation

The basic factors underlying motivation are no secret. Although these factors are well known and understood, they are all too often not applied. They can be divided into two categories, those that relate primarily to how students feel (affective factors) and those that relate to how students think (cognitive factors). A list of these basic factors follows:

Affective Factors	*Cognitive Factors*
Interest	Purpose for reading
Attitudes	Short-term goals
	Reading level
	Knowledge of results
	Success
	Usefulness of knowledge

Although these factors will be discussed separately, they operate together to bring about a motivated student.

Affective Factors

The affective factors which influence motivation are interest and attitudes. These two factors interact to create a good or bad feeling in the learner about something and/or someone.

---

*Indicates core Enabling Activity

Interest refers to a curiosity or a concern about something—in this case a subject area. For most students, interest in a subject area does not bloom overnight like a spring flower; but rather it is developed in a subject area after many exposures to those intricacies that strike their curiosity. A social studies teacher who compares and contrasts the marriage customs and ceremonies in different countries with junior and senior high school girls is appealing to their curiosity. Likewise, a mathematics teacher who deals with the consumption and cost of gasoline to determine cost per mile of automobile operation is appealing to the curiosity of high school boys. Interest in a subject area is developed by teachers through continually relating the content of their courses to the curiosities of their students. This requires not only knowledge of the content area but knowledge of the broader realm of the daily interests of students. The teacher who builds interest knows both his content area and his students; he can relate one to the other.

Parents and teachers—in that order—have the most pronounced effect upon students' attitudes toward academic education. Parents create the initial attitude. Teachers refine the attitude toward school in general and their subject areas in particular. An attitude is a disposition or mental set toward something, which might be a subject area and/or a teacher. Attitudes may be either positive or negative. Students with positive attitudes toward their subject areas can be seen in the hallways carrying the subject textbook. They can also be seen in the libraries studying. Usually their assignments are complete and on time. Students with a negative attitude are also seen in the hallways. They are the students who carry few books, no notebook paper, and whose pencils always remain sharp. They too go to the library—to look at a newspaper, magazine, or to sleep. In class their assignments are rarely completed and these students can usually be seen sitting in a reclined position with a dazed look on their faces. In order to create a positive attitude toward a subject area, a teacher has to be a special person. Through his actions he must relay to his students a feeling of concern for them as individuals. He must be willing to accept their academic, emotional, and social level of development. He must be supportive of their smallest achievement and try his best to withhold his criticism. Attitude, like interest, is a pervasive quality that is developed only after a long period of pleasurable experiences. Finally, teachers who think positively about their students generally create students who think positively about their teachers and the content they teach.

Cognitive Factors

The cognitive factors which influence motivation are purpose, short-term goals, adjustment for reading level, knowledge of results, success, and usefulness of knowledge. These six factors interact to stimulate the cognitive or thinking processes of the learner.

In order to be motivating, assignments must be given with a purpose. The purpose is a teacher's specific direction in an assignment. The teacher who at the end of a class tells his students to read from the text pages 27–54 for tomorrow is providing a very unrealistic purpose for learning. The student perceives the purpose as getting to page 54. Once she reaches page 54, she feels she has achieved her purpose. However, the teacher does not feel she has achieved her purpose until she can satisfactorily answer the questions that he will raise over the material on the following day. Unfortunately for the student, in this example, she will not find out what her purposes are for reading until the teacher begins to ask questions on the following day. Now suppose that a student who completes her assignment and reads pages 27–54 comes to class and is asked a few questions by the teacher. Suppose further that she is unable to answer the questions because she did not read the material for those purposes. In this case, the teacher would probably assume that the student did not read the material since she could not answer the questions. After a few such assignments, the student discontinues reading any assignments. A better way for you to handle such an assignment would be to write on the chalkboard two, three, or more questions directed at the important points to be obtained from the reading. Then you tell the student to read whatever is necessary to answer the questions. This would provide specific purposes for reading and alert the student to precisely what is to be obtained from the reading assignment.

Short-term goals are another important cognitive factor. When the goals are short range, students perceive them as taking very little time and are therefore less reluctant to do the assignment. When you provide your students with a number of questions for which to read, you are providing them with short-term goals. Each question becomes a goal in itself and before long the students complete their assignment not realizing the lapse of time or the amount of effort expended. The students probably read as much when assigned to read a specific number of pages, such as pages 27–54 in the previous example. The difference is that they know specifically what to read for and each question became a goal by itself which makes the assignment appear shorter.

The reading levels of all students need to be considered when making reading assignments. Assigning the same text material to students who read above, at, and below grade level is one way of making the reading assignment nonmotivating for perhaps the above and surely the below average reader. One way to avoid this pitfall is to select a number of textual materials with a range of readabilities. Module 3 provides suggestions for determining the suitability of material for various students. Module 1 suggests ways of determining readability and Module 2 ways of altering the reading level. Given enough time, a school or county librarian can locate many materials on various reading levels. You may want to provide the librarian with the Graph for Estimating Readability to assist him in locating materials suitable for your students.

No student achieves unless he knows what he has done right and *specifically* what he has done wrong. Being told by a geography teacher that he used the right process to determine the latitude and longitude of Chicago on a globe tells the student how to do the same for Orlando, Florida. Pointing out the specific error made in the process and providing specific instructions help the student obtain the correct answer next time. Some teachers fail to tell students when they are correct but consistently tell them when they are wrong. Knowing what is wrong tells you how not to respond the next time but gives *no* clue on how to respond next time. Relative to the present discussion, the best advice for motivating students is to emphasize the positive and de-emphasize the negative. When you do emphasize the negative—BE SPECIFIC.

In life, most people gravitate toward those vocations and avocations where they meet success. When we meet with repeated failure, we withdraw from the situation physically and mentally. Teachers who make reading assignments without providing a purpose are probably insuring that their students meet with failure when the assignment is due. A student could easily have read the material for one purpose while the teacher assigned it for another. A few such reoccurrences of this experience and another subject area mental dropout is created. Repeat the experience across subject areas and you may produce a physical dropout from school. The importance of success in motivation can be summed up by the statement, ''No greater is a feeling, than a feeling of success!''

''Knowledge for knowledge's sake is garbage!'' If you do not like the brashness of this statement, we will supply you with the name of the student who made this contribution and you can take it up with him. But he did make a point when he said this to his teacher. Knowledge acquired with no suggested application to daily problems or interests is fleeting knowledge indeed! For example, every teacher knows it is important to teach students the new vocabulary in her subject area. Now if vocabulary is taught by the teacher but no stress is placed upon application and use in the classroom, how long will the vocabulary last in the minds of students? And will the students be interested in additional vocabulary study? Finding ways of relating content to life is not easy. But it is essential, not only for motivation, but also for retention.

There are other factors, too, including the physical and cultural. The condition of the school plant and home also influence motivation. However, these factors often fall outside the realm of a classroom teacher. For the most part, the classroom teacher can only manipulate the affective and cognitive factors discussed in this Study Guide. As a result, manipulating these factors will not bring about success with every student but should increase the motivation of many. In education, as in life, every little bit helps!

At the end of this Study Guide there are two forms you should find valuable. The first entitled ''What Motivates Me?'' consists of a number of questions about motivating factors to which students answer YES or NO. It will take your students about ten minutes to complete. An analysis of your students' answers will help you identify the important motivational factors from the perception of your students. As an alternative, the statements on this form may be used as key statements for a class discussion of motivation.

The second form at the end of this Study Guide is entitled ''My Teacher.'' This form contains a number of questions about you as a motivator of students and as a teacher. If you wish to learn something about yourself, reproduce copies of this form and distribute them to your students. The form will take approximately ten minutes for your students to complete. An analysis of the YES and NO responses will reveal the degree to which you are considering motivation factors when you prepare your reading assignments and lesson plans.

You are now familiar with a number of factors that affect motivation. If you can create a motivation strategy using the core factors from those identified in this Study Guide, you are ready for Enabling Element 4. If not, Enabling Element 3 should prove interesting as well as valuable.

What Motivates Me

Name _____ Class _____ Date _____

Directions: Read each of the following statements carefully and circle
YES or NO for each one. Your answers will tell your
teacher something about what motivates you to learn.

1. I read my assignments only when class time is   YES NO
   provided to do so.

2. I like to know what I am to learn from an assign- YES NO
   ment.

3. I prefer one long assignment to two short assign- YES NO
   ments.

4. The more I like a subject the more likely I will   YES NO
   complete my reading assignment.

5. I like to be told if my answers to questions are   YES NO
   correct or incorrect.

6. When it is noisy in the classroom, it is difficult to YES NO
   complete my reading assignments.

7. I complete my reading assignments even if the   YES NO
   material is difficult for me to understand.

8. I like to read about things I can make or use in my YES NO
   daily life.

9. Other people moving around or talking in the class- YES NO
   room make it hard for me to concentrate.

10. I like to be able to answer correctly questions asked YES NO
    by my teacher.

11. When I do something right, someone should tell   YES NO
    me so.

12. I like long reading assignments.   YES NO

13. I like to receive a reward when I complete my   YES NO
    reading assignment.

14. When I am right the teacher can tell everyone;   YES NO
    when I am wrong she should tell just me.

15. I like to help my teachers select my reading as-   YES NO
    signments.

My Teacher

Name _____ Class _____ Date _____

Directions: Your teacher would like to know more about himself as a
teacher. Please read each of the following questions and
then circle YES or NO after each question.

1. Does your teacher make fun of you when you are   YES   NO
   having difficulty reading?

2. Does your teacher often get you so interested in   YES   NO
   your reading assignment that you talk about the
   assignment outside of class?

3. When your teacher finishes telling you about your   YES   NO
   reading assignment, do you sometimes feel you
   want to go to the library to find out more about the
   assignment?

4. Does your teacher make material which looks hard   YES   NO
   to read seem easier to read?

5. Does your teacher tell you what you are to learn   YES   NO
   from your reading assignment before the assignment is due?

6. Does your teacher ask interesting questions over   YES   NO
   the reading assignments?

7. Does your teacher help you find material you can   YES   NO
   read for your assignments?

8. Does your teacher give reading assignments from   YES   NO
   materials that are too difficult to understand?

9. Does your teacher explain or define the new words   YES   NO
   in reading assignments?

10. Does your teacher tell you when you did a good job   YES   NO
    on your reading assignment?

11. When you are reading, does your teacher try to   YES   NO
    keep down the noise level in the classroom?

12. Does your teacher give reading assignments that   YES   NO
    are too long?

13. Does your teacher help you see the value of reading   YES   NO
    assignments to your daily life or to daily events?

14. Does your teacher ever ask you what you would   YES   NO
    like to read to complete your assignment?

15. Does your teacher ever let you decide how much   YES   NO
    reading you need to do to complete your assign-
    ment?

16. Does your teacher know what you are interested in   YES   NO
    reading?

Enabling Element 3
A Motivation Strategy

Specific Objective 3

You will list the core factors in a motivation strategy and prepare a mnemonic device to be used for retaining the core factors in memory.

Enabling Activities

*1. Read Study Guide 3, entitled "A Motivation Strategy," to identify the core components of such a strategy for reluctant readers.

*2. Read Study Guide 3 to acquire a mnemonic device useful for remembering the strategy presented in this Study Guide.

3. Examine some of your subject area textbooks to determine if any motivation suggestions are provided. If your subject area books are like many others, you will find few suggestions on motivation; however, your textbook may be one of those where the authors provide not only suggestions but also a motivational strategy such as the one provided in this module. If this is the case, you may want to try both strategies to see which is most effective.

4. Discuss with colleagues the strategy provided in this module. Chances are they are also using the same strategy. A great deal can be learned from discussions of motivation.

5. There are many textbooks and popular paperbacks available on the topic of motivation. You may find it beneficial to read one of these to further your understanding and ultimately enhance your techniques for handling students. Look at the bibliography for suggestions.

---

*Indicates core Enabling Activities

Study Guide 3
A Motivation Strategy

In Study Guide 2 a number of factors associated with motivation were identified. All of these contribute to a student's state of motivation and therefore are important. However, it is probably not reasonable to expect that most teachers will keep in mind the eight or more factors mentioned in Study Guide 2. Therefore, in this module a brief but powerful four-step motivational strategy is presented.

The four-step motivational strategy is designed for general use when making reading assignments and employs the use of a mnemonic device that makes the strategy easier to remember. The strategy was developed by first identifying the many major factors that contribute to a student's state of motivation. Second, the factors were reduced to four core factors. When these core factors are considered in lesson planning, they will increase the probability of motivated students. To assist you in remembering the motivation strategy, the first letter from the key word in each of the core factors has been used to make up another word called an acronym.

The key letters, four core components of the motivation strategy, and implications for motivation follow:

P Students acquire more meaning from what they read when they are provided with a *P*URPOSE for reading. Providing students with purposes for reading defines what specific information and understandings are to be obtained as they read. Setting a purpose for reading also makes material more meaningful to the reader. Assignments which are purposeful and meaningful are motivating.

A Students must acquire a positive *A*TTITUDE toward reading. This quality is developed through associations with teachers who have positive attitudes toward their students. Negative attitudes and reinforcement cause students to withdraw from teachers, their subject areas, and their assignments. Being an eternal optimist is difficult but nevertheless essential to teachers who wish to motivate students and teach important skills.

R Students must be made aware of *R*ESULTS through a teacher's stipulation of right and wrong responses. Providing students with knowledge of right and wrong is one way a student learns

what he should and should not do the next time he finds himself
in a similar situation.

S Students, like teachers, do not repeat experiences unless they
   meet with some *S*UCCESS. Every student needs to find some
   success in every lesson you teach and in every assignment you
   make. Accumulations of successes increase the likelihood of
   motivation for future assignments.

Additional suggestions for implementing each core component can be
found at the end of this Study Guide.

Now if you will look at the acronym formed by the first letter of
each key word in the core factors you will see that it is a familiar word.
Par is what most golfers hope to obtain on every hole on the golf course.
PARS are what the golfer accumulates to signify satisfactory performance. Since satisfactory performance is every teacher's goal for every
learner, PARS might be a useful acronym and mnemonic device for
remembering the four core factors in the motivational strategy provided
in this module.

You now have a strategy that can be applied when you make
reading assignments. This strategy should be helpful for motivating
many of the reluctant readers in your classroom. To further help you
implement the strategy, a number of suggested activities are provided.
The activities are listed under the core component descriptors—
*P*urpose, *A*ttitude, *R*esults, and *S*uccess.

Activities For Implementing the Motivation Strategy

Purpose

Purpose provides direction for and meaning from what is read.
Purposes for reading can be established through a number of activities.

1. Prepare a number of questions to be used for setting up a
   purpose and guiding students' reading. Write the questions on
   the chalkboard and leave them there for the duration of the
   assignment.

2. Prepare a number of true and false questions over the assignment. Duplicate the questions and distribute them to your students. Ask the students to read their assignment and to answer
   the true–false questions.

3. Preview the reading assignment with the class. Ask the students to create questions based upon their previewing that can be used to guide their reading of the assignment. List the questions on the blackboard, or duplicate the questions and distribute them prior to the reading of the assignment. Module 7 on study strategies provides guidelines for creating questions through previewing.

4. Divide your class into small groups. Have each small group preview the reading assignment and prepare a number of questions over the assignment. Collect the questions and duplicate those you feel are most important. Distribute these prior to the reading of the assignment.

5. Check the teacher's manual of your textbook to see which questions the authors feel a student should be able to answer at the end of a specific unit or assignment. Share these questions with your students after they have previewed the assignment and created their own questions. Through discussion, agree upon a set of questions which will be used to guide the students' reading of the assignment. Assign factual type questions to the less able readers and inferential questions to the more able readers.

6. Have each student preview the reading assignment and draw up his own purposes or questions for reading. Then have him read the assignment to achieve his own purposes. Afterwards, conduct a class discussion of the reading assignment and determine the agreement on reading purposes. Have the students explain their previewing techniques and their interest in the topic. Their interests will probably explain the different purposes.

Attitudes

Teachers have a responsibility to create positive dispositions toward school in general and their subject matter areas specifically. Positive attitudes are developed through teacher-pupil interactions.

1. Demonstrate to your students that you are aware of what they know as well as what they do not know. This is a demonstration of your concern for them as individuals.

2. Recognition of the many excellent responses your students make builds positive attitudes and motivation.

3. Avoid berating and degrading students. This builds negative attitudes toward the individual teacher and ultimately toward education in general.

4. Teachers who berate their school and their colleagues in front of students build negative associations in the minds of their students. These negative associations ultimately turn into negative attitudes toward teachers and schools.

5. Speak positively about your subject area. It is difficult for students to become interested in a subject for which the teacher demonstrates no enthusiasm.

Results

Immediate and frequent knowledge of results is instrumental to motivation.

1. Prepare sheets which can be used for checking one's own answers. These sheets will provide immediate and frequent feedback to the student. Such feedback initiates motivation.

2. Be sure that the learning from one assignment is added to previous learning so students can see their total growth in the subject area.

3. Overemphasizing right or wrong responses does not contribute to motivation. If the student is right too often, he is not likely to be challenged. If the student is wrong too often, he is likely to become frustrated and give up the task. A teacher should emphasize rights more than wrongs while always keeping in mind that one way in which students learn is from their errors.

4. When emphasizing what a student did wrong, be sure to follow the emphasis with instruction that specifically tells a student what he needs to do to be right.

5. Students with poor attitudes toward subject areas need to have their correct responses recognized by their teachers in the presence of their classmates. Although teacher recognition is always important, peer approval means the most.

Success

Success breeds success. Without it there is no motivation.

1. Find a task in your subject area that every student can accomplish successfully every day.

2. Display the successes of poorly motivated students in your classroom for others to see.

3. Individual assignments on a contractual basis are a good way to make sure that students meet with success in every assignment.

4. If you and the student agree upon purposes for reading assignments, successes for the student are insured.

5. Provide students with reading materials at their reading level.

6. Allow students to read more or less depending upon their interest in a topic.

7. Contract with students for a certain grade and a certain quality of performance in a reading assignment.

8. Pair a good and a reluctant reader to work cooperatively on an assignment.

You have now completed Study Guide 3 and are ready to apply the motivation strategy to a reading assignment. If you already know how to do this, go directly to the Post-test. If you are not sure of how to incorporate the motivation strategy into daily reading assignments, Enabling Element 4 will show you how this is done.

Enabling Element 4
Preparing Reading Assignments

Specific Objective 4

You will incorporate a motivation strategy into a subject area reading assignment.

Enabling Activities

*1. Read Study Guide 4, "Preparing Reading Assignments," to familiarize yourself with the procedure for incorporating a motivation strategy into your daily lesson plan.

*2. Examine the subject area reading assignment provided. Incorporate the motivation strategy into this assignment to enhance its appeal.

3. Examine the reading assignments suggested by the author(s) of your textbook. Do these provide any material which can be used as one of the components of the motivation strategy?

*4. Sometimes authors provide discussion questions at the end of a unit. If your textbook has such questions, examine them. Determine if they can be assigned before students begin reading in order to establish reading purposes.

*5. Incorporate the strategy presented in this module into one of your reading assignments. Be sure to evaluate the effectiveness of the lesson as a result.

Study Guide 4
Preparing Reading Assignments

The purpose of this Study Guide is to explain and demonstrate how the motivation strategy introduced in Study Guide 3 can be used to enhance

---

*Indicates core Enabling Activities

the appeal of reading assignments. An assignment is an important part of a lesson plan. If it is not completed by the student, he will not have the necessary information for the following discussion. Due to a lack of information, the student will be unable to answer the teacher's questions which means an "F" for the day. Such marks eventually lead to a failing grade for the grading period. Assignments are often not completed because they are not planned and presented in such a way as to create a need or motivate the potential reader.

An examination of subject area teachers' plan books often reveals that reading assignments are given as follows:

Pages 127–152 for Tuesday. Continue discussion on WWII.

When the teachers' manual for textbooks are examined, reading assignments such as the following often appear:

Pp. 127–152. This chapter describes the events leading up to the involvement of the United States in World War II. Important events, dates, places, and people are brought into perspective.

Both examples of reading assignments are not likely to appeal to your students. A few changes by the subject area teacher will make the assignment more motivating. Let's incorporate the motivation strategy (PARS) into this reading assignment to see how the likelihood is increased for achieving a motivated state in your students.

First, we will need to obtain a *general purpose* for reading the assignment. Remember that the general topic under discussion is the events leading to the involvement of the United States in World War II. So our general purpose may be stated as the following question:

General Purpose for Reading

What are the major events which led to the involvement of the United States in World War II?

This is a broad purpose that provides the student with direction in his reading assignment. Without such a broad purpose, students could become bogged down in details and lose sight of the broad organization of the reading assignment.

Second, *specific purposes* are needed to assist students in obtaining definite facts that eventually can be used to compile a list of major events leading to the involvement of the United States in World War II. These purposes serve as precise teacher directions for reading the textbook. Each question also serves as a short-range goal.

To get the reading assignment under way, all the teacher needs to do is to assign the general and specific purposes along with a beginning page number. The students are directed to read and obtain the necessary information without a terminal page number. The following sample questions are arranged in the order of their discussion in the reading material and are designed to bring the reader into contact with *major events* asked for in the general purpose question.

Specific Purposes for Reading

1. After World War I, the victorious Allies met in Paris, France, to arrange the terms of the peace treaty to be signed by the defeated Germans. Why were the German people unhappy with the terms of this peace treaty?
2. What was the economic and political situation in Germany following the signing of the peace treaty?
3. What conditions were present that allowed Hitler to come to power in Germany?
4. Why did Germany, Italy, and Japan join forces in World War II?
5. What was the reaction in the United States when Germany invaded Austria? Czechoslovakia? Poland?
6. What was the reaction in the United States when Germany invaded and conquered France and beat the British at Dunkirk?
7. Who were the candidates in the 1940 presidential election?
8. The winner of the 1940 presidential election interpreted his victory as a mandate from the American people to send aid to friendly war-torn European countries. Why was this a significant event?
9. What did the Lend-Lease Act signal to the Germans, Italians, and Japanese?
10. What single event was responsible for the direct involvement of the United States in World War II?

The second component in the motivation strategy is *teacher attitudes*. Such beliefs regarding students and subject area are expressed by actions or dispositions. Although these attitudes and ensuing actions cannot be written like purposes into lesson plans, they are equally as important. The teacher who differentiates reading assignments according to her knowledge of students' reading levels and interests, emphasizes *right* responses, avoids ridicule and degradation, and demonstrates enthusiasm for her subject area is building motivation and positive attitudes toward school and subject matter.

The third component is *knowledge of results*. As was mentioned earlier in this Study Guide, immediate and frequent knowledge of results is instrumental to motivation. This component is easily incorporated into the reading assignment or lesson plan. After agreeing on questions to define purpose for reading, tell your students how they will be able to check upon the answers they obtain. You may want to consider providing prepared answers to the questions used for setting purposes. The students can then read the answers immediately after they complete their reading assignment. If their answers differ, provide them with an opportunity to reread parts of their assignment to see where they were misled. An alternative procedure for providing immediate feedback is to pair or small group students for comparing and discussing answers. Another technique you may wish to try is individual conferences with students to discuss and clarify their answers. Still another way is the customary class discussion of answers. For reluctant readers, reading assignments should be read partly in class and partly outside of class. Students who have a tendency not to complete assignments are often encouraged to do so when provided with an opportunity to start the assignment in class. This is especially true if provisions are made to show the reluctant readers how much progress they have made with their assignments in class, and to assure them they are obtaining the desired information.

The fourth component is *success*. If you have established purposes for reading, demonstrated your belief in the dignity of your students and the value of your subject area, and made arrangements for immediate feedback, you have done most of what is necessary to insure that every reader will meet with some success. To further insure success, you may want to include in your reading assignment or lesson plan a few of the suggestions from the SUCCESS subsection of Activities for Implementing the Motivation Strategy. A reading contract for a specified grade is a good way to insure success and motivate reluctant readers. You could ask reluctant readers to read their assignments for fewer purposes. Still another is to assign only one purpose per period of reading time and to keep the reading unit short. Pairing a good student with a reluctant reader is an additional way to insure success. Remember, success breeds success and enhances motivation but success must be planned for by the teacher. Planning success is essential for reluctant readers and cannot be left to chance.

You now see how the motivation strategy can be used to enhance the appeal of a reading assignment. Often some changes in the nature of reading assignments and in our attitudes are necessary to achieve motivated students.

Practicum Exercise

Now it is your turn to modify a reading assignment. To complete this section all you need is a sheet of paper and a writing instrument. Answer each question in order and then compare your answers with those provided in Answers to the Practicum Exercise which follow.

Reading Assignment

Mr. Hernandez, an 11th grade biology teacher, is about to make a reading assignment to his students. The topic presently under discussion is the circulatory system of the human body. Pages 117–131 in the textbook discuss this topic. Mr. Hernandez has many reluctant readers in his class who consistently do not complete their reading assignments.

How would you advise Mr. Hernandez to prepare this reading assignment to enhance motivation?

Write down your answers to the following questions and when you are through, compare them with the answers provided.

1. What are the key letters in the mnemonic device and key words in the motivation strategy that can be incorporated into this reading assignment?

2. The topic under study is the circulatory system which includes the heart, blood, and blood vessels. What suggestions regarding *purpose* do you have for Mr. Hernandez?

3. What about the manner in which Mr. Hernandez makes the assignment? What are the important teacher attitude considerations?

4. Once Mr. Hernandez's students have completed their assignment, how can he provide for immediate feedback on results?

5. Mr. Hernandez has a reluctant reader for whom he wants to guarantee considerable success. Do you have any suggestions for him?

When you have all your answers written down, compare them with the following answers.

Answers to the Practicum Exercise

1. The basic mnemonic device is PARS. The key words are *P*urpose, *A*ttitude, *R*esults, and *S*uccess.

2. Mr. Hernandez needs to set one general reading purpose which relates to the broad topic—the circulatory system. Then he needs to have approximately three specific reading purposes, one for each of the major components of the circulatory system—heart, blood, blood vessels. Reading purposes are probably best stated in the question form as this provides specific and clear direction for students.

3. If Mr. Hernandez takes into consideration his students' reading levels and interests, he is demonstrating a concern for students as individuals. If he is supportive of students' reading efforts no matter how meager, and emphasizes their growth no matter how small, he is demonstrating his concern for individuals. By doing these things and showing an enthusiasm for his subject area, he is building positive attitudes toward school, teachers, and subject area.

4. Knowledge of results can be provided immediately after students have completed their reading assignments by (a) providing self-correction answer keys, (b) placing students in pairs or small groups for comparing answers and discussion, or (c) teacher-pupil conferences. You may have thought of additional acceptable techniques which provide immediate feedback.

5. Success can be guaranteed through (a) teacher-student work contracts where the amount and quality of work is agreed upon in advance, (b) a grade contract guaranteeing an agreed upon grade for a specified quantity and/or quality of work, (c) pairing a reluctant and good reader to work together in completing the assignment, (d) providing a single, short-range purpose for reading at or below the reading level of the reluctant reader, or (e) providing class time for reading the assignment.

If your answers agree with the sample answers in content or intention—congratulations! You have reached the end of this Study Guide and should now be ready for the Post-test.

One word of caution about motivation strategies before we close. Motivation strategies, like most other strategies, do not achieve their height of effectiveness until they have been applied consistently over a long period of time. The reason for this is simple. Motivation factors are not discreet entities but rather interrelated factors. When manipulated by a teacher, each factor interacts with other factors. Ultimately the cumulative effect is that a need is created in even some of the most reluctant readers. This effect takes time to achieve so do not become disappointed or give up using the strategy if your results are not immediate.

Final Comment

From this module you have acquired a motivation strategy that should help you turn on more students in your subject area. The application of this strategy is left up to you as a teacher. No one may ever know if you apply or forget the strategy. But it is our hope that you will feel a professional and ethical responsibility to apply the motivational strategy presented in this module. If you do, we feel you will accomplish more of your instructional objectives and many of your students will remember you as someone who cared.

Post-test

Directions: Read each of the following statements and complete each Post-test item as directed.

1. Write a one-word synonym for motivation. List two sources of motivation.
2. List the eight major affective and cognitive factors influencing motivation.
3. Find the core factors in the motivation strategy presented in this module. Write the motivation acronym presented in this module?
4. List and explain the application of this strategy to the following subject area reading assignment to enhance its appeal.

Reading Assignment

> Mr. Davis is a physical education teacher interested in familiarizing his classes with football theory. He is about to assign to be read pages 22–31 from a basic textbook in sports. The current topic under study is the fundamentals of football which consists of such subtopics as (a) time and periods of play, (b) kickoff, (c) scrimmage, (d) passing, (e) downs, and (f) scoring.

Answers to the Post-test

1. Some appropriate synonyms for motivation are *need* and *desire*. Two sources of motivation are intrinsic motivation (from within) and extrinsic motivation (from without).
2. The major affective and cognitive factors are:

Affective	*Cognitive*
Interest	Purpose
Attitude	Short-term goals
	Adjustments for reading levels
	Success
	Usefulness of knowledge
	Knowledge of results

3. The core factors in the motivational strategy introduced in this module are: PURPOSE, ATTITUDE, RESULTS, and SUCCESS.
   The key word mnemonic device to aid retention of the core factors is the acronym PARS.
4. The procedure for modifying the ''Fundamentals of Football'' reading assignment is:
   First, establish PURPOSE.
   > Prepare general and specific purposes for reading assignment.

   Second, adjust your ATTITUDE.
   > Consider the needs and interests of individual students, be supportive of individual efforts, and be enthusiastic about your subject area.

   Third, provide RESULTS.
   > Provide immediate knowledge of results through self-correction devices, small group discussions, or teacher-pupil conferences.

Fourth, insure SUCCESS.
See to it that every individual student succeeds on some part of the reading assignment.

If any of your answers and the sample answers disagree in content or intention, recycle through the discussion of the specific components or the example reading assignment on U.S. involvement in World War II.
If you are still having difficulty, see your instructor.

Selected Bibliography

Ausubel, D. P. "A Teaching Strategy for Culturally Deprived Pupils: Cognitive and Motivational Considerations." In *Teaching Reading in High School: Selected Articles*. Edited by R. Karlin. Indianapolis: Bobbs-Merrill, 1969.

Darling, D. "Evaluating the Affective Dimension of Reading." *Perspectives in Reading,* Edited by T. C. Barrett. Newark, Delaware: International Reading Association, 8, 1967.

Dinkmeyer, D., and Dreisurs, R. *Encouraging Children to Learn: The Encouragement Process.* Englewood Cliffs, New Jersey: Prentice-Hall, 1963.

Estes, T. H. "A Scale to Measure Attitudes Toward Reading." *Journal of Reading,* 1971, *15* (2), 135–38.

Hunt, J. M. "Experience and the Development of Motivation." In *Readings in Educational Psychology*. Edited by H. W. Bernard and W. C. Huckins. Cleveland: World, 1967.

Hovious, M. "Motivating Junior High Readers." *Journal of Reading,* 1974, *17* (5), 373–75.

Hunter, M. *Motivation.* El Segundo, California: Tip Publications, 1971.

Kohl, H. R. *Teaching the Unteachables.* New York: New York Review, 1967.

Krathwohl, D. R. et al. *Taxonomy of Educational Objectives: Handbook II, Affective Domain.* New York: David McKay, 1964.

Marx, M. H., and Tombaugh, T. N. *Motivation.* San Francisco: Chandler, 1967.

Mouly, G. J. *Psychology for Effective Teaching.* New York: Holt, Rinehart and Winston, 1973.

Mueller, D. L. "Teacher Attitudes Toward Reading." *Journal of Reading,* 1973, *17* (3), 202–5.

Ransbury, M. K. "An Assessment of Reading Attitude." *Journal of Reading,* 1973, *17* (1), 25–28.

Thomson, M. K. "Motivation in School Learning," In Skinner, C. E., ed
Educational Psychology. Englewood Cliffs, New Jersey: Prentice-Hall,
1959.

Waples, D. *What Reading Does to People*. Chicago, Illinois: University of
Chicago, 1967.

Weiss, M. J. *Reading in the Secondary Schools*. New York: Odyssey, 1961.

Module 10

Identifying and Helping Problem Readers

CONTENTS

Prospectus

Rationale

One problem that constantly frustrates content area teachers is students who are reading far below grade level. Oftentimes these students appear uninterested, rebellious, withdrawn, slow or unmotivated. Usually students who are poor readers do not complete assignments, attempt to copy from other students, and fail to take part in class discussions. You may wonder why these students even come to school.

This module is designed to (1) help you develop a better understanding of such students and (2) provide practical suggestions for helping and referring students who are experiencing reading problems. The students with reading problems can survive—and learn—in content area classes. Their teachers must understand the symptoms and causes of reading problems, identify factors which may be interfering with the students' responsiveness to reading, be aware of sources of help, and have ideas for teaching students who cannot read commonly used written materials. These competencies, along with the commitment to help students succeed, will enable students to perform better and learn more in their content areas.

Objectives

TERMINAL OBJECTIVE: You will identify problem readers and factors which may be interfering with their responsiveness to reading tasks, and adapt your instructional procedures to help problem readers succeed in your content areas.

Specific Objectives:

1. You will define the term *problem reader* and list five behaviors typical of students classified as problem readers.

2. You will list and explain by categories those factors that may cause reading failure.

3. You will use nontesting devices to identify factors that may cause reading failure.

4. You will indicate appropriate referral sources for students who manifest certain symptoms, state guidelines and techniques for adapting instruction to help problem readers succeed in the content classes.

Resources And Time Required

All materials required for completion of this module are included. It would be most helpful if you talked with the school nurse, librarian, reading specialists, guidance counselor, school psychologist, and assistant principal in charge of curriculum to determine what specific support sources are available. Some discussions with the various resource personnel will enhance your accomplishment of the objectives in this module. The estimated time to complete the starred core Enabling Activities is two to four hours.

Directions: For each question, determine the word that indicates your belief regarding your competency. If you are in doubt, choose NO.

1. Undoubtedly you have problem readers in your classes. Can you define the term *problem reader* and list five behaviors typical of such readers?   YES NO

2. There are many factors that determine how well students learn to read. Can you state and explain six major factors that influence reading achievement?   YES NO

3. Content teachers share the responsibility for determining factors which may be interfering with students' responsiveness to reading. Do you have an observation checklist, personal inventory, and other nontesting devices which can be used to identify possible causes of reading failure? Are you using them?   YES NO

4. All teachers can help problem readers succeed if appropriate assistance is provided. Do you know the specialists to whom problem readers should be referred? Do you have guidelines and techniques to help problem readers succeed in your classes?   YES NO

Branching Program Alternatives for
Pre-test Responses

1. In general, problem readers are students who are reading two years below their expected reading level. If you are not sure of the typical behaviors of problem readers, complete Enabling Element 1. If you are familiar with the behaviors, you are ready for Enabling Element 2 to learn about factors which contribute to reading failure.

2. The six major factors that influence reading achievement are similar to those that influence success in any academic area. If you are familiar with the six factors (physical, language, environment, aptitude, social-emotional problems, and previous education), then go right on to Enabling Element 3. See Enabling Element 2 if you need to refresh your memory or learn a mnemonic device to help you remember the factors.

3. If you have your own checklist, personal inventory, and other nontesting devices that you are using to identify possible causes of reading failure, go to Enabling Element 4. If you need such nontesting instruments, Enabling Element 3 includes sample devices.

4. Do you know to whom you should refer a student who exhibits certain educationally inhibiting behaviors, and are you aware of guidelines and techniques for helping problem readers in your classroom? Enabling Element 4 is designed to alleviate teacher and student frustration by providing alternative strategies to help such students. If you want to ''make it through the day,'' as well as actually help students succeed, do Enabling Element 4.

Enabling Element 1
Characteristics of Problem Readers

Specific Objective 1

You will define the term *problem reader* and list five behaviors typical of students classified as problem readers.

Enabling Activities

*1. Read Study Guide 1, "Characteristics of Problem Readers," to determine their typical behaviors and also to learn a general definition of the term.

2. At a teachers' meeting, discuss who is responsible for teaching basic reading skills to those students who are reading less than two years below expected reading level. Will English teachers assume this responsibility? Should special developmental reading classes be established? Are there sufficient reading classes in your school, considering the number of students who read two years below their expected grade level?

3. List the names of ten students you have or have had who can be classified as problem readers. After each name, write two or three adjectives which describe them as students. Analyze your list to determine what common characteristics the students have or had. Also, think about the differences among the students and list possible reasons for the differences. Why is it that some students learn to cope better with their problems?

4. Look at achievement scores in reading if they are available for your students. Using the definition of problem readers in this module, approximately how many problem readers do you have?

---

*Indicates core Enabling Activities

*5. Do the Practicum Exercise to summarize the characteristics of these readers.

Study Guide 1
Characteristics of Problem Readers

By the time students enter middle or secondary schools, they should be able to use an appropriate strategy for attacking unfamiliar words, as well as comprehend different types of written materials and have an extensive reading vocabulary. They are learning how to use a study strategy and flexible reading rate and how to demonstrate considerable skill in reading orally. Hopefully the students are developing many and varied tastes and interests in reading and are beginning to critically evaluate what they read. Finally, it is hoped students who enter middle and secondary schools will consider reading as an important source of pleasure and knowledge.

Obviously, not all students exhibit these behaviors when they complete elementary school. Some students are behind even in the first grade. A student's reading disability may be mild, moderate or severe depending upon his expected level of reading performance. Most reading specialists believe a student who is reading two years below his expected reading level can be identified as a "problem reader." These students are in need of remedial reading instruction in a special class within the school or at a private reading clinic. It is important that all classroom teachers be aware of the characteristics of problem readers so these students can be referred for special reading instruction and then aided in classes.

Characteristics of Problem Readers

A summary of the characteristics of problem readers follows. Of course a student will not exhibit all of these behaviors; however, an array of behaviors will be evident. It is worth a special note to remind you that these characteristics are often apparent because reading materials are inappropriately assigned to students. For example, if a student has an eighth-grade reading level and the textbook is written at the eleventh-

---

*Indicates core Enabling Activities

grade reading level, these characteristics will be manifested by that student. To prevent this from occurring we suggest you use an Informal Suitability Survey (Module 3).

A problem reader usually has faulty or inadequate word recognition skills. She fails to use context clues in combination with other skills such as phonics and structural analysis. She tends to skip or guess at words which are unfamiliar rather than analyzing the word to see if there is a prefix, suffix, stem, or familiar sound pattern.

The student usually has difficulty with comprehension. Her reading vocabulary is limited; thus, she fails to get meaning from the reading. Also, she generally fails to set purposes for reading, read by thought units, or identify the author's organization or purpose.

A problem reader also exhibits other inappropriate behaviors. She may repeat many words when reading orally, confuse common words, read word by word rather than in thought units, and become overly tense or nervous when reading.

Of course the reader who is deficient in applying content-area related reading skills generally does not have the knowledge of the specialized vocabulary or symbols. She usually fails to adjust her rate to the selection and has not developed the specialized skills such as those required to read tables. graphs or diagrams. She usually does not have a particular strategy for studying or note taking, but rather avoids these activities.

In general, a problem reader appears to be uninterested and perhaps lazy. She does not read assigned materials which are content-area related. She may withdraw when asked to read orally or overact by making fun of the situation. Often attendance is irregular, which further hinders her academic progress.

It usually does not take content teachers long to recognize problem readers. You can identify them early if you use an Informal Suitability Survey and reading skills tests, which were described in Modules 3 and 4 respectively. If not, when you make reading assignments, administer quizzes, or ask students to read in class, some of the above characteristics will be evident. Your next task—if you really want to help students—is to try to identify possible causes of reading failure so your attempts at helping problem readers will be fruitful. Enabling Element 2 will help you understand why some students manifest these characteristics. Before going on to Enabling Element 2, you may find it valuable to summarize the characteristics of problem readers.

Practicum Exercise

Prepare a summary list of the characteristics of problem readers.

Enabling Element 2
Possible Causes of Reading Failure

Specific Objective 2

You will list and explain by categories those factors that may cause reading failure.

Enabling Activities

*1. Read Study Guide 2, "Possible Causes of Reading Failure." Identify and be able to explain the six major factors which influence reading achievement.

2. In addition to discussing how emotional problems can cause reading failure, discuss how reading failure can influence emotional problems.

3. Often elementary school teachers receive the total blame for reading failure. Discuss why this is unjust.

*4. Usually a student fails in reading due to a number of interrelated factors. Describe some students who can be classified as problem readers and indicate the various factors that may be working together to cause the reading problems.

5. Some reading specialists believe the environment is the most important factor which influences reading achievement. Do you agree with this statement? Can parents of middle school and secondary school students help their children in reading? In what ways? How can these suggestions be communicated to parents?

---

*Indicates core Enabling Activities

Study Guide 2
Possible Causes of Reading Failure

Content teachers can be of valuable assistance if they know some of the reasons why students fail to read as well as expected. This information can be used to help problem readers succeed even though they are experiencing reading problems. As you read the descriptions of possible causes of reading failure, try to think of ways you can identify these factors in your students. Remember that problems are often caused by two or more interrelated factors rather than by one isolated factor.

Physical

A number of physical factors correlate with failure in reading. Disabilities in vision and hearing can produce reading problems. For example, a student may have difficulty obtaining a clear image from materials printed on the chalkboard or in the textbook. Reduced visual acuity, fusion difficulty, and eye muscle control problems are just a few of the visual disabilities that correlate with reading failure. Likewise, the student with insufficient hearing or discrimination usually has problems in reading because he misunderstands the teacher's directions and explanations.

The general health of the student is also an important factor in learning to read. Students who have not had a proper diet or sufficient rest may experience difficulty in reading, which is a highly abstract task requiring a high degree of concentration. These students generally have poor attendance and may have experienced many childhood illnesses, which resulted in extended absences from school. In some cases, specific illnesses such as glandular disturbances or thyroid dysfunctions may hinder academic achievement. Other students may take inappropriate drugs or substances which influence their hearing, vision, and general health.

Language Development

The relationship between language development and success in reading is obvious. Students who have a meager vocabulary, poorly developed sound–symbol relationships, and a weak grasp of the grammar base of the language have considerable difficulty with reading.

Not all students grow in height and weight at the same rate. Likewise, not all students develop the language facility at the same time or have excellent models of language. Students who mature slowly are likely to arrive at school too immature for the academic task of reading. Likewise, students who are disadvantaged in that they have not heard standard English, experience difficulty when they read language patterns and words which are unfamiliar. Thus, some students fall behind in reading—and remain behind—because of the maturational factors and substandard language models.

Environment

Reading requires students to bring meaning to printed symbols. Meaning is only possible, however, when students have had some experiences which are related to what they are reading. Students who have not had many real or vicarious experiences are at a disadvantage when reading. For an example, if a student is reading a selection concerning a country he has visited, he is likely to get more meaning from what he is reading than another student who has never been out of the city in which he was born.

Parents are also a part of the environment and set an example for their children. Those parents who read frequently and enjoy reading as a source of information and pleasure are most likely to convey these attitudes to their children. Conversely, students who come from homes where there are no reading materials may experience difficulty in learning to read because this task is not valued.

Aptitude for Reading

There is a high positive correlation between reading achievement and intelligence among high school students and adults because many of the factors that are measured with present day intelligence tests are the same factors that are required for success in reading. For example, most intelligence tests measure visual memory, auditory memory, the ability to make judgments, and general information and vocabulary. Of course all of these factors are very important in learning to read. A student who does not seem to have the aptitude for learning to read as well as some other students usually falls behind in reading. It should be remembered, however, that students with less than average intelligence can still learn to read as long as opportunities are provided and the instructional methods are adapted to their aptitudes.

Social-Emotional Problems

Social-emotional factors also influence reading achievement. Some students fail in reading because they are overwhelmed with social and emotional problems resulting from poor relationships with friends and family. Reading difficulties sometimes result from personal problems brought about by inapporpriate relationships with siblings and peers. Symptoms associated with social and emotional problems such as a short attention span, preoccupation, and lack of desire to stay with a task are the same behaviors which are associated with academic failure.

Educational

Schools have also caused many reading problems among students. It is common to hear high school teachers blame elementary school teachers for poor reading instruction, and sometimes this is true. It should be remembered, however, that many factors influence poor reading achievement. Previous teachers may have used unsuitable materials, methods, or in fact neglected some students who attended irregularly and seemed turned off by reading. With large numbers of students in the classroom, teachers find it impossible to provide for all the individual differences and cannot do as much as they would like to do, or need to do, to help each student. The result is that students' reading levels and needs for specific skills have not been properly determined and/or remediated.

PLEASE Remember the Factors

These six factors work together to either help or hinder progress in reading. It is essential that teachers consider all of them when determining why some students have failed to learn to read as well as expected.

A mnemonic device which may help you remember these factors is the acronym PLEASE. Each letter in this acronym represents one of the major factors influencing reading achievement:

P—physical—health, hearing, vision, nutrition

L—language factors—vocabulary, grammar, sentence structure

E—environment—home, attitudes toward reading, motivation

A—aptitude—visual memory, auditory memory, judgment, general information

S—social-emotional—relationships with peers, family, and self

E—education—quality of teaching, appropriateness of materials, class size

Perhaps you will remember this acronym because it is the plea made by problem readers—Please! Your task is to *PLEASE observe, PLEASE refer,* and *PLEASE help* problem readers. The other study guides in this module will aid you as you perform these tasks.

Enabling Element 3
Using Nontesting Devices to
Identify Possible Causes of Reading Failure

Specific Objective 3

You will use nontesting devices to identify factors that may cause reading failure.

Enabling Activities

*1. Read Study Guide 3, "Using Nontesting Devices to Identify Possible Causes of Reading Failure." Compare the advantages and disadvantages of the different devices which you can use to identify possible causes of reading failure.

*2. Try the Observational Checklist with some of the students in your class who are problem readers. Can you identify some explanations for the reading failures of these students? Remember, the more you use the checklist the more automatic your observations will become. Periodically reread the checklist to refresh your memory.

3. Duplicate the Incomplete Sentences and Personal Inventory and have your students complete them. Think of ways of using this information for adapting instruction.

4. Talk with teachers in your building to determine who will use the different devices. It is suggested that all teachers use the checklist as a guide to observing and talking with students, while others who have the major responsibility for certain students, such as homeroom teachers, use the Personal Inventory and Incomplete Sentences. Adapt these suggestions to your particular school.

5. Share some of the results of the Personal Inventories with the school librarian. Responses to items 7, 9, 13, and 20, may

---

*Indicates core Enabling Activities

provide valuable information for selecting books, magazines, and other materials for the library or media center.

Study Guide 3
Using Nontesting Devices to Identify
Possible Causes of Reading Failure

If the factors which seem to be interfering with students' responsiveness to reading can be identified, then students can be given appropriate help. Even though content area teachers are not expected to provide remedial reading instruction for problem readers, they can be of valuable assistance in determining the factors that are hindering progress. Four useful devices for identifying PLEASE factors are included in this module.

Teachers need to employ different techniques for gathering information about problems because students are different. Some students are eager to talk with teachers; talking and listening to these students is appropriate. Others will avoid talking about themselves. In these cases, the teacher must be able to observe or use paper and pencil inventories to gather information. Presented in this Study Guide are an Observational Checklist, guidelines for interviewing students, and two paper and pencil inventories.

Using an Observational Checklist

The following checklist is designed to provide guidelines for observing students who are experiencing reading difficulties. If you read the checklist periodically you will be sure to have these factors and specific behaviors paramount in your mind as you are observing students. Keep in mind the mnemonic device which was presented in Study Guide 2: PLEASE. Each one of the letters in this acronym refers to one of the major reasons for reading failure:

P-physical factors, L-language development, E-environmental factors, A-aptitude, S-social-emotional, E-educational factors. Some observable behaviors are listed for each one of these factors.

A Checklist for Identifying Possible Causes of Reading Failure

Directions: Which of the major area(s) seem to be interfering with the students' responsiveness to reading? Underline specific behaviors you observe and add comments as necessary.

_____ P—*Physical Factors*

When the student is reading, does she:
lose her place
rub her eyes
blink excessively
tilt her head so as to use only one eye
complain of blurred print, headaches, or watering eyes
When you speak to the student, does she:
tilt her head
cup her ear
appear inattentive
ask you to repeat directions
Does she appear well rested and generally healthy?
What is her attendance record?
Comments:

_____ L—*Language Factors*

When she speaks, does she:
have a meager vocabulary
have poor sentence structure
Does the student make frequent spelling errors that indicate
a lack of knowledge of sound–symbol relationships?
Does she have a past history of poor performance in
language-related courses?
If you have had occasions to talk with the parents and
siblings, did you notice anything helpful for interpreting
the student's language background?
Comments:

_____ E—*Environmental*

        Does the student talk about places she has visited or events that she has experienced?

        Do you know if the student has any books, magazines, or other reading materials of her own?

        Do the parents seem interested in the student and accept her?

        Is education valued by the family?

        Comments:

_____ A—*Aptitude Factors*

        Does the student ask questions?

        Does she have a fairly good background of information?

        Is she able to draw conclusions and make sound judgments based on given facts?

        Does the student learn things rapidly and remember what she has learned?

        Is the student able to see similarities and differences in concepts?

        Comments:

_____ S—*Social-Emotional Factors*

        Is the student accepted by her family and peers?

        Is she able to get along with others?

        Does she have a positive self concept?

        Is she able to control her emotions and concentrate long enough to complete a task?

        Comments:

_____ E—*Educational Factors*

Does the student have positive or negative attitudes toward the school?

Does she have purposes for learning?

Has the student experienced success or failure in most academic areas?

Has the student been enrolled in any remedial reading programs?

Are the materials available appropriate for the student?

Comments:

You are not expected to complete this checklist for each of your students. The purpose of the checklist is to guide your observations of students as you try to identify possible causes that may be hindering them. Often your observations are the ones that are the keys for identifying the causes of reading problems. PLEASE keep these factors in mind so you can help identify possible reasons for students' lack of responsiveness to instruction.

Using a Personal Inventory

Consider using or adapting the following Personal Inventory if you would like to quickly gather more information about your students. You can administer a Personal Inventory to the students for whom you have the major responsibility. As you read the items notice they are designed to gather information concerning the six major factors which influence reading achievement and academic progress in general.

Notice the directions indicate a student can leave blank those items he does not wish to answer. You should note these items and then use observation as a device to gather more information concerning the items. As with all devices, remember the responses indicate the feelings of the students on that particular day. This is a sample of behavior which must be combined with other samples before any conclusions or judgments are made.

After administering the inventory, use the guidelines provided for interpreting the information. Keep in mind, however, that some questions may elicit responses which provide information concerning two or more factors.

Personal Inventory

Name _____ Date _____

Address _____ Age _____

Telephone _____

Directions: The following questions are designed to help me get to know you. Write your answers in the blanks provided. If you are not sure of some answer, or do not want to answer some question, simply leave it blank.

1. What other schools have you attended? _____

   _____

2. Are you supposed to wear glasses? _____ If yes, when did you first get them?_____

   _____

3. Do your eyes bother you when you read or write? _____ In what way? _____

   _____

4. Is your hearing (circle one) excellent, good, fair, or poor?

5. Is your health (circle one) excellent, good, fair, or poor?

6. How many hours do you sleep each day? _____

   _____

7. Do you read for pleasure? _____ If yes, name some of the recent books or magazines you have read. _____

   _____

8. Is your reading (circle one) excellent, good, fair, or poor?

9. What is the most interesting topic you like to study? _____

   _____

10. What is the least interesting topic that you must study? _____

    _____

11. How long do you usually spend studying outside of school? ___

12. List some of the places that you have visited outside of (city) ___

    _____

    _____

13. What interests do you have outside of school? _____
    _____
    _____

14. What school activities do you enjoy? _____
    _____
    _____

15. How do you get along with your parents? _____
    _____
    _____
    _____

16. Circle the word that shows how most teachers think of you as a
    student: excellent, good, fair, or poor.

17. Is your vocabulary: excellent, good, fair or poor?

18. Is your spelling: excellent, good, fair, or poor?

19. Do you have a place to study at home? Please describe it.
    _____
    _____

20. What kinds of responsibilities would you like to have as an adult?
    _____
    _____
    _____
    _____

21. Check the words that usually describe you:

    _____ serious   _____ unhappy
    _____ angry   _____ friendly
    _____ intelligent   _____ boastful
    _____ capable   _____ cheerful
    _____ unfriendly   _____ fair
    _____ mature   _____ immature
    _____ sensitive   _____ snobbish

    _____ witty   _____ flexible
    _____ ugly   _____ handsome/beautiful
    _____ calm   _____ stubborn
    _____ cooperative   _____ complaining
    _____ hostile   _____ boring
    _____ noisy   _____ selfish
    _____ kind   _____ shy

You may add other words that describe you if you would like. __

22. Why do some people like you? _____

_____

_____

23. Are there some people who do not like you? _____
    Why? _____

_____

24. What is your father's occupation? _____
    What is your mother's occupation? _____

25. What language is usually spoken in your home? _____

_____

26. Do your parents talk with you about school? _____ If so, what
    kinds of things do they ask? _____

_____

_____

Guide to Interpreting Information From the Personal Inventory

Major Factor	*Questions Designed to Provide Information*
Physical	2, 3, 4, 5, 6
Language	8, 17, 18, 25
Environment	12, 19, 24, 26
Aptitude	9, 10, 13, 20
Social-Emotional	15, 21, 22, 23
Education	1, 7, 11, 14, 16

Incomplete Sentences

Some teachers like to use incomplete sentences such as those which follow to gather information about students. The teacher who has the major responsibility for certain students may be the one who will administer the incomplete sentences. When interpreting responses to incomplete sentences it should be remembered that the student's responses only represent her feelings on a particular day. Before making any rash judgments, more information should be gathered by consulting the guidance counselor, cumulative records, personal inventory, other teachers, and information from the talks you might have with the student.

Incomplete Sentences

Name _____ Date _____

Directions: Quickly complete the following sentences. Write down the first thing that enters your mind. There are no right or wrong answers.

1. Reading is _____
2. I like to _____
3. My friends _____
4. I feel _____
5. The best magazine _____
6. Elementary school was _____
7. My eyes _____
8. My ears _____
9. My parents _____
10. Education is _____
11. I have been to _____
12. I wish I could _____
13. When I read to others _____
14. I am liked by _____
15. School is _____
16. My teachers _____
17. Books are _____
18. I sleep _____
19. When I finish school _____
20. My home _____
21. I need help in _____

22. My best subject is _____

23. Spelling is _____

24. Teachers usually _____

Although responses vary, in general you will find the following guides useful as you analyze the responses to the incomplete sentences. Certain responses will necessarily fit more than one classification; however, we have tried to make them as discrete as possible. For example, one student may complete item 4 with "I feel tired" when another student may say, "I feel lonely." In the first case the item refers to a physical factor, and the second response concerns the social-emotional factors. It will be necessary to adapt the following guidelines to the students' responses.

Guidelines for Analyzing the
Incomplete Sentence Responses

Factor	*Sentence Number Which May Provide Information*
Physical	4, 7, 8, 18
Language	1, 13, 17, 23
Environment	5, 10, 11, 13, 20
Aptitude	12, 19, 21, 22
Social-Emotional	2, 3, 9, 14
Education	6, 15, 16, 24

Talking and Listening to Students

Some students are eager to share information with their teachers if the teachers seem interested in them. Talking to and listening to students can be a useful technique to gather information concerning the six factors which influence reading achievement. All teachers have some responsibility to listen to students because different students relate better to different teachers. If all the teachers on the staff are aware of the importance of listening to students, and are perceptive as they listen and talk to students, the staff will be better able to help them. For example, some students will relate to the physical education teacher on the field and may be turned off completely by the English teacher in the classroom; whereas, another student will relate better to the English teacher and avoid face to face encounters with the physical education teacher.

Many of the questions which are listed in the Personal Inventory form can be used in talking with students. Of course, the questions will be phrased differently and asked in a natural sequence as the conversation develops. If the teacher is aware of the six major categories, however, it is possible to organize the responses of the students into meaningful categories for interpretation.

When talking to students you must be sincere and present an attitude of concern. Ask questions in such a way that the student realizes you are not "meddling in his affairs," but rather trying to help him. You will want to aid the student in accepting himself as he is, and yet provide a ray of hope for improvement. Help the students realize reading and success in academic areas are important, but that there are other important things in life too. Sample questions which you can use to gather information are listed below. Again, the importance of having a natural conversation with the student is emphasized.

Sample Questions Which Can Be
Used When Talking With Students

Physical Ability. Have you ever had any trouble with seeing or hearing? What illnesses have you had? How many hours do you sleep in a day?

Language. What language do your parents speak? Did they graduate from high school? College? Do you have any problems in learning to spell, read, or write?

Environment. What places have you visited while on vacation? How do your parents feel about your school activities? Can you study at home?

Aptitude. What things do you do best? Do you want to do better in school? Why? Do you think you can learn to read better?

Social-Emotional. Who are your best friends? How well do you get along with your family? What kinds of things make you happy? Frustrated? Sad?

Education. What kind of student were you in elementary school? Have you ever been in a special reading class? Do your teachers generally like you?

Final Comment

In addition to using these nontesting devices to determine possible causes of reading failure, you can also use some of the reading skills tests which were presented in Module 4 on diagnosing particular reading skills. These skill tests will help you further identify special reading difficulties which may be remediable. Likewise, if you use an Informal Suitability Survey, you will be doing your part to help find appropriate materials for problem readers. One testing or nontesting device simply is not sufficient. You need a battery of devices to enable you to gather information that will in turn enable you to help students. For practical ideas on what to do with information that you have gathered, go on to Enabling Element 4.

Enabling Element 4
Referring and Helping Problem Readers

Specific Objective 4

You will indicate appropriate referral sources for students who manifest certain symptoms and state guidelines and techniques for adapting instruction to help problem readers succeed in the content classes.

Enabling Activities

*1. Read Study Guide 4, "Referring and Helping Problem Readers." Identify possible resource persons to whom problem readers can be referred. Also note ways that you can help such students in your classes.

*2. Talk with the school nurse, psychologist, and guidance counselors to determine the specific services they offer and the procedures for initiating referral. Ask about professional services which are free to those who do not have an adequate income.

*3. Talk with the reading specialist and developmental reading teachers to determine what reading services are offered in the school. What other types of reading instruction should be offered?

4. Discuss guidelines for referring students for special help. What are the school and county guidelines for referring problem readers? You should not refer students to specialists outside the school without the advice and consent of the appropriate person. Often the guidance counselor, assistant principal, school psychologist, or some other resource person is able to use more

---

*Indicates core Enabling Activities

elaborate screening devices to determine if referrals are in fact necessary.

5. Talk with your colleagues about ways of involving parents in home-school tutoring programs with problem readers.

6. Read the Teacher Daily Dozen Checklist. Note one item which you would like to improve. Brainstorm with your colleagues and review previous modules to determine specific ways which you can implement the behavior.

Study Guide 4
Referring and Helping Problem Readers

If you have identified problem readers and perhaps determined some of the factors which may be interfering with their responsiveness to reading, what is the next step? Should you discontinue teaching your content area and begin teaching reading? Obviously, this is not possible nor desirable.

There are two ways content teachers can help problem readers: (1) You need to refer students to the proper sources of help. You are not expected to teach beginning reading skills, diagnose or prescribe glasses, or hearing aids, or act as a full time guidance counselor. You need and must have the help of specialists! (2) Even though you are not expected to teach primary grade reading skills, there are some adaptations which you can make in your instructional strategies to help problem readers. In other words, you do have some responsibility to help students who are reading two years or more below their expected grade level succeed in your content area while they are trying to overcome their reading deficiencies. Problem readers can succeed in content areas if you make these minor adaptations. Suggestions for referral and ideas for adapting instructional strategies are presented for each one of the major factors that influences reading achievement. PLEASE use referrals and the following guidelines and techniques—they help!

Helping Students with Physical Problems

1. Refer the student to the school nurse for further screening. Perhaps a visual, hearing, or health problem has been missed or

has developed recently. If drug or substance abuse is evident, refer the student to the school counselor.

2. Encourage the student to wear glasses or a hearing aid if prescribed. Help the student accept herself as she is by being honest with her concerning any physical limitations.

3. Suggest short periods of work when doing close work, such as reading and writing. Direct the student to set a time limit for studying.

4. Have the student sit near the chalkboard, screen, or generally where the action is. Do not pay too much attention to her so as to make her feel awkward and unusual.

5. If necessary, contact the librarian to see if books with larger print are available. You might also see if cassettes are available or could be made for those students who have a difficult time reading, but yet are able to listen and comprehend.

6. Remember not to turn your back on students when speaking or to put your hands in front of your face. Often teachers are not conscious of habits that may interfere with their teaching effectiveness. Evaluate yourself continuously to see if you are articulating, and maintaining good eye contact.

7. It might be helpful to write key vocabulary words on the chalkboard and discuss the meanings and pronunciations of the words using the suggestions in Modules 5 and 8.

8. If the student is experiencing health problems which are hindering her attendance, you might ask the visiting teacher to contact the parents. It may be necessary to adjust the assignments and number of credits according to the capabilities of the student.

Helping Students with Language Problems

1. Refer the student to a remedial reading specialist or remedial English classes. When doing so, share the information you have gathered about the student's reading skills and habits.

2. Give oral tests if possible. Often you can administer tests orally while the other students are taking the written exams. If this is not possible, see if a parent volunteer can help you.

3. Provide information on cassettes or have others read to students for whom suitable materials are not available. Often students can listen and understand what they may not be able to read.

4. Repeat the student's responses using correct grammar and good sentence structure. Realize you alone are not going to change the student's use of language overnight; however, if all teachers make conscientious efforts, and if the student desires to improve, it is possible to change language patterns.

5. Use many visual materials to expand concepts. The old saying ''a picture is worth a thousand words'' may be trite, but it is very true.

6. Correct spelling errors by going over the frequently missed words. Point out the sounds that may be confusing to the students.

7. To help students increase their vocabularies at higher levels, use the ideas in Module 5. Many problem readers only have specific understandings of words.

8. Suggest some self-study books which are designed to improve spelling, reading or writing. Many times these books include practical exercises and essential information which can be of valuable assistance for improving spelling, writing, and reading.

Helping Students with Environmental Problems

1. Use many visual and auditory aids to help the students develop concepts. Students can develop many concepts through vicarious experiences when direct experiences are not possible.

2. Refer the student to the guidance counselor if physical abuse is evident. Child abuse agencies rely on teachers for referrals; however, you should talk with the appropriate authority before making referrals to outside agencies.

3. Praise the student sincerely for ideas, good suggestions, and so forth. Do not overdo the praise so as to make the student feel that you really do not have confidence in her.

4. Be available to parents if they express concern. Many times parents are interested in their children and want them to do better.

5. Have confidence in the student. Expect her to do her best and show disappointment when you do not get her best efforts.

6. Make the students aware of the various resources that are available to them at school and public libraries. If you use many reading materials in your classes, arrange visits to the libraries to inform students of what materials are available and how to locate them. Provide opportunities for the students to browse and use some of the materials which are interesting to them.

7. Help students realize the value of having a place for study and good study habits. Provide specific suggestions on how they can study in your content area. Suggest places in the school or community where they can study and at the same time enjoy the company of other people if desired.

8. Read or tell stories about famous people who have been successful even though they came from a detrimental environment. Oftentimes magazines and newspaper articles include such examples. Remember you are not going to change attitudes in one day; however, if you take advantage of teaching opportunities on a daily basis, the change will occur.

Helping Students with Social-Emotional Problems

1. Refer the student to the guidance counselor or school psychologist. Some students have problems which require special analysis and guidance. After the student has met with the guidance counselor and/or the school psychologist, talk with them to determine what recommendations they have for helping the student in the classroom.

2. Avoid antagonizing the student. Avoid that which tends to ''set off'' the student.

3. Determine the student's strengths and praise her sincerely. At the same time, help the problem reader face her weaknesses and set goals for improving herself.

4. Be ready to listen to the student. Not all students are ready to talk; but when they do, they are generally trying to get advice from you.

5. Give responsibility which is of interest to the student. Differentiate your assignments according to interests and abilities.

6. Accept the student as she is. You may not like what she does, but you can still like her as a person.

7. Use discussion groups and group dynamic techniques to help students develop skill in working with and accepting others. Often students form stereotypes and develop cliques which hinder social activities. It is important for teachers to help students appreciate the differences in their classmates.

8. Help students plan schedules which allow time for social involvement as well as studying. Help the students accept the fact that most students enjoy socializing and yet must spend some of the time studying if they are going to succeed academically. Plan flexible schedules with the students.

Helping Students with Less Aptitude for Reading

1. Refer the student to the school psychologist for an individual intelligence test to determine special aptitudes. An I.Q. score is not as meaningful as the scores for factors of intelligence which the test measures. Determine special areas in which the student might have a better aptitude, such as in visual or auditory memory, and then capitalize on this strength as you teach the student or give suggestions for studying.

2. Use many visual materials, first hand experiences, and concrete objects when teaching. Keep in mind that reading is a highly abstract task which requires the person to form mental images from the printed symbols. Many times students who demonstrate low aptitude have not had as many experiences as others.

3. Adjust materials to capabilities according to results of the Informal Suitability Survey.

4. Grade on an individual rate of progress if at all possible.

5. Encourage the students by creating pride in achievement. Help students realize the value of a job well done.

6. Help the students develop confidence in what they can do and be, rather than emphasizing what they cannot do or become. Remember there are aptitudes for many different types of skills.

7. Remember the importance of repetition and practice. Most students, and especially those with low aptitude toward reading, need many practice and reinforcement activities to learn new concepts or skills.

8. Identify the most important concepts, attitudes, and skills which you believe students need to have in your content area. Concentrate on these objectives so that the students will learn the things most helpful in life.

Helping Students from Educationally Poor Backgrounds

1. Make sure you are providing materials which the students are capable of reading. Apply some of your newly developed skills in administering and interpreting Informal Suitability Surveys.

2. Use the different teaching strategies that were suggested for word meaning and word pronunciation skills. Since vocabulary is an important factor for comprehension, identify the most important specialized words in your content area and emphasize these. Have the students keep a record of new words they are learning.

3. If you need to use many materials which require reading, have an excellent reader put the most important sections of the commonly required reading materials on cassettes. These might be kept in the library or classroom for use by poor readers. Use audio-visual aids which will help the students develop concepts without reading.

4. Summarize the most important material on a handout written at a low reading level. Review Module 2 for specific suggestions on how to write materials at specified reading levels.

5. Ask the librarian or department chairman for books or other supplemental materials written at lower reading levels which also contain the concepts and skills you are trying to teach. You

may want to establish centers that focus on interesting topics or skills.

6. Introduce assignments with a purpose so the students will have specific information to find. Discuss with them how the assignments will help and demonstrate to them strategies for studying.

7. Have more involvement activities during class sessions. Students can learn from each other while they do group research and have discussions. Simulation type activities in which students actually apply newly acquired skills or concepts are very appropriate for problem readers. Role playing and dramatization can also be helpful in making your class sessions come alive.

8. Use the textbook illustrations, pictures, and charts to explain the content of your subject area. Often graphic aids along with your comments or questions can provide the essential information found in the text. Supplement this material by inviting resource people to your classroom.

9. Outline or teach the students to outline some of the most important information in the course. Many times comprehension is aided if the thoughts are well organized as is required when outlining. A skill group might help to teach this skill or other important skills that problem readers have not developed. See Module 4 for more specific directions.

Remember you are certainly not expected to change problem readers into mature readers in the short period of time that you have with them. However, you should have a positive attitude toward problem readers and believe that they can succeed in your classes if you make the minor adaptations that were suggested above. Your attitude and effective teaching techniques will enable problem readers to develop better concepts via success; and this, too, will help them grow in reading achievement.

Putting It All Together

Keep in mind that usually more than one factor influences reading achievement. A student may be plagued by social-emotional problems that are triggered by physical problems. These two problems may in turn result in educational problems for the student. The following checklist is designed to help you "put it all together to get the job done" as you try to help problem readers. Notice the checklist which follows is a Daily Dozen Checklist rather than a series of steps that you can follow in helping problem readers. The emphasis is on *continuous* effective teaching as the prescription for helping problem readers in your classroom. Use a checklist to continually evaluate yourself to make sure you are not contributing to the delinquency of problem readers. This is what teaching content area related reading skills is all about!

Teacher Daily Dozen Checklist

_____ 1. Am I using materials which the students are capable of handling? Do I use my department chairman and librarian as resources for getting such materials?

_____ 2. Have I identified the most important concepts for my students? Am I teaching the concepts, skills, and attitudes which will make their lives better?

_____ 3. Am I using a variety of activities in the classroom rather than just reading? Do I use activities such as simulation, role playing, resource people, discussions, and audiovisual aids?

_____ 4. Do I differentiate my assignments according to the needs of the students? After having used Informal Suitability Surveys, am I using the information to provide appropriate materials? Do I give suggestions for students on how to read the materials?

_____ 5. Do I accept my students as they are? Do I avoid labeling them? Have I determined their most important strengths and are my instructional techniques designed to maximize them?

_____ 6. Do I refer students who need specialized help? Am I aware of the support services which are available in the school and community?

_____ 7. Do I identify and demonstrate enthusiasm for my content area? Am I stimulating the students' interests and curiosity?

_____ 8. Am I continuously observing students to determine factors which may be helping or hindering their academic achievement? Have I used this information to actually help the students?

_____ 9. Do I take time for myself? Am I able to enjoy many experiences outside of school which will make me a better teacher in the classroom?

_____ 10. Am I actually helping my students increase their vocabularies and develop appropriate strategies for word pronunciation, comprehension, and study?

_____ 11. Am I aware of the reading skills which are required for reading materials in my content area? Do I help students learn to read these specialized types of materials or am I just assuming that anyone can read them? Do I use skills groups and skill centers to provide for individual differences?

_____ 12. Am I implementing the PARS (Module 9) strategy for motivating reluctant readers? Is my attitude one which will be influencing the students to succeed in my classes? Do I have faith in students?

Directions: The following questions are designed to measure your accomplishments of the objectives in this module. Read each item and respond as directed.

1. Define the term *problem reader* and list five typical behaviors of problem readers.
2. List the six major factors that influence reading achievement. After each factor, provide a specific example of how it can help or hinder reading achievement.
3. Read the following description of a fifteen-year-old problem reader and identify two factors that may be causing the reading failure.

When Tom comes to your class he seems to want to "goof off." He doesn't pay attention when you are talking and never completes the assignments you make. When you provide time for him to begin his textbook reading assignment in class, he doesn't even open his book. You found the major textbook was too difficult for him when you surveyed the suitability of the textbook for students. Yet when you read the textbook he is able to understand with one hundred percent accuracy.

According to Tom's cumulative record he received a prescription for glasses when he was in the fourth grade, yet you have never seen him wear them. As you think back, you have noticed that he squints when looking at the chalkboard.

Even though Tom fools around in class once in awhile, he does ask good questions. He is friendly and outgoing in his manner; however, you noticed he doesn't have many close friends in this class. He is always courteous when you talk with him individually.

When Tom's homeroom teacher administered the incomplete sentences (Study Guide 3) to the class, Tom was one of the first students to complete the sentences. Read his responses that follow.

Tom's Responses to the Incomplete Sentences

1. Reading is a rip off.
2. I like to watch television.
3. My friends are OK.
4. I don't like these questions.
5. The best magazine is *Popular Mechanics.*
6. Elementary school was fun.
7. My eyes are OK.
8. My ears are on my head.
9. My parents work.
10. Education is a drag.
11. I have been to New York.
12. I wish I could find a job.
13. When I read to others I get nervous.
14. I am liked by my dog.
15. School is a drag.
16. My teachers are smart.
17. Books are hard.
18. I sleep in on Saturdays.
19. When I finish school I will make more money.
20. My home is near the expressway.
21. I need help in math.
22. My best subject is shop.
23. Spelling is OK.
24. Teachers usually like me.

4. Indicate two possible referral sources and two ways you could help Tom in your class.

Answers to the Post-test

1. A problem reader can be defined as a student who is reading two years below his expected reading level. Their behavior varies because there are many different skills involved in reading; however, the following behaviors are frequently typical of problem readers:

   a. Lacks systematic method for determining unknown words.

   b. Neglects to set purposes for reading.

   c. Experiences difficulty in comprehending materials.

   d. Cannot vary rate according to the nature of the reading materials.

   e. Becomes tense and makes many errors when asked to read orally.

   f. Has not developed a study strategy or specialized reading skills necessary for success in content areas.

   g. Has a limited vocabulary in speaking, writing, listening and reading.

   h. Displays a negative attitude towards reading assignments.

2. The six factors that influence reading achievement are:

   a. Physical

   b. Language Development

   c. Environment

   d. Aptitude

   e. Social-Emotional Problems

   f. Education

      Physical factors can help or hinder reading achievement in many ways. Excellent visual and auditory skills are prerequisites for the reading task. Likewise, good physical health enables a person to learn. If a student has visual, health and/or auditory problems, the chances for success in reading are limited.

Language development can influence reading achievement, too. Students who were generally slow in the development of language skills, or do not have adequate models to learn standard English, fall behind during the early years of school. Concentrated efforts to improve language can help the student become a better reader.

The environment is one of the most important factors in reading achievement. The student who does not have books or other reading material along with a place to study at home is hindered. Progress in reading is made more difficult by parents who do not support the schools or the student. Conversely, parents who overprotect their child or put him under too much pressure can hinder achievement, too.

Reading is highly correlated with intelligence as measured by present-day academic aptitude tests. The student who is below average in those factors that influence reading (visual memory, auditory memory, and vocabulary) experiences difficulty in learning to read because reading requires these aptitudes.

Social-emotional factors can help or hinder reading achievement. Reading requires a great deal of concentration and thinking. The student who is plagued with social-emotional concerns may not be able to put forth the concentration which is required. Also, if the student feels that he is not capable of learning, he will have a more difficult time learning to read.

Students who are fortunate enough to have enthusiastic, dedicated teachers who diagnose to determine appropriate objectives and activities will have a better chance of succeeding in reading. Teachers who neglect the problem reader contribute further to the cause.

3. A visual defect may be influencing Tom's responsiveness to instruction. Glasses were prescribed when he was in the fourth grade, but he does not wear them. He seems to avoid accepting this limitation according to his response to item 7. According to the description, Tom does not have friends in your class. Likewise, his responses to items 4 and 14 may indicate possible social-emotional problems. It could be he is "goofing off" to gain acceptance from peers. Also, he may not be wearing his glasses because he does not want to appear different from his

peers. The interaction effects of poor vision and lack of appropriate peer relationships could be contributing to his lack of responsiveness to instruction.

4. At this time Tom should be referred to the school reading specialist to determine the extent of his reading disability and to suggest instructional materials which would be most beneficial for him. You might also refer Tom to his counselor, who might provide some insights to his acting out behavior and negative self-concept. The school nurse could screen his vision again and talk with him about the visual defect. Try to give attention to Tom and motivate him by using the questions he asks in class. Involve him in activities which do not require reading. Perhaps you might have Tom listen to some tapes which include sections of the textbook which you would like him to understand. If possible, relate some of your content area objectives to Tom's interest in cars, math, and industrial arts.

Final Comment

This module was written to provide you with some explanations why certain students are problem readers. The techniques for adapting instruction for such students are outlined in this module and were extended in previous modules. These techniques will enable you to help the problem reader develop the skills and knowledge of your content area. It is hoped that you will apply the ideas in this module to help problem readers become more successful in your classes. Simply because a student is a problem reader, it does not follow that he cannot succeed in school. Of course, his success depends upon the most important factor in the educational process—you!

If you have completed all Post-test items correctly, you are finished with the module. If not, see your instructor for help or return through the Enabling Elements as needed.

Selected Bibliography

Aukerman, R. C. *Reading in the Secondary School Classroom*. New York: McGraw-Hill, 1972.

Behrens, H. D., and Maynard, G. *The Changing Child: Readings in Child Development*. Glennview, Illinois: Scott Foresman, 1972.

Cushenbery, D. C. *Remedial Reading in the Secondary School*. West Nyack, New York: Parker, 1972.

Farr, R. *Reading: What Can Be Measured?* Newark, Delaware: International Reading Association, 1969.

Forgan, H. *Help Your Child Learn to Read*. Toronto: Pagurian Press Ltd., 1975.

Hafner, L. E. *Improving Reading in Middle and Secondary Schools,* 2d ed. New York: Macmillan, 1974.

Karlin, R. *Teaching Reading in High School*. 2nd ed. Indianapolis: Bobbs-Merrill, 1972.

Leeds, D. S. "The Role of Self-Concept in the Psychological Development of the Individual." *Reading World,* December, 1971, 161–76.

Marksheffel, N. D. *Better Reading in the Secondary School*. New York: Ronald, 1966.

Ramsey, W. Z., ed. "Organization for Individual Differences." *Perspectives in Reading,* Newark, Delaware: International Reading Association, 1967, 9.

Rossman, J. F. "Remedial Readers: Did Parents Read to Them at Home?" *Journal of Reading,* 1974, *17,* 622–25.

Schubert, D. G., and Torgerson, T. L. *Improving the Reading Program*. Dubuque, Iowa: William C. Brown, 1972.

Strang, R. *Reading Diagnosis and Remediation*. Newark, Delaware: International Reading Association, 1968.

Strang, R; McCullough, C. M.; and Traxler, A. C. *The Improvement of Reading*. New York: McGraw-Hill, 1967.

Wilson, R. M. *Diagnostic and Remedial Reading for Classroom and Clinic*. Columbus, Ohio: Charles E. Merrill, 1972.

Bibliographies For Secondary School Reading

Publications Every Secondary School Should Have

Artley, S. A. *Trends and Practices in Secondary Reading*. Newark, Delaware: International Reading Association, 1963.

Bamman, H. A., Hogan, U., and Greene, C. E. *Reading Instruction in the Secondary Schools*. New York: David McKay, 1961.

Berger, A., and Hartig, H. *The Reading Materials Handbook*. Oshkosh, Wisconsin: The Academia Press, 1969.

Blanton, W., and Farr, R. *Reading Tests for Secondary Grades*. Newark, Delaware: International Reading Association, 1972.

Burmeister, L. E. *Reading Strategies for Secondary School Teachers*. Reading, Massachusetts: Addison-Wesley, 1974.

Cheyney, A. B. "Teaching Reading Skills Through the Newspaper." *Reading Aids Series*. Edited by C. T. Mangrum. Newark, Delaware: International Reading Association, 1971, *50*.

Cushenbery, D. C. *Remedial Reading in the Secondary School*. West Nyack, New York: Parker, 1972.

Duggins, J. *Teaching Reading for Human Values in High School*. Columbus, Ohio: Charles E. Merrill, 1972.

Early, M., ed. "Reading Instruction in Secondary Schools." *Perspectives in Reading, No. 2*. Newark, Delaware: International Reading Association, 1964.

Fader, D., and McNeil, E. B. *Hooked on Books*. New York: Berkley, 1968.

Florida Reading Quarterly. Florida State Reading Council, School of Education, Florida Atlantic University, Boca Raton, Florida.

Hafner, L. E. *Improving Reading in Middle and Secondary Schools*, 2d ed. New York: Macmillan, 1974.

Hawkins, T. *Benjamin: Reading and Beyond*. Columbus, Ohio: Charles E. Merrill, 1972.

Herber, H. L. *Teaching Reading in Content Areas*. Englewood Cliffs, New Jersey: Prentice-Hall, 1970.

372

Herber, H., ed. "Developing Study Skills in Secondary Schools." *Perspectives in Reading, No. 4.* Newark, Delaware: International Reading Association, 1965.

Journal of Reading. International Reading Association. Newark, Delaware.

Journal of the Reading Specialist. College Reading Association. Reading Clinic, Syracuse University, Syracuse, New York.

Karlin, R. *Teaching Reading in High School,* 2d ed. Indianapolis, Indiana: Bobbs-Merrill, 1972.

Laffey, J. L., ed. *Reading in the Content Areas.* Newark, Delaware: International Reading Association—ERIC/CRIER, 1972.

Marksheffel, N. D. *Better Reading in the Secondary School.* New York: Ronald Press, 1966.

Massey, W. J., and Moore, V. D. *Helping High School Students to Read Better.* New York: Holt, Rinehart and Winston, 1965.

Newton, J. *Reading in Your School.* New York: McGraw-Hill, 1965.

Olson, A. V., and Ames, W. S., eds. *Teaching Reading Skills in Secondary Schools: Readings.* Scranton, Pennsylvania: Intext Publishing Company, 1970.

Plenty, R. C. *Reading Ability and High School Dropouts.* New York: Bureau of Publications, Teachers College, Columbia University, 1956.

Pescosolido, J., and Gervase, C. *Reading Expectancy and Readability.* Dubuque, Iowa: Kendall/Hunt, 1971.

Proceedings of the College Reading Association. Reading and Language Arts Center, Syracuse University, Syracuse, New York.

Reading: Grades 7–8–9. New York: New York City Board of Education, 1959.

Reading Improvement. Project Innovation, Box 566, Chula Vista, California, 92010.

Reading in Florida Secondary Schools. Bulletin 35C, Tallahassee, Florida: Florida State Department of Education, 1966.

Reading News Report. 11 West 42nd Street, New York, New York, 10036.

Robinson, H. A. *Teaching Reading and Study Strategies: The Content Areas.* Boston: Allyn and Bacon, 1975.

Robinson, H. A., and Rauch, S. J. eds. "Corrective Reading in the High School Program." *Perspectives in Reading, No. 6.* Newark, Delaware: International Reading Association, 1966.

Robinson, H. A., and Thomas, E. G. eds. *Fusing Reading Skills and Content.*

Newark, Delaware: International Reading Association, 1969.

Sargent, E. E.; Huus, H., and Andressen, O. *"How to Read A Book." Reading Aids Series.* Newark, Delaware: International Reading Association, 1970.

Shaw, P. B. *Effective Reading and Learning.* New York: Thomas Y. Crowell, 1956.

Shepherd, D. L. *Comprehensive High School Reading Methods.* Columbus, Ohio: Charles E. Merrill, 1973.

Simpson, E. A. *Helping High School Students Read Better.* Chicago, Illinois: Science Research Associates, 1954.

Spache, G. D. *Good Reading for Disadvantaged Readers.* Champaign, Illinois: Garrard, 1970.

Spache, G. D. *Good Reading for Poor Readers.* Champaign, Illinois: Garrard Publishing, 1970.

Stewart, L. J.; Heller, F. M.; and Alberty, E. J. *Improving Reading in the Junior High School.* New York: Appleton-Century-Crofts, 1957.

Umans, S. *New Trends in Reading Instruction.* New York: Teachers College Press, 1963.

Weiss, M. J. *Reading in the Secondary Schools.* New York: The Odyssey Press, 1961.

Willard, C. B. *Your Reading: A Book List for Junior High Schools.* New York: Signet, 1966.

Yearbooks of the National Reading Conference. College of Education, University of Georgia, Athens, Georgia.

Bibliographies for Content Areas

Art

Olson, A. V., and Ames, W. S., eds. *Teaching Reading Skills in Secondary Schools: Readings.* Scranton, Pennsylvania: Intext Publishing Company, 1970. p. 115.

Shepherd, D. L. *Comprehensive High School Reading Methods.* Columbus, Ohio: Charles E. Merrill, 1973. pp. 288–89.

Thomas, E. L. and Robinson, H.A. *Improving Reading in Every Class: A Sourcebook for Teachers.* Boston, Massachusetts: Allyn and Bacon, 1972. pp. 455–64.

Business Education

Aukerman, R. C. *Reading in the Secondary School Classroom.* New York: McGraw-Hill, 1972. pp. 233–63.

Shepherd, D. L. *Comprehensive High School Reading Methods.* Columbus, Ohio: Charles E. Merrill, 1973. pp. 277–82.

Strang, R.; McCullough, C. M. and Traxler, A. E. *The Improvement of Reading,* 4th ed. New York: McGraw-Hill, 1967. pp. 361–65.

Thomas, E. L., and Robinson, H. A. *Improving Reading in Every Class: A Sourcebook for Teachers.* Boston: Allyn and Bacon, 1972. pp. 363–88.

The English Language Arts

Aukerman, R. C. *Reading in the Secondary School Classroom.* New York: McGraw-Hill, 1972. pp. 137–62.

Burton, D. L. *Literature Study in High Schools.* New York: Holt, Rinehart, and Winston, 1959.

Ciardi, J. *How Does a Poem Mean?* Boston, Massachusetts: Houghton Mifflin, 1960.

Dechant, E. *Reading Improvement in the Secondary School.* Englewood Cliffs, New Jersey: Prentice-Hall, 1973. pp. 301–304.

Emery, R. C., and Houshower, M. B. *High Interest-Easy Reading for Junior and Senior High School Reluctant Readers.* Champaign, Illinois: National Council of Teachers of English, 1965.

Hafner, L. E. *Improving Reading in Middle and Secondary Schools: Selected Readings,* 2d ed. New York: Macmillan, 1974. pp. 346–74.

Hook, J. N. *The Teaching of High School English.* New York: Ronald Press, 1965.

Herber, H. L. *Teaching Reading in Content Areas.* Englewood Cliffs, New Jersey: Prentice-Hall, 1970. pp. 219–30.

Megaliff, C. *The Junior Novel.* C. W. Post College of Long Island University, Port Washington, New York, 1964.

Olson, A. V., and Ames, W. S., eds. *Teaching Reading Skills in Secondary Schools: Readings.* Scranton, Pennsylvania: Intext Publishing Company, 1970. pp. 102–107; 183–215.

Shepherd, D. L. *Comprehensive High School Reading Methods.* Columbus, Ohio: Charles E. Merrill, 1973. pp. 169–84.

Squire, J. *Responses of Adolescents While Reading Four Short Stories.* Champaign, Illinois: National Council of Teachers of English, 1964.

Strang, R.; McCullough, C. M.; and Traxler, A. E. *The Improvement of Reading,* 4th ed. New York: McGraw-Hill, 1967. pp. 300–21.

Umans, S. *New Trends in Reading Instruction.* New York: Teachers College Press, 1963. pp. 19–26.

Weiss, M. J. *The English Teacher's Reader*. New York: Odyssey, 1962.

Foreign Language

Shepherd, D. L. *Comprehensive High School Reading Methods*. Columbus, Ohio: Charles E. Merrill, 1973. pp. 285–88.

Strang, R.; McCullough, C. M.; and Traxler, A. E. *The Improvement of Reading*, 4th ed. New York: McGraw-Hill, 1967. pp. 365–69.

Thomas, E. L., and Robinson, H. A. *Improving Reading in Every Class: A Sourcebook for Teachers*. Boston, Massachusetts: Allyn and Bacon, 1972. pp. 389–416.

Health

Karlin, R. *Teaching Reading in High School*, 2d ed. Indianapolis, Indiana: Bobbs-Merrill, 1972. pp. 305–07.

Olson, A. V., and Ames, W. S. eds. *Teaching Reading Skills in Secondary Schools: Readings*. Scranton, Pennsylvania: Intext Publishing Company, 1970. pp. 115–16.

Shepherd, D. L. *Comprehensive High School Reading Methods*. Columbus, Ohio: Charles E. Merrill, 1973. pp. 290–91.

Homemaking

Aukerman, R. C. *Reading in the Secondary School Classroom*. New York: McGraw-Hill, 1972. pp. 265–88.

Shepherd, D. L. *Comprehensive High School Reading Methods*. Columbus, Ohio: Charles E. Merrill, 1973. pp. 282–85.

Strang, R.; McCullough, C. M.; and Traxler, A. E. *The Improvement of Reading*, 4th ed. New York: McGraw-Hill, 1967. pp. 369–74.

Thomas, E. L., and Robinson, H. A. *Improving Reading in Every Class: A Sourcebook for Teachers*. Boston, Massachusetts: Allyn and Bacon, 1972. pp. 417–36.

Industrial Arts

Aukerman, R. C. *Reading in the Secondary School Classroom*. New York: McGraw-Hill, 1972. pp. 233–63.

Dechant, E. *Reading Improvement in the Secondary School*. Englewood Cliffs, New Jersey: Prentice-Hall, 1973. pp. 311–12.

Hafner, L. E. *Improving Reading in Middle and Secondary Schools: Selected Readings*, 2d ed. New York: Macmillan, 1974. pp. 276–304.

Karlin, R. *Teaching Reading in High School*, 2d ed. Indianapolis, Indiana: Bobbs-Merrill, 1972. pp. 305–07.

Olson, A. V., and Ames, W. S., eds. *Teaching Reading Skills in Secondary*

Schools: Readings. Scranton, Pennsylvania: Intext Educational Publishers, 1970. p. 114.

Shepherd, D. L. *Comprehensive High School Reading Methods.* Columbus, Ohio: Charles E. Merrill, 1973. pp. 282--85.

Strang, R.; McCullough, C. M.; and Traxler, A. E. *The Improvement of Reading,* 4th ed. New York: McGraw-Hill, 1967. pp. 374–75.

Thomas, E. L., and Robinson, H. A. *Improving Reading in Every Class: A Sourcebook for Teachers.* Boston, Massachusetts: Allyn and Bacon, 1972. pp. 341–62.

Umans, S. *New Trends in Reading Instruction.* New York: Teachers College Press, 1963. pp. 42–45.

Mathematics

Aukerman, R. C. *Reading in the Secondary School Classroom.* New York: McGraw-Hill, 1972. pp. 189–232.

Dechant, E. *Reading Improvement in the Secondary School.* Englewood Cliffs, New Jersey: Prentice-Hall, 1973. pp. 306–09.

Hafner, L. E. *Improving Reading in Middle and Secondary Schools: Selected Readings,* 2d ed. New York: Macmillan, 1974. pp. 320–46.

Herber, H. L. *Teaching Reading in Content Areas.* Englewood Cliffs, New Jersey: Prentice-Hall, 1970. pp. 265–68.

Olson, A. V., and Ames, W. S., eds. *Teaching Reading Skills in Secondary Schools: Readings.* Scranton, Pennsylvania: Intext Publishing Company, 1970. pp. 107–10.

Shepherd, D. L. *Comprehensive High School Reading Methods.* Columbus, Ohio: Charles E. Merrill, 1973. pp. 251–72.

Strang, R.; McCullough, C. M.; and Traxler, A. E. *The Improvement of Reading,* 4th ed. New York: McGraw-Hill, 1967. pp. 336–43.

Thomas, E. L., and Robinson, H. A. *Improving Reading in Every Class: A Sourcebook for Teachers.* Boston, Massachusetts: Allyn and Bacon, 1972. pp. 277–325.

Umans, S. *New Trends in Reading Instruction.* New York: Teachers College Press, 1963. pp. 33–37.

Music

Olson, A. V., and Ames, W. S., eds. *Teaching Reading Skills in Secondary Schools: Readings.* Scranton, Pennsylvania: Intext Publishing Company, 1970. pp. 114–15.

Shepherd, D. L. *Comprehensive High School Reading Methods.* Columbus, Ohio: Charles E. Merrill, 1973. pp. 289–90.

Strang, R.; McCullough, C. M.; and Traxler, A. E. *The Improvement of Reading*, 4th ed. New York: McGraw-Hill, 1967. pp. 375–77.

Thomas, E. L., and Robinson, H. A. *Improving Reading in Every Class: A Sourcebook for Teachers*. Boston, Massachusetts: Allyn and Bacon, 1972. pp. 437–446.

Physical Education

Olson, A. V., and Ames, W. S., eds. *Teaching Reading Skills in Secondary Schools: Readings*. Scranton, Pennsylvania: Intext Publishing Company, 1970. p. 115.

Shepherd, D. L. *Comprehensive High School Reading Methods*. Columbus, Ohio: Charles E. Merrill, 1973. pp. 290–91.

Thomas, E. L., and Robinson, H. A. *Improving Reading in Every Class: A Sourcebook for Teachers*. Boston, Massachusetts: Allyn and Bacon, 1972. pp. 465–71.

Science

Aukerman, R. C. *Reading in the Secondary School Classroom*. New York: McGraw-Hill, 1972. pp. 163–87.

Dechant, E. *Reading Improvement in the Secondary School*. Englewood Cliffs, New Jersey: Prentice-Hall, 1973. pp. 309–11.

Hafner, L. E. *Improving Reading in Middle and Secondary Schools: Selected Readings*, 2d ed. New York: Macmillan Publishing, 1974. pp. 304–20.

Karlin, R. *Teaching Reading in High School*, 2d ed. Indianapolis, Indiana: Bobbs-Merrill, 1972. pp. 300–302.

Olson, A.V., and Ames, W. S., eds. *Teaching Reading Skills in Secondary Schools: Readings*. Scranton, Pennsylvania: Intext Publishing Company, 1970, pp. 110–12.

Shepherd, D. L. *Comprehensive High School Reading Methods*. Columbus, Ohio: Charles E. Merrill, 1973. pp. 213–49.

Shepherd, D. L. *Effective Reading in Science*. New York: Harper and Row, 1960.

Strang, R.; McCullough, C. M.; and Traxler, A. E. *The Improvement of Reading*, 4th ed. New York: McGraw-Hill, 1967. pp. 322–36.

Thomas, E. L., and Robinson, H. A. *Improving Reading in Every Class: A Sourcebook for Teachers*, 4th ed. Boston, Massachusetts: Allyn and Bacon, 1972. pp. 327–39.

Thurber, W. A., and Collette, A. T. *Teaching Science in Today's Secondary School*. Boston, Massachusetts: Allyn and Bacon, 1964.

Social Studies

Aukerman, R. C. *Reading in the Secondary School Classroom.* New York: McGraw-Hill, 1972. pp. 99–135.

Carpenter, H. M. ed. *Skill Development in the Social Studies.* 33rd Yearbook, National Council for the Social Studies, Washington, D.C., 1963.

Dechant, E. *Reading Improvement in the Secondary School.* Englewood Cliffs, New Jersey: Prentice-Hall, 1973. pp. 304–06.

Hafner, L. E. *Improving Reading in Middle and Secondary Schools: Selected Readings.* 2d ed. New York: Macmillan, 1974. pp. 374–98.

Herber, H. L. *Teaching Reading in Content Areas.* Englewood Cliffs, New Jersey: Prentice-Hall, 1970. pp. 231–64.

Karlin, R. *Teaching Reading in High School.* 2d ed. Indianapolis, Indiana: Bobbs-Merrill, 1972. pp. 302–04.

Lowenstein, M. R. *Teaching Social Studies in Junior and Senior High Schools.* Chicago, Illinois: Rand McNally, 1963.

Preston, R. C. *Guiding the Social Studies Reading of High School Students.* Bulletin No. 34, National Council for the Social Studies, Washington, D.C., 1963.

Shepherd, D. L. *Comprehensive High School Reading Methods.* Columbus, Ohio: Charles E. Merrill, 1973. pp. 187–210.

Shepherd, D. L. *Effective Reading in the Social Studies.* New York: Harper and Row, 1961.

Strang, R.; McCullough, C. M.; and Traxler, A. E. *The Improvement of Reading,* 4th ed. New York: McGraw-Hill, 1967. pp. 344–59.

Umans, S. *New Trends in Reading Instruction.* New York: Teachers College Press, 1963. pp. 27–32.